CREATING SIGNIFICANT LEARNING EXPERIENCES

CREATING SIGNIFICANT LEARNING EXPERIENCES

An Integrated Approach to Designing College Courses

L. Dee Fink

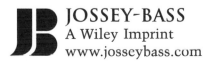

JOSSEY-BASS
A Wiley Imprint
www.josseybass.com

Published by Jossey-Bass
A Wiley Imprint
989 Market Street, San Francisco, CA 94103-1741   www.josseybass.com

Jossey-Bass books and products are available through most bookstores. To contact Jossey-Bass directly call our Customer Care Department within the U.S. at 800-956-7739, outside the U.S. at 317-572-3986 or fax 317-572-4002.

Jossey-Bass also publishes its books in a variety of electronic formats. Some content that appears in print may not be available in electronic books.

Library of Congress Cataloging-in-Publication Data

Fink, L. Dee, 1940–
   Creating significant learning experiences: an integrated approach to designing college courses/L. Dee Fink.—1st ed.
       p. cm. — (Jossey-Bass higher and adult education series)
Includes bibliographical references and index.
   ISBN 0-7879-6055-1 (alk. paper)
   1. College teaching—United States. 2. Education, Higher—United States—Curricula. I. Title. II. Series.
   LB2331 .F495 2003
     378.1'2—dc21

2002153519

Printed in the United States of America
FIRST EDITION
HB Printing   10 9 8 7 6 5

THE JOSSEY-BASS
HIGHER AND ADULT EDUCATION SERIES

TABLE OF CONTENTS

This Book is Dedicated to:

Steve Paul
(1952–2001)

and

the hundreds of teachers who have inspired me
because of how much they *care*

PREFACE

This book has been written in response to two widespread problems that I see in much of college teaching today. The first is that the majority of college teachers do not seem to have learning goals that go much beyond an understand-and-remember type of learning. A few extend into certain aspects of application learning—such things as problem solving, thinking, and decision making. But even those that offer a decent version of application learning are notable by their exception. As a result, sitting in many courses gives one the feeling that teachers are doing an information dump. They have collected and organized all the information and ideas they have on a given topic and are dumping their knowledge onto (and they hope into) the heads of their listeners. When these courses are over, one has the scary feeling that the students are also about to engage in some information dumping of their own.

The second problem is that most teachers seem to have difficulty figuring out what teaching activities they might use besides the two traditional standbys: lecturing and leading discussions. Studies have been done where someone goes into college classrooms and measures what teachers actually do. The number of times that a teacher even asks a question in a one-hour class period is remarkably low. In-depth, sustained discussions where students respond to other students as well as to the teacher are extremely rare. Although the language and vision of active learning have become a significant movement in North America, professional practice still lags woefully behind.

The fact that teachers have these problems is not entirely their fault. They are put through graduate programs that by and large dishonor the challenge and complexity of good teaching. Graduate students' time and attention is almost exclusively directed to the challenge and complexity of doing good research. Then, once the graduating Ph.D. students assume full-time positions as college professors, they are told to "just teach" if they've joined a teaching institution, or to "get busy with research and publishing" if their institution has research aspirations. Seldom if ever are they provided with the means to learn how to be better teachers. And the reward system delivers a clear message, especially at larger institutions: "Your number one priority is to get some publications out!"

Central Message

The whole point of this book is to offer ideas that can improve the way teaching is normally practiced in higher education. For this to happen, readers who teach will need to see, first, that there are ways of teaching that are different, significantly different, from what they are doing now. Second, they will need to be persuaded that these new and different ways of teaching will result in good things happening, both for their students and for themselves. Third, they will need guidance in figuring out *how* to teach in new and different ways. Finally, their institutions and other important organizations in higher education will need to recognize the worth of this effort and provide a proper level of encouragement and support. My hope is that this book will succeed in addressing all four needs and thereby help teachers find new and better ways to engage in one of the most important and potentially satisfying professions in the world.

To accomplish this goal, I lay out a new vision of what teaching and learning can be, based on three major ideas: significant learning, integrated course design, and better organizational support.

Significant Learning

The first idea is a new taxonomy of significant learning that offers teachers a set of terms for formulating learning goals for their courses. This taxonomy goes beyond understand-and-remember and even beyond application learning. For teachers and institutions that want to provide a learning-centered education, this taxonomy offers a road map to a variety of significant kinds of learning.

Integrated Course Design

The book also contains a model of integrated course design. This model builds on and incorporates many ideas that already exist in the published literature on instructional design and good teaching. But I have presented these ideas in a new way that will make it easier for teachers and instructional designers to see what they can actually do—and have students do—to promote such things as significant learning, active learning, and educative assessment. By emphasizing the integrated nature of instructional design, the model also shows that the real power of these ideas will come only when they are properly linked with each other. Having students engage in an experiential exercise, for example, becomes much more potent when it is linked with reflective dialogue. Authentic assessment becomes even more meaningful when it is linked to opportunities for students to engage in self-assessment. When the two concepts of significant learning and integrated course design are linked, teachers will have powerful new tools to analyze and reshape their own teaching. These tools will allow them to more fully understand what it is they are doing now that is worthwhile, *why* that is worthwhile, and what else they can do to make their teaching even more effective.

Better Organizational Support

The first two ideas are intended primarily for teachers. But learning about and implementing new ideas on teaching requires time, effort, and support. This means college teachers will need strong support for changing how they teach, stronger support than most have at the present time. Chapter Six presents some recommendations for better institutional support, linked to six specific needs of faculty. Most of the support needed will have to come from the faculty's home institution. But a number of other organizations also significantly influence how faculty work, so their role in supporting better teaching is also examined.

Plan of the Book

The general plan of this book is as follows. First I will describe what I see happening in higher education at the present time (Chapter One). This situation, as I see it, calls for substantial changes in the way we teach but at the same time offers numerous new ideas on how this might be done. Then I will lay out two of the major ideas in this book. The first is a taxonomy of significant learning that provides us with a new language for setting learning goals (Chapter Two). Following this, the key ideas of integrated course design are presented to give teachers new tools for achieving a more challenging set of learning goals (Chapters Three and Four).

Teachers may still feel the need for suggestions on how to change the way they teach, so this issue is addressed in Chapter Five. Assuming faculty are ready to make this kind of personal and individual change, they will need better organizational support from the various organizations that influence how they work (Chapter Six). Finally, in Chapter Seven, I share my dream of what higher education would be like if all the groups involved in this enterprise aligned themselves to support more significant learning during the transformation of higher education that lies ahead of us at the dawn of the twenty-first century.

Web Site on Significant Learning

I also invite readers to visit a Web site on significant learning that has been set up to keep the conversation going. The main goal of the Web site is to allow teachers to ask questions and share successes, and to archive valuable materials and ideas for promoting significant learning in all educational contexts.

The structure of this Web site will undoubtedly evolve over time. But it will initially contain a discussion list, materials to assist teachers in the design process, and a description of courses that promote significant learning.

The URL for this Web site is http://www.significantlearning.org.

Acknowledgments

To paraphrase a modern aphorism: "It takes a village to write a book." That has never been more true of a book than of this one. A very important part of my village consists of the other people who have written about college teaching. The key ideas presented here build on a number of classic works in higher education and incorporate exciting ideas from several contemporary publications. A quick look through the text, the list of references, and the suggested readings in Appendix B will illustrate how deeply my own education is indebted to the published works of others.

Others have contributed in an even more direct fashion. While the questions and ideas presented here have been brewing for many years, several insights crystallized in 1996 when I was teaching a course titled "Instructional Strategies in Adult and Higher Education" at the University of Oklahoma. The response of the graduate students in that class prompted me to undertake an intense journey of searching, reading, creating, discussing, testing, and revising of ideas.

Along the way, a number of individuals were instrumental in furthering that journey. Steve Paul, an exceptional music educator then at Oklahoma and later at the University of Arizona, pushed me in a series of conversations that lasted a year and a half and resulted in the initial outline of the key ideas presented here. Bill McKeachie, the person who more than anyone else legitimized scholarly work on college teaching, provided important encouragement during the early stages of this journey, a time when I was unsure about the worth of the ideas and my own ability to put them in book form. Tom Angelo generously took time from a very busy schedule to read an early draft and pointed out some needed changes.

During the last few years, faculty at my own institution and elsewhere have listened to these ideas in informal conversations and in formal workshops. Although this is a task that never ends, their response has brought me a long way toward understanding what needs to be said to make these ideas meaningful to people who care about teaching and who want to teach well. One faculty member in particular, John Furneaux, a physics professor at Oklahoma, not only listened but offered his own course as a lab for testing the worth of the ideas. The results of that experiment are shared in Chapter Five.

I also wish to pay tribute to two people who served as mentors to me at various times early in my life: Thomas Ludlum and William Pattison. Both of them modeled a level of intellectual and humane excellence that has served as a guidepost throughout my personal and professional life.

Lynn Sorenson, formerly at Oklahoma and now associate director of the Faculty Center at Brigham Young University, generously gave of her time and expertise in suggesting changes that made this book more coherent and readable.

Finally, I must mention the influence of Arletta Knight, who also works in the field of instructional development and who has given me marvelous feedback on multiple drafts of the manuscript. She offered continuous moral encouragement and extremely valuable suggestions on changes that would help the book make better sense to others. I am extremely fortunate to have such a person in my life—and to have such a person as my wife!

THE AUTHOR

L. Dee Fink is director of the Instructional Development Program and an adjunct professor of geography at the University of Oklahoma. He received his Ph.D. and M.A. degrees from the University of Chicago and his B.A. from Capital University. When he first came to Oklahoma from graduate school in 1976, he taught courses in geography and higher education. In 1979 he proposed and established the Instructional Development Program and has served as its director ever since. At Oklahoma he was also a faculty member for fifteen years in the College of Liberal Studies, a special program of interdisciplinary studies for adult, nonresidential students and served as the first director of Oklahoma's Gateway to College Learning, a course intended to orient freshmen to college.

His work as an instructional consultant for over twenty years provides the primary basis for the ideas in this book. He has observed the classroom teaching of hundreds of faculty members, consulted with them individually to enhance student learning in their courses and solve teaching problems, and led numerous faculty discussions and workshops. These consulting experiences, in addition to his own teaching experience, have given him an intimate feel for the situation, thoughts, feelings, and actions of college teachers.

He has also been active nationally and internationally in faculty development. He initiated the Great Plains regional consortium for faculty developers in 1981, has been a member of the Professional and Organizational Development (POD) Network in Higher Education for over twenty years, has served on the POD Executive Committee, and has codirected the workshop on "Getting Started in Faculty Development" at the annual POD conference since the early 1990s. He has served on the editorial boards of the ASHE-ERIC Higher Education Reports and the *Journal of Staff, Program, and Organization Development*. In 2002, he was elected president of the POD network, which is the premier faculty development organization in North America.

In 1989 he was a recipient of the AAHE's Jaime Escalante "Stand and Deliver" Award, and in 1992 he received the Outstanding Faculty Award from the College of Liberal Studies at the University of Oklahoma.

One of his first major publications was an empirical study of a hundred beginning college teachers that appeared in Jossey-Bass's *New Directions for Teaching and Learning* no. 17, in 1984. Since then he has published numerous articles and book chapters on college teaching, evaluating college teaching, new faculty members, and instructional development programs. He is also coeditor of *Team-Based Learning* (Praeger, 2002). The URL for his professional Web site is http://www.ou.edu/idp/dfink.htm.

CREATING SIGNIFICANT LEARNING EXPERIENCES

CHAPTER ONE

CREATING SIGNIFICANT LEARNING EXPERIENCES

The Key to Quality in Educational Programs

We won't meet the needs for more and better higher education until professors become designers of learning experiences and not teachers.

—LARRY SPENCE (2001)

Every year, in the United States alone, more than five hundred thousand college teachers prepare to teach classes, and more than fifteen million students come to learn. Most of us teach four to eight courses a year. As we engage in this task, we have two options. We can continue to follow traditional ways of teaching, repeating the same practices that we and others in our disciplines have used for years. Or we can dare to dream about doing something different, something special in our courses that would significantly improve the quality of student learning. This option leads to the question faced by teachers everywhere and at all levels of education: Should we make the effort to change, or not?

Given the scale of education and its significance for individual lives and society at large, the response of teachers to this perennial question is of immense importance. What are the factors affecting our response? This chapter and this book will present some ideas on this question. As Spence asserts in the quote that opens the chapter, I too will argue that college teachers need to learn how to design courses more effectively for higher education to significantly improve the quality of its educational programs.

The primary intent of this opening chapter is to describe the unusual and exciting situation in higher education at the present time. A variety of developments have created an extremely strong need to improve the quality of our educational programs. At the same time a wealth of new ideas on teaching have emerged in the last few decades that offer college teachers unusual opportunities to make a creative response to this situation. Near the end of this chapter I will present the reasons why course design, in my view, is the right place to integrate several of these new ideas and, at the same time, constitutes the single most significant change most teachers can make to improve the quality of their teaching and of student learning.

How Satisfactory Are Current Forms of Instruction?

When examined from outside the academy, our present teaching practices appear to be not only adequate but even quite good. The demand for our services remains high. The percentage of graduating high school students that choose to come to college is over 50 percent and continues to rise. The percentage of adults enrolling in some kind of higher education program also remains strong and growing. And American higher education continues to be very attractive to students from around the world.

But when we examine the situation from *inside* the academy and look at the quality of student learning, we find a more disturbing picture. How well are college students learning what they should be learning? People obviously have different views about what they think students ought to be learning in college, but most people would be concerned about the following results from a Gallup survey of college seniors (Heller, 1989):

- 42 percent were unaware that the Koran is the sacred scripture of Islam.
- 42 percent could not locate the Civil War between 1850 and 1900.
- 31 percent placed Reconstruction after World War II.

However, while it is disturbing that almost half of our college graduates are not acquiring even a rudimentary level of general knowledge, many would argue, myself included, that "memorized knowledge" is not the primary goal of higher education. Colleges and universities should be focusing their efforts on developing people who can engage in complex thinking and reasoning. How are we doing on that score?

Amiran (1989) conducted an extensive and multifaceted study of college student performance on tests on reflexive thinking and metacognition and came to the following conclusions:

- *Reading:* Students could identify the main points and supporting evidence in essays, but they showed little growth during their college years in their ability to identify the implications of the essay, articulate the author's assumptions, or to see the relationship between the article and their own lives and society.

- *Reflexive thinking:* Few students proved adept at reflexive thinking. They lack problem-solving and reasoning skills and are very weak in recognizing the assumptions that have to be made to solve given problems.
- *Scientific reasoning:* Students know little about scientific reasoning, empirical scientific methodology, the importance of establishing a control for establishing cause-effect relationships, or researcher bias.
- *Historical reasoning:* Students were weak both in terms of establishing a chronology of events and in terms of seeing causal relationships between or among events.

This data suggests that higher education is currently turning out graduates who neither have a good general knowledge nor know how to engage in the kind of complex thinking and reasoning that society today needs. Why might this be?

Cause of These Shortcomings

The basic problem is that, although faculty members want their students to achieve higher kinds of learning, they continue to use a form of teaching that is not effective at promoting such learning. When interviewed, faculty often make reference to higher-level learning goals such as critical thinking. But they have traditionally relied heavily on lecturing as their main form of teaching. In one study of eighteen hundred faculty in five different types of institutions (including small private colleges), 73–83 percent chose lectures as their primary method of instruction (Blackburn and others, 1980). Although those percentages have probably dropped slightly in the last decade, my interactions with faculty suggest that lecturing is still by far the dominant mode of teaching.

What kinds of results does lecturing, even good lecturing, produce? A long history of research indicates lecturing has limited effectiveness in helping students

- Retain information after a course is over.
- Develop an ability to transfer knowledge to novel situations.
- Develop skill in thinking or problem solving.
- Achieve affective outcomes, such as motivation for additional learning or a change in attitude.

In a carefully designed test at Norwich University in England, teachers gave a lecture specifically designed to be effective (McLeish, 1968). Students were given a test on their recall of facts, theory, and application of the content. They were allowed to use their own lecture notes and even a printed summary of the lecture. At the end of the lecture, the average level of the students' recall of information was 42 percent. One week later, even with the benefit of taking the same test a second time, students' recall had dropped to 20 percent.

In another study in the United States, students who took a year-long, two-semester course on introductory economics were compared with students who had never had the course at all (Saunders, 1980). Over twelve hundred students in the two groups were given a test on the content of the course.

At the end of the course, students who took the course scored only 20 percent higher than students who had never had the course. Two years later, the difference was 15 percent. Seven years later, the difference was only 10 percent.

Collectively the results from these and other studies (many of which are summarized in an excellent study by Lion Gardiner, 1994) suggest that our current instructional procedures are not working very well. Students are not learning even basic general knowledge, they are not developing higher-level cognitive skills, and they are not retaining their knowledge very well. In fact, there is no significant difference between students who take courses and students who do not.

Are People Concerned About These Problems?

Clearly not everyone is concerned about the results of present forms of instructional practice; otherwise there would be greater pressure to make substantial changes. On the other hand, when one looks carefully at the reactions of many faculty, students, and the public to the quality of student learning, one finds an awareness, perhaps even a growing awareness, that something is not right.

Faculty Concerns. When I talk to faculty, many say their biggest concern is low student attendance in class. Many see daily class attendance running around 50 percent by mid-semester in their lower division courses. But they report other problems as well. Students do not complete reading assignments. The energy level in class discussions is low. Students focus on grades rather than on learning. Textbooks keep getting larger and larger, which means teachers have to work harder and harder to cover the material. Many say they have lost their joy in teaching. And when they try to change, they often feel unsupported by students, colleagues, and the whole institution.

Student Concerns. Students, for their part, have similar concerns. They often complain about courses not being very interesting, that they just sit and take notes and then cram for exam after exam. They have difficulty seeing the value or significance of what they are learning. They too see the textbooks getting larger and larger; for them this means greater cost as well as more material that they have to learn, master, or memorize for the test.

In one extensive study of student reaction to the instruction they were receiving (summarized in Courts and McInerney, 1993, pp. 33–38), students' most common criticism was focused on the quality of education they were receiving, the way teachers teach, and the level of performance expected of the students. By far the most common concern was directed specifically at the tendency of teachers to rely primarily on lectures and workbook exercises to transmit information, on the absence of interaction, and on the lack of what student after student referred to as "hands-on learning." Additional conclusions included the following:

- Students were not self-directed learners. They were not confident in their ability to approach a problem and figure it out on their own.
- The students evidenced a powerful sense that they were not learning as much as they should be.
- Many of the students voiced a belief that their college teachers do not really care much about them or about promoting their learning or interacting with them.
- The result? Students do not engage fully or energetically in learning something they do not want to learn or see no reason for learning.

My conversations with students on my own campus and elsewhere indicate that they also are feeling very fragmented and isolated. The fragmented feeling comes from their observation that their courses do not connect to each other; there is "this course" and "that course" but no coherent education. Their feelings of isolation come from not having much interaction with other students, either in class or out of class, about course-related matters. The net result? Low intellectual effort by students. While most college teachers say they expect two hours of out-of-class study time for each hour of class, students are spending much less than this. Teachers' expectations would mean that a full-time student who is enrolled in five three-credit-hour courses would need to study thirty hours per week. However, studies of actual student study time repeatedly indicate that most students spend six hours or less per week—for all their courses combined. They spend much more time socializing, working, or watching TV (several studies, cited in Gardiner, 1994, p. 52).

Public Concerns. The public is also beginning to be concerned about what they perceive to be the poor quality of higher education in this country. This is a significant part of the impetus behind the move in many state legislatures to set up accountability programs and even performance-based appropriations. The *Chronicle* *of Higher Education* reported a few years ago (Carnevale, Johnson, and Edwards, 1998) that, as of that date, "11 states tie some appropriations to measures of public institutions' performance, and 15 more are likely to follow suit within the next five years." Two years later the *Chronicle* contained an article about a proposal by the Board of Regents for the whole University of Texas system to set up competency tests (Schmidt, 2000). The article noted that a "growing number of states [were looking] to the large-scale administering of competency tests as a means of setting standards for public colleges, or students, or both." The National Center for Higher Education Management Systems (NCHEMS) was quoted as reporting that, in the past two years, there has been a "significant increase in the number of states seriously considering—or actively piloting—standardized testing as a deliberate element of higher education policy."

Clearly many people believe we need to improve the quality of higher education. But what is the change that needs to be made?

Base Need: Significant Learning Experiences for Students

Beneath each of these several levels of concern is a fundamental need, and that is for students to have a significant learning experience. If this could happen more frequently and more consistently in higher education, everyone—faculty, students, parents, institutions, and society at large—would be more satisfied with the quality of higher education than they are at the present time.

Significant Learning Experiences

One way of focusing this issue is to search for ways of providing students with significant learning experiences. If we can find ways to identify and create learning experiences that students and others can agree are truly significant, we will have made important progress in our effort to improve the quality of higher education. What might such learning experiences be like?

The central idea of this phrase is that teaching should result in something others can look at and say: "That learning experience resulted in something that is truly significant in terms of the students' lives." How can we properly define and characterize that kind of learning experience?

It would seem that a proper definition requires us to recognize that a significant learning experience has both a *process* and an *outcome* dimension. And each of these dimensions has two features, as shown in Exhibit 1.1.

In a powerful learning experience, students will be engaged in their own learning, there will be a high energy level associated with it, and the whole process

EXHIBIT 1.1. CHARACTERISTICS OF SIGNIFICANT LEARNING EXPERIENCES.

Process:

- *Engaged:* Students are engaged in their learning.
- *High energy:* Class has a high energy level.

Results, Impact, Outcomes:

- *Significant and lasting change:* Course results in significant changes in the students, changes that continue after the course is over and even after the students have graduated.
- *Value in life:* What the students learn has a high potential for being of value in their lives after the course is over, by enhancing their individual lives, preparing them to participate in multiple communities, or preparing them for the world of work.

will have important outcomes or results. Not only will students be learning throughout the course, by the end of the course they will clearly have changed in some important way—they will have learned something important. And that learning will have the potential for changing their lives in an important way. It has been my observation that all significant learning offers one or more of the following values:

- *Enhancing our individual life:* developing an ability to enjoy good art and music, developing a thoughtful philosophy of life, and so on.
- *Enabling us to contribute to the many communities of which we will be a part:* family, local community, nation state, religion, special interest groups, the world.
- *Preparing us for the world of work:* developing the knowledge, skills, and attitudes necessary for being effective in one or more professional fields.

An Analogy

As a person who enjoys good restaurants, I see an analogy between what restaurants have to do to provide a high-quality dining experience and what colleges have to do to provide a high-quality educational experience. Without meaning to slight other important factors, three key aspects of a good dining experience are an inviting menu, well-prepared food, and prompt and thoughtful service. If any one of these ingredients is missing, the quality of the dining experience is significantly lowered. But the quality of the food is especially important: this is the fundamental reason for going to a restaurant in the first place. If the food is not well prepared, the restaurant is going to have problems, no matter how exciting the menu or how friendly the waiters.

Similarly, in higher education, colleges need to assemble good curricula, good instruction, and good faculty who can interact well with students. If any one of these is not done well, the quality of the educational experience suffers significantly. Again, though, the quality of the instruction is critically important. This is the fundamental reason people go to college. If the instruction is not done well, it does not matter how exciting the course titles in the curriculum or how kind the faculty; the overall learning experience will be deficient.

If we propose to change and improve higher education so that students will have more significant learning experiences, both the faculty and the institutions will have to make some big changes. Is this possible and likely?

Faculty: Ready for Change?

The question that all faculty face is this: Should I spend the time and effort to learn about and implement new ways of teaching? Essentially all faculty members feel more than fully loaded already with all their present teaching, research, and service obligations. So suggesting that faculty members take on a substantial new task aimed at their own professional development is no small issue. Their response to this question, then, would appear to rest on the issue of whether there is a good basis for saying, "Yes, I should invest in learning how to teach better." Is there a potential benefit that has sufficient value and sufficient likelihood of happening, that would justify the time and effort required?

The answer to this question lies inside faculty. It is my experience and belief that nearly all faculty have deep inner dreams of what they would like their teaching to be like—and those dreams are significantly different from their ordinary, everyday experiences in the classroom. If some way could be found to encourage faculty to dream their dreams and to have a realistic hope of making these dreams a reality, they would have the basis they need for saying, "Yes, it is worthwhile for me to invest in learning how to be a better teacher."

Do they have such dreams? They not only do have dreams, they have wonderful dreams. I have been giving numerous workshops on the subject of designing courses since 2001 from California to Connecticut, in large state universities, regional colleges, small private colleges, special-purpose institutions, and community colleges. The task of designing something is inherently creative, so I ask faculty to exercise their creativity by "dreaming and imagining" for a moment.

Imagine yourself teaching in a perfect situation, where the students will do anything and everything you ask of them. They will read everything and write everything you ask them to. They will do it on time and do it well. In this special situation, you can do anything you want as a teacher and have any kind of impact on students that you desire. The only limitation is your own imagination.

Question: In your deepest, fondest dreams, what kind of impact would you most like to have on your students? That is, when the course is over and it is now one or two years later, what would you like to be true about students who have had your courses that is not true of others? What is the distinctive educational impact you would like for your teaching and your courses to have on your students?

The creative energy that teachers pour into answering this question is immense, and the answers themselves are absolutely marvelous to behold. Typical responses include statements such as the following:

My dream is that students, one to two years after the course is over, will be able to. . .

- Apply and use what they learn in real-life situations.
- Find ways to make the world better, be able to make a difference.
- Develop a deep curiosity.
- Engage in lifelong learning.
- Experience the "Joy of Learning."
- Take pride in what they have done and can accomplish, in whatever discipline or line of work they choose.
- See the importance of community building, both at work and in their personal lives.
- See the connections between themselves and their own beliefs, values, and actions and those of others.
- Think about problems and issues in integrated ways, rather than in separated and compartmentalized ways. Students will see connections between multiple perspectives.
- See the need for change in the world and be a change agent.
- Be creative problem solvers.
- Develop key skills in life, such as communication skills.
- Understand and be able to use the basic principles of my course.
- Stay positive, despite the setbacks and challenges of life and work.
- Mentor others.
- Continue to grow as critical thinkers.
- Value continuous improvement.

Following this dreaming exercise, I also ask faculty to individually make an artistic representation of their dream. This can be in whatever form they choose; it can be a picture, a poem, a song, a mime, a simple dramatization, or whatever. Making a picture is the most common response, but almost every workshop has elicited all the other forms as well. Then participants are asked to share their dreams and the artistic representations in small groups. Following this, each group selects something to share with the whole set of participants.

The process of illustrating and sharing dreams has the effect of enlarging and enhancing them in valuable ways. An example of this is the dream of Gina Masequesmay, a professor of Asian American studies at California State University at Northridge. She described her individual dream in the following way:

> My dream is for my students to be able *to think critically,* to incorporate this thinking in their daily lives, and to *share that knowledge and compassion with others* in order to work towards a just world for all.
>
> To be able to think critically is to first realize that knowledge/truth is conditioned by power. What that means is that one's understanding of the world is biased by one's social location in society, and therefore, all perspectives are partial. In order to have a fuller view of what is really happening in the world, one needs to step outside of one's biased/cultural lens that limits one's view and to be reflective of this process of attempting to be "critical" as opposed to accepting authority without questions.

The rest of her group then added their dreams to hers. They integrated critical thinking, compassion, and sharing with the dreams of reflexive thinking, continuity over time, and the goal of developing this learning in a step-by-step process.

These are exciting dreams. If we can find ways to do whatever needs to be done to make such dreams a reality, higher education will be a more exciting experience and students will graduate with a very different kind of education than seems to be the norm at the present time.

Dreams such as these, though, raise the question of whether institutions of higher education, the places where faculty work and where these events all take place, are ready to change in ways that will support faculty change more effectively.

Institutional Change: Coming, Ready or Not!

Faculty members are not likely to make the decision to change without support from their institutions. They need to feel that their institutions truly value better learning and better teaching and are willing to provide faculty with what they need in order to learn new ways of teaching: time, encouragement, institutional centers that can provide the ideas that faculty need, reward, and so on. Are institutions ready to change? The view in many circles is that such change is not an option or a choice for institutions; it is inevitable. Change is going to happen, whether institutions are ready for it or not. What is the nature of this change and what is driving it?

The Forces Driving Institutional Change

During the last decade or so, a number of voices have been predicting that higher education is about to undergo major change and have spoken as advocates of that change. What they see coming is a structural change, prompted in part but not solely by new technology. Included in this change is the need for a new vision of what constitutes "good learning" and the kind of pedagogy that will generate that kind of learning.

One of the voices is that of Dolence and Norris, whose short but visionary report, *Transforming Higher Education* (1995), presents the general view that society is undergoing a fundamental transformation from the Industrial Age to the Information Age. One consequence of that change is that most social institutions will also be transformed, including higher education. Society and individual learners now have different needs, in terms of both what people need to learn and how they can and should learn. Dolence and Norris's formulation of the different characteristics associated with learning in the Industrial Age and the Information Age are shown in Exhibit 1.2.

Based in part on the special capabilities of information technology, the primary force that will drive change in higher education is the fact that traditional institutions are about to lose their "exclusive franchise," that is, their monopoly on providing postsecondary learning. New providers have already appeared and are competing effectively for students: corporate universities, the University of Phoenix (offering a combination of classes at distributed sites and online courses; see http://www.uophx.edu), and Virtual University (a completely online university; see http://vu.org). Universities that stick to the Industrial Age or factory model will probably continue to exist but will increasingly be at a competitive disadvantage. Traditional universities are insufficiently flexible, they focus on processes and outputs (graduates) rather than on outcomes (significant learning), and they operate in a way that generates high cost (Dolence and Norris, 1995, p. 11). If the new vendors succeed in unbundling the degree package and offering students a high-quality learning experience focused on what learners need and want, offering certification of that learning, and doing so at greater convenience or lower cost, or both—they will attract a significant amount of enrollment away from traditional

EXHIBIT 1.2. HIGHER EDUCATION IN THE INDUSTRIAL AGE AND THE INFORMATION AGE.

Industrial Age:	Information Age:
Teaching franchise	Learning franchise
Provider-driven, a set time for learning	Individualized learning
Information infrastructure as support tool	Information infrastructure as the fundamental instrument of transformation
Individual technologies	Technology synergies
Time out for education	Just-in-time learning
Continuing education	Perpetual learning
Separate learning systems	Fused learning systems
Traditional courses, degrees, and academic calendars	Unbundled learning experiences based on learner needs
Teaching and certification of mastery are combined	Learning and certification of mastery are related, yet separable, issues
Front-end, lump-sum payment based on length of academic process	Point-of-access payment for exchange of intellectual property based on value added
Collections of fragmented, narrow, and proprietary systems	Seamless, integrated comprehensive and open systems
Bureaucratic systems	Self-informing, self-correcting systems
Rigid, predesigned processes	Families of transactions customizable to the needs of learners, faculty, and staff
Technology push	Learning vision pull

Source: Dolence and Norris, 1995, p. 4. Used by permission.

institutions, and deservedly so. Unless, of course, traditional institutions make some significant changes and offer programs that meet these same requirements. Either way, the key requirement will be the ability to offer a high-quality learning experience. The advantage will go to those institutions that learn how to do that better, sooner, and at least cost (calculated in terms of time and effort as well as money).

Does anyone else think these changes are likely to happen? Frank Newman, former president of the Education Commission of the States, believes higher education is entering a period of major change and has recently summarized and identified four major forces that are driving this change. (The comments that follow are adapted from the Futures Project Web site: http://www.futuresproject.org, accessed in the summer of 2000.) In Newman's view, the first of the four forces driving many of the other changes is *information technology*. This technology is now sufficiently widespread and sufficiently sophisticated such that whole courses and curricula offered completely online are rapidly becoming commonplace. The unique capabilities of information technology are stimulating a second force for change, the rapid emergence of *new providers* of educational services. Corporate organizations and for-profit educational companies are growing rapidly in their offerings of discrete learning packages as well as traditional degree programs. This combination of new providers and new modes of delivering educational services is leading to the third force for change: the *globalization of higher education*. Educational institutions both in the United States and elsewhere are marketing and offering their courses and degree programs worldwide. One highly visible example of this is Cardean University, a consortium of four American universities (Chicago, Stanford, Columbia, and Carnegie Mellon) and the London School of Economics, that is offering business degrees globally.

Finally the foregoing changes also interact with *new kinds of students*. In the United States, increasing numbers of older students, minority students, and first-generation students continue to seek higher education. In addition, traditional kinds of students are coming into higher education with a greater familiarity with computers and often with part-time jobs. Some of these students will be looking for traditional kinds of educational experiences; others will stay at home and seek their education in a new form of delivery from a provider who can be located anywhere in the world.

Newman predicts that, as a result of these four forces for change, a much higher level of competition than in the past will characterize higher education in the future and the whole enterprise will become much more learning-centered. To the degree that he is correct in this prediction, institutions of higher education will face significant new pressures to become more open to change. And if this happens, leaders in colleges and universities may be more ready than in times past to make significant changes in the way they operate.

Leading Toward the Right Kind of Change

As administrative and faculty leaders face this era of major change, the question clearly is not whether they should change but *what kind* of change they should attempt to make. Historically, higher education in the United States has responded to calls for change when these voices became strong enough. This happened, for example, in the mid-1800s when land-grant universities were established for the purpose of providing a more application-oriented education, in the late 1800s when universities introduced discipline-based research and departments, and in the mid-1900s when society called for greater access to higher education by non-traditional kinds of students.

Since the 1980s a similar chorus of voices has been calling for another change, a change in how students learn and especially in what they learn. In a sense, these voices are describing the dreams that others in society have for higher education, and these dreams are coming from both national organizations and from well-informed individuals.

National Organizations. One of the earliest voices to catch national attention on this subject came from a study group in the National Institute of Education. Their report, *Involvement in Learning* (1984), acknowledged the positive changes that have occurred in American higher education but also expressed their concern about some problems: problems in student achievement, a shift in undergraduate programs toward narrow specialization, a decline in the attractiveness of faculty careers, and others. They also noted that traditional ways of measuring excellence were inadequate because they focused on resources and inputs, not on "what students actually learn and how much they grow as a result of higher education" (p. 15). The group then urged institutions of higher education to produce demonstrable improvements, not only of "student knowledge" but also in students' "capabilities, skills, and attitudes between entrance and graduation" (p. 15). This was one of the earliest and strongest calls for college courses to go beyond "content learning."

One year later the Association of American Colleges (AAC) sponsored a Project on Redefining the Meaning and Purpose of Baccalaureate Degrees. The language and tone of this report was stronger and even more critical than the NIE report. The opening statement sounded a wake-up call to American higher education:

> The educational failures of the United States are emerging as a major concern of the 1980s. . . . Our report addresses the crisis in American education as it is revealed in the decay of the college course of study and in the role of college faculties in creating and nurturing that decay. . . .
>
> As for what passes for a college curriculum, almost anything goes. We have reached a point where we are more confident about the length of a college education than about its content or purpose [AAC, 1985, pp. 1–2].

The members of the project group went on to describe a minimum required curriculum that was strikingly different from the by-now-familiar "major and general distribution requirements." They proposed a new kind of curriculum, the central theme of which was that students should learn "how to learn" (p. 24).

In a similar vein, a report by the National Association of State Universities and Land-Grant Colleges called on these universities to be proactive in helping all students develop essential life skills and important values in higher education.

We want to stress that values deserve special attention in this effort. The highest educational challenge we face revolves around developing character, conscience, citizenship, tolerance, civility, and individual and social responsibility in our students. We dare not ignore this obligation in a society that sometimes gives the impression that virtues such as these are discretionary. These should be part of the standard equipment of our graduates, not options [NASULGC, 1997, pp. 12–13].

At about the same time, Campus Compact, an organization devoted to the promotion of service learning in higher education, cosponsored a meeting at the Wingspread Conference Center in Wisconsin on "The Civic Responsibilities of Research Universities." In a statement called the "Wingspread Declaration" (Campus Compact, 1998), the conferees proclaimed their belief that "research universities must prepare students to be responsible citizens and enable faculty to develop and put their knowledge to work for the betterment of their communities." If one wants to prepare students for "responsible and engaged citizenship," what should students learn? They should be "learning the skills, developing the habits and identities and acquiring the knowledge to contribute to the general welfare (on campus, in communities, and in the world)."

Pre-Professional Education. A number of studies have been conducted in various fields of pre-professional education to determine what graduates in those particular fields should know and how changing times have changed what students need to learn. In a major study of business education, Porter and McKibbin (1988) surveyed both business college deans and corporate CEOs to see what changes people in these roles thought were needed in both undergraduate and graduate business education. Their recommendations, among other things, called for more attention to people skills—both managing people and leadership—along with integrating corporate and community activities and preparing for lifelong or continuous learning.

More recently the engineering profession's accreditation body (Accreditation Board for Engineering and Technology, commonly known as ABET) has taken the need for new kinds of learning a step further and incorporated specific kinds of learning into their accreditation standards (http://www.abet.org/criteria.html; accessed May 2002). The new standards (known as "ABET 2000" because they are required for accreditation after the year 2000) identify specific kinds of learning that engineering students should have achieved by graduation. These include specific engineering skills or competencies (for example, being able to design a system that meets the client's needs), general professional skills (for example, being able to communicate effectively), and broad professional perspectives (for example, understand the impact of engineering solutions in a global and societal context).

At about the same time an advisory committee in the National Science Foundation examined the state of undergraduate education in science, math, engineering, and technology (SMET). Titled *Shaping the Future*, the report observed that while America's basic research in science, math, and engineering is world class, its education is still not (1996, p. iii). Given the importance of science, math, engineering, and technology in the modern world generally and in this field of work in particular, problems in SMET education are quite serious. What should students learn? The authors called on SMET faculty to meet the new expectations of today's society by building certain attitudes and skills. Specifically, they urged faculty to promote new kinds of learning, for example, developing the skills of communication, teamwork, and lifelong learning (p. iv).

Individual Calls for New Kinds of Learning. In addition to these calls by national and professional organizations for changes in what students learn, a number of people who are careful observers of higher education have published major statements calling for the same thing. One of these is a book by Lion Gardiner (1994) called *Redesigning Higher Education*. After completing a major study on the topic, Gardiner noted that leaders in business, industry, and government have identified several important kinds of learning needed by citizens and workers in the years ahead. He labeled these as "critical competencies" and his list included the following personal characteristics, skills, and dispositions (p. 7):

- Conscientiousness, personal responsibility, and dependability
- The ability to act in a principled, ethical fashion
- Skill in oral and written communication
- Interpersonal and team skills
- Skill in critical thinking and in solving complex problems
- Respect for people different from oneself
- The ability to adapt to change
- The ability and desire for lifelong learning

Richard Paul has focused on one of these critical competencies, critical thinking, in his work as director of the Center for Critical Thinking at Sonoma State University in California. In *Critical Thinking* (1993), he argues that we live in a world with two important characteristics: it is changing rapidly and it is becoming more complex. Based on this view, he concludes that "the work of the future is the work of the mind, intellectual work, work that involves reasoning and intellectual self-discipline" (p. 13). As a result, Paul argues, we all need to parent differently, work differently, and educate differently.

Although the majority of professors in higher education would like to believe they promote critical thinking, a survey of 140 college teachers by Paul and his colleagues led them to believe that most teachers promote only a shallow form of critical thinking. Their study found that the vast majority, 75–80 percent, *say* they value and do things in their classrooms to promote critical thinking. However, only a small minority (19 percent) are able to give a clear explanation of what critical thinking is. Only 9 percent are clearly teaching for critical thinking on a typical day in class, and only a very small minority (8 percent) are able to identify important criteria and standards by which they evaluate the quality of their students' thinking (Paul, Elder, and Bartell, 1997).

This may be the reason why so many employers still claim that their college graduate hires do not think well, write well, or communicate well.

Are Significantly Better Kinds of Learning Really Possible?

It's clear that participants in higher education and leaders in society do see a need for colleges and universities to provide educational programs that result in different and more significant kinds of learning. But this raises the question of whether it is in fact possible to change the quality of teaching and learning significantly. Can we really do better than we are doing now?

As it turns out, the scholars, practitioners, and theorists of college teaching have been very active in the last few decades generating numerous ideas about new and better ways of teaching. These new ideas give us the tools we need to fashion new kinds of learning for our students.

New Paradigms for Teaching

A number of writers have been announcing a paradigm shift in terms of how higher education views pedagogy. In a widely read and cited article, Barr and Tagg (1995) describe what they believe to be a major change already taking place in American higher education. This change is a paradigm shift in which institutions are thinking less about providing instruction (the teaching paradigm) and more about producing learning (the learning paradigm). Their article goes on to note the implications of such a shift for the complete operation of undergraduate education:

Mission and purpose: from improving the quality of instruction to improving the quality of learning

Criteria for success: from "quality of entering students" to "quality of exiting students"

Teaching and learning structures: from "covering material" to "specific learning results"

Learning theory: from "learning is cumulative and linear" to "learning is a nesting and interaction of frameworks"

Productivity and funding: from defining productivity in terms of "cost per hour of instruction per student" to "cost per unit of learning per student"

Nature of roles: from "faculty being primarily lecturers" to "faculty being primarily designers of learning methods and environments"

The authors state their belief that this shift is both "needed and wanted." I would agree entirely. The only adjustment I would make is that the real need is not just for institutions to "produce learning" but to "produce *significant* learning."

In a similar vein William Campbell and Karl Smith (1997) have presented a comparison of what they call "old and new paradigms" for college teaching (see Exhibit 1.3). The views in the new paradigm reflect many of the themes emphasized for some time by innovative educators in instructional development programs in this country and elsewhere.

Frank Smith has also written about two kinds of learning in a provocative book about "learning and forgetting" (1998). He describes what he calls the "classic" view of learning that sees learning as continual, effortless, and never forgotten. This is the kind of learning that occurs naturally in everyone's life all the time. This stands in contrast to the "official" view that sees learning as occasional, hard work, and easily forgotten. This is the kind that occurs much too often in formal schooling. He argues, "We can only learn from activities that are interesting and comprehensible to us; in other words, activities that are satisfying. If this is not the case, only inefficient rote learning, or memorization, is available to us and forgetting is inevitable" (p. 87).

In a set of initiatives that began in the 1970s, researchers in Sweden, Great Britain, and Australia semi-independently developed the idea that teachers, educational assessors, and researchers should pay attention to the *experience* of student learning, not just to the activities (Marton, Hounsell, and Entwistle, 1984, 1997). Their observations reveal that some students exhibit a "deep approach to learning" while others use a "surface approach." In the former, students seek a personal, meaningful understanding of the material being studied while the latter are content to simply reproduce the information presented during the course (1997, p. x).

EXHIBIT 1.3. OLD AND NEW PARADIGMS FOR COLLEGE TEACHING.

	Old Paradigm	New Paradigm
Knowledge	Transferred from faculty to students	Jointly constructed by students and faculty
Student	Passive vessel to be filled by faculty's knowledge	Active constructor, discoverer, transformer of knowledge
Mode of learning	Memorizing	Relating
Faculty purpose	Classify and sort students	Develop students' competencies and talents
Student growth, goals	Students strive to complete requirements, achieve certification within a discipline	Students strive to focus on continual lifelong learning within a broader system
Relationships	Impersonal relationship among students and between faculty and students	Personal relationship among students and between faculty and students
Context	Competitive, individualistic	Cooperative learning in classroom and cooperative teams among faculty
Climate	Conformity, cultural uniformity	Diversity and personal esteem; cultural diversity and commonality
Power	Faculty holds and exercises power, authority, and control	Students are empowered; power is shared among students and between students and faculty
Assessment	Norm-referenced (that is, grading on the curve); typically use multiple-choice items; student rating of instruction at end of course	Criterion-referenced (that is, grading to predefined standards); typically use performances and portfolios; continual assessment of instruction
Ways of knowing	Logical-scientific	Narrative
Epistemology	Reductionist; facts and memorization	Constructivist; inquiry and invention
Technology use	Drill and practice; textbook substitute; chalk-and-talk substitute	Problem solving, communication, collaboration, information access, expression
Teaching assumption	Any expert can teach	Teaching is complex and requires considerable training

Source: Campbell and Smith, 1997, pp. 275–276. Used by permission.

An awareness of this distinction implies that teachers need to think about the impact of how they teach and assess, and not just on *how much* students learn but on the *quality* of that learning (p. x, my emphasis).

Now that we have all these new perspectives and paradigms, what can or should teachers do differently? What new ways of teaching and learning have been developed that can augment the traditional practices of lecture and class discussion?

New Forms of Teaching

During the last two decades teachers have been experimenting with and exploring a number of alternative approaches that fall under the general heading of active and experiential learning. Despite the fact that these efforts have proceeded in a more or less uncoordinated fashion, teachers—supported by an increasing number of campus-based teaching/learning centers—have found value in the following ways of teaching and learning.

A number of books summarize the new ideas on teaching and learning that have emerged in the last few decades. Among the ones I have found useful are *Teaching and Learning on the Edge of the Millennium*, edited by M. Svinicki (1999); *Changing College Classrooms*, edited by D. Halpern (1994); *Teaching Tips*, by W. McKeachie and others (1999); *Tools for Teaching*, by B. Davis (1993); *New Paradigms for College Teaching*, edited by W. Campbell and K. Smith (1997); and *Better Teaching, More Learning*, by J. Davis (1993).

Role-Playing, Simulation, Debate, and Case Studies. Although these are discrete teaching activities rather than more general teaching strategies, together they offer students an experience that has significant psychological and social as well as intellectual dimensions. In any case they provide a clear alternative to teaching as "dispensing information" (Bonwell and Eison, 1991).

Writing to Learn. Teachers have used writing for many years—but primarily to assess learning, as with term papers and essay questions on tests, rather than as an integral part of the learning process. The whole writing-across-the-curriculum effort made the argument that writing activities can also enhance the process and quality of student learning (Zinsser, 1988; Bean, 1996).

Small Group Learning. The last decade or so has seen a dramatic increase in the use of small groups, sometimes in the form of temporary groups (as with cooperative learning) and sometimes in the form of permanent groups that develop into high-performance teams (team-based learning). Given the right kind of structure and assignments, small groups can create powerful kinds of learning—about the subject, the problem-solving process, oneself, working with others, cross-cultural awareness, and so on (Johnson, Johnson, and Smith, 1991; Millis and Cottell, 1998; Michaelsen, Knight, and Fink, 2002).

Assessment as Learning. Teachers have of course been assessing students as long as formal education has existed. But more recently educators have been finding ways to incorporate assessment activities as part of the learning process itself. Alverno College uses learning portfolios and the resources of its extensive Assessment Center to give continuous developmental feedback to students about their learning, as part of what the staff call "student assessment as learning" (Mentkowski, 1999). At the level of individual courses, the now-popular Classroom Assessment Techniques serve the same purpose: feedback, usually ungraded, is provided frequently so students can enhance the quality of their learning and teachers can assess the effectiveness of different teaching and learning techniques and strategies (Angelo and Cross, 1993).

Problem-Based Learning. One of the more powerful teaching strategies to emerge in recent times is problem-based learning. In this strategy, the problem comes first. Used somewhat widely in medical schools and to a lesser extent in other professional schools, students learn in a way that simulates actual working conditions as closely as possible. Students, like professionals, encounter an open-ended, ill-defined problem. They must learn to make a preliminary analysis, gather information or data, assess the relevance of the new information, propose a solution, and assess the quality of their tentative solution. Evidence indicates that students learn how to analyze and solve problems much more effectively this way, compared, for example, to the traditional medical school curriculum of "learn all the facts" for two years and only then proceed to learn how to apply the by-now half-forgotten facts (Wilkerson and Gijselaers, 1996; Duch, Groh, and Allen, 2001).

Service Learning. Although it has a number of historical predecessors, service learning has emerged rapidly during the 1990s as a way of linking higher education with a felt need for more community involvement, both by students and by the institution itself. The basic idea is that students enroll in a course on a given topic, and then during the course engage in some kind of related activity in the community. By adding an experience component that involves both service to others and a chance to observe significant community problems or issues, students add a whole new dimension of quality to their learning (Jacoby, 1996; Rhoads and Howard, 1998; Zlotkowski, 1998).

Online Learning. Clearly the new kid on the block in terms of alternative ways of learning, online learning nonetheless has already displayed the potential to change the whole structure of higher education. By putting learning material on a CD-ROM or Web site, or by creating opportunities for electronic communication among the teacher and students, institutions offering online learning can provide learning on demand, literally anywhere, anytime. Despite valid questions about the impact of the loss of the residential experience, online learning is here to stay and is growing rapidly. The key issue, which remains to be answered, is how to ensure that this mode of delivering educational programs will result in high-quality learning.

The number of new ideas has become so great that what is needed now is a conceptual framework that will organize these ideas and show more clearly how they relate to one another. In my view, this is the reason we need a thorough understanding of the course design process.

The Significance of Learning About Course Design

What is it that faculty need to learn about and can learn about that will enable them to provide a higher-quality learning experience for students? In my view, four general aspects of teaching—sketched in Figure 1.1—are involved in all teaching, regardless of whether that teaching is effective or ineffective, traditional or innovative. All teachers need to have some knowledge of the subject matter, make decisions about the design of their instruction, interact with students, and

FIGURE 1.1. THE FOUR COMPONENTS OF TEACHING.

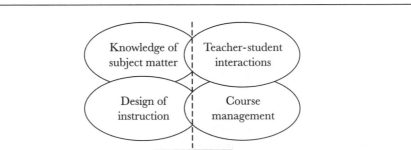

manage course events. The first two in general take place before the course begins; the other two after it begins.

This view implies that teachers who want to improve their teaching can do so by improving their competence in one or more of these four aspects of teaching. Improving any one of these aspects of teaching will clearly be of value. However, based on my several years of experience working with faculty, I see differences in the degree to which each of these factors is likely to make a major difference in the quality of one's teaching.

For example, most college faculty members have a good command of their subject matter, thanks to that being the dominant focus in graduate school and in the faculty selection procedures at most institutions. Although it is true that some faculty could benefit from rethinking what beginning learners need to learn (as opposed to advanced learners like themselves), overall, knowledge of subject matter is not a major bottleneck to better teaching and learning in higher education.

"Teacher-student interactions" is an umbrella term that refers to all the different ways teachers interact with their students: lecturing, leading class discussions, meeting with individual students during office hours, communicating by e-mail, and so on. This aspect of teaching, by my observation, is a skill that runs the full spectrum from poor to excellent. Some faculty members have a personality and a set of social skills that make it easy for them to interact naturally with students in a way that enhances learning. Others need to learn how to be more dynamic, establish better credibility, and otherwise relate better with their students. For a significant percentage of college teachers, learning how to improve their interactions with students would be a major advance. For the others, this is not a primary problem.

"Course management" refers to being organized and ready for the different events in a course, for example, by having assignments ready when they are needed, grading and returning exams promptly, having grade information ready when a student requests it, and so on. Occasionally I see situations where this is a serious problem. But for most professors, course management is not a major problem.

"Design of instruction," on the other hand, is a skill for which few college-level teachers have extensive training. Some have been fortunate enough to learn about the design of learning experiences because they went through teacher training as an undergraduate, had a course on this subject as a graduate student, or have participated in an in-service faculty development program on instructional design. But most faculty members simply follow the traditional ways of teaching in their particular discipline. They lack the conceptual tools they need to significantly rethink and reconstruct the set of teaching and learning activities they use. In my experience, of these four basic aspects of teaching, faculty knowledge about course design is the most significant bottleneck to better teaching and learning in higher education.

Potential Impact on Problems Faced by Teachers

Looking at this same issue another way, it also seems that course design has the greatest potential for solving the problems that faculty frequently face in their teaching. To test this proposition, it's useful to look at three common problems and ask which of three possible responses is likely to be of most value.

Getting Students to Prepare Before Class. Teachers frequently complain that they cannot get students to do their reading and other homework assignments before coming to class. Hence the class is unprepared for working on challenging problems and questions. What might a faculty member do to address this problem?

- Assign bigger penalties for not doing the readings beforehand.
- Give students a pep talk.
- Redesign the course to give students a reason to do the readings.

All three options are potentially helpful. But most people select the redesign option as most likely to solve the preparation problem and thereby position students to engage in a more significant learning experience.

Student Boredom. Another common problem is that students are bored, either with the teacher's lectures or with the whole course. If the teacher wants to do something about student boredom in a way that would have the biggest impact on the quality of student learning, which of the following options, based on the three of the four aspects of teaching, would most likely accomplish this goal?

- Enhance the teacher's lecturing skills.
- Insert more material from cutting-edge research.
- Redesign the course to replace lecturing with more active learning.

Each of these responses has the potential to reduce student boredom. But when I present this question in workshops for teachers, participants almost always select the third option, and I would wholeheartedly agree. Redesigning the course to incorporate more active learning has the greatest potential not only to solve the student boredom problem but also to increase the quality of student learning.

Poor Retention of Knowledge. To test this general proposition one more time, a third problem that teachers sometimes confront is that their students seem to learn the material in a course, as evidenced by exam scores. But then they seem unable to retain this knowledge when they move on to other courses. What could a teacher do to solve this problem?

- Make the tests better (or tougher).
- Give students a refresher course during inter-session.
- Redesign the course to give students more experience with using what they have learned.

Most research would support the third option again, in the expectation that opportunities to apply knowledge will lead to deeper understanding and greater retention of the learning. And this means redesigning the course to provide more application opportunities.

Overall Significance of Learning About Course Design

If faculty members can learn effective procedures for designing courses, it will have value for a variety of reasons. It will give them the tools they need to move much closer to making their dreams a reality. It will allow them to address many of the classroom problems they face as teachers. It will provide an organizing framework for understanding the role and significance of many of the new ideas on teaching. And it will provide institution leaders with a needed direction for improving the quality of educational curricula and the quality of instruction in the courses within those curricula.

While I clearly understand and acknowledge the important role that content knowledge and interacting well with students have in teaching, I have become convinced over the years that learning how to design courses is the missing link that can integrate new ideas about teaching, solve major teaching problems, and allow institutions to offer better support for faculty and better educational programs for students (and society).

An Invitation to a New Way of Thinking About Teaching

I began this chapter by noting that college teachers everywhere continually face the question of whether to keep teaching the way they always have or to learn how to change and improve. I built a case for change by describing the need for better learning by students, the availability of new and seemingly better ideas about college teaching, and the fact that institutions are in a period of change and hence may be able to provide better support for faculty change. In my view, this all adds up to an invitation to change and to develop new ways of thinking about teaching and learning. The situation has never been better for faculty to learn and to begin to find the intellectual and institutional support they need to create the kinds of learning experiences for students that faculty in fact wish for in their own special dreams.

This book is an attempt to organize and present some ideas about one fundamental part of the whole change process—that of designing instruction. If faculty can learn how to design their courses more effectively, students are much more likely to have significant learning experiences, the kind that are being called for in many parts of society today.

But this book is also about dreams. My dream is that faculty will be encouraged to embrace their own dreams about teaching and learning. But I hope they will not only dream of something special happening; they will also come to believe *it is possible to make it happen.*

To get this process started, Chapter Two introduces a language for articulating learning goals that will allow faculty and other educational leaders to more effectively describe the kinds of learning that they value and dream about.

CHAPTER TWO

A TAXONOMY OF SIGNIFICANT LEARNING

If learning is regarded not as the acquisition of information, but as a search for meaning and coherence in one's life and, if an emphasis is placed on what is learned *and its* personal significance to the learner, *rather than* how much is learned, *researchers would gain valuable new insights into both the mechanisms of learning and the relative advantages of teacher-controlled and learner-controlled modes of learning.*

—PHILIP CANDY (1991)

Some years ago I was visiting with my doctor during an annual physical, and we started talking about the quality of our country's schools and colleges. As a man concerned about public affairs, he expressed a feeling that seems to be widespread in society at the present time, that "students don't seem to be learning much these days." My response was, "No, they are learning things. They just aren't learning the 'right' things, the things that they need to be learning."

The distinction I was trying to make that day—and the distinction that Candy makes so well in the opening quote—is the difference between a content-centered and a learning-centered approach to teaching. If higher education hopes to craft a more meaningful way of educating students, as advocated by the multiple constituencies cited in the preceding chapter, then college professors will need to find a new and better way of teaching, one that focuses on the *quality* of student learning. How can we begin the process of doing this?

For the past twenty years, I have been working with faculty members as an instructional consultant at the University of Oklahoma to assist them in finding ways to improve their teaching and their students' learning. As we worked at that task, we found ourselves on a journey that seemed to parallel the national effort described in Chapter One: searching for better ways of providing significant learning experiences for our students.

Before long we realized that we needed to find or create a new set of concepts and terms to describe those experiences. We needed a language that could accurately and fully describe the kind of impact we wanted to have on students' lives. This new language would need to be applicable across a wide range of disciplines and learning situations. It would also have to satisfy the felt needs of the several major constituencies in higher education: faculty members, students, administrators, disciplinary associations, employer groups, and so on.

This chapter describes a new "taxonomy of significant learning" that encompasses a wide range of different kinds of learning. It includes the types of learning that many constituencies (students, faculty, professional associations, commentators on the educational needs of modern society, and so on and on) deem to be significant. It goes on to show how to create course goals based on the taxonomy and describe how the taxonomy reflects the kinds of learning described and advocated in the literature on college teaching. It also points out the paradigm shift embedded in this taxonomy and addresses a number of questions associated with such a fundamental change in perspective.

Beginning the Journey

My own search for better ideas on teaching began a number of years ago when I was waiting in an office on campus one day and a receptionist asked me: "Given all your experience of observing other people's courses, what do you think makes a good course 'good'?" After recovering from the embarrassed realization that I did not have a ready answer for this innocent but profound question, I began working on a reply and eventually developed a list that I capriciously called "Fink's Five Principles of Fine Teaching." The last three items on this list have been modified from time to time, but the first two have always remained at the top of the list. The current list is as follows:

Good courses are courses that. . .

- Challenge students to significant kinds of learning.
- Use active forms of learning.
- Have teachers who *care*—about the subject, their students, and about teaching and learning.
- Have teachers who *interact well* with students.
- Have a good system of feedback, assessment, and grading.

This list simply reflects my view that, if someone's teaching successfully meets these criteria, its impact is going to be good, no matter what else is bad about it—even if a teacher is not a great lecturer or well organized. Conversely, if someone's teaching does not meet these five criteria, that teaching is poor, no matter what else is good about it.

The single most important item on this list, in my view, has always been the first one. If students have indeed been challenged to and have achieved something that can meaningfully be called "significant learning," then the learning experience has been good, no matter what else is bad about the course. The bottom line is that significant learning has been achieved. This then leads to the question: What kinds of learning can be said to constitute significant learning?

What Makes Learning Significant?

When teachers face the task of describing what they want students to get out of their course and when they want something that would take them beyond their own thinking, some turn to the well-known taxonomy of educational objectives formulated by Benjamin Bloom and his associates in the 1950s. Although there are in fact three taxonomies (cognitive, affective, and psychomotor), teachers refer to the one in the cognitive domain most frequently (Bloom, 1956). The cognitive taxonomy consists of six kinds of learning arranged in a hierarchical sequence. These are, from the highest to the lowest

- Evaluation
- Synthesis
- Analysis
- Application
- Comprehension
- Knowledge (meaning the ability to recall information)

Teachers have used this taxonomy both as a framework for formulating course objectives and as a basis for testing student learning.

There is no question about the value of what Bloom and his associates accomplished by creating this taxonomy. Any model that commands this kind of respect half a century later is extraordinary. However, as noted in Chapter One, individuals and organizations involved in higher education are expressing a need for important kinds of learning that do not emerge easily from the Bloom taxonomy, for example: learning how to learn, leadership and interpersonal skills, ethics, communication skills, character, tolerance, and the ability to adapt to change. My interpretation of the aforementioned statements is that they are expressing a need for *new kinds* of learning, kinds that go well beyond the cognitive domain of Bloom's taxonomy and even beyond cognitive learning itself. This suggests that the time may have arrived when we need a new and broader taxonomy of significant learning. With an awareness of this need in mind, I have reviewed descriptions of quality teaching and learning and have attempted the task of creating a new taxonomy, one that describes various ways in which learning can be significant and represents my effort to synthesize several decades of conversations with students and teachers on this topic.

In the process of constructing this taxonomy, I was guided by a particular perspective on learning: I defined learning in terms of change. For learning to occur, there has to be some kind of change in the learner. No change, no learning. And significant learning requires that there be some kind of lasting change that is important in terms of the learner's life. With this perspective in mind, I created a taxonomy based on the six kinds of significant learning shown in Figure 2.1.

FIGURE 2.1. TAXONOMY OF SIGNIFICANT LEARNING.

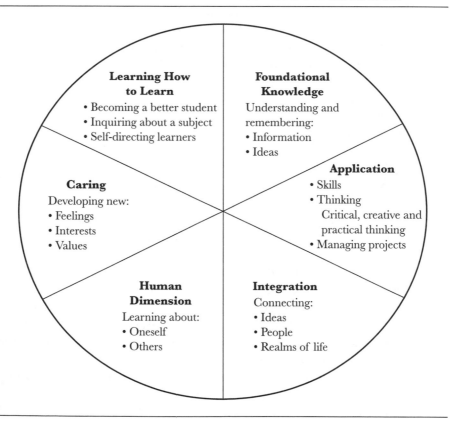

Major Categories in the Taxonomy of Significant Learning

Each category of significant learning contains several more specific kinds of learning that are related in some way and have a distinct value for the learner.

Foundational Knowledge. At the base of most other kinds of learning is the need for students to know something. *Knowing,* as used here, refers to students' ability to understand and remember specific information and ideas. It is important for people today to have some valid basic knowledge, for example, about science, history, literature, geography, and other aspects of their world. They also need to understand major ideas or perspectives, for example, what evolution is (and what it is not), what capitalism is (and is not), and so forth.

Special value: Foundational knowledge provides the *basic understanding* that is necessary for other kinds of learning.

Application. Besides picking up facts and ideas, students often learn how to engage in some new kind of action, which may be intellectual, physical, or social. Learning how to engage in various kinds of thinking (critical, creative, practical) is an important form of application learning. But this category of significant learning also includes developing certain skills (such as communication or playing the piano) or learning how to manage complex projects.

Special value: Application learning allows other kinds of learning to become *useful.*

Integration. When students are able to see and understand the connections between different things, an important kind of learning has occurred. Sometimes they make connections between specific ideas, between whole realms of ideas, between people, or between different realms of life (say, between school and work or between school and leisure life).

Special value: The act of making new connections gives learners a new form of *power,* especially intellectual power.

Human Dimension. When students learn something important about themselves or about others, it enables them to function and interact more effectively. They discover the personal and social implications of what they have learned. What they learn or the way in which they learn sometimes gives students a new understanding of themselves (self-image) or a new vision of what they want to become (self-ideal). At other times, they acquire a better understanding of others: how and why others act the way they do, or how the learner can interact more effectively with others.

Special value: This kind of learning informs students about *the human significance* of what they are learning.

Caring. Sometimes a learning experience changes the degree to which students care about something. This may be reflected in the form of new feelings, interests, or values. Any of these changes means students now care about something to a greater degree than they did before, or in a different way.

Special value: When students care about something, they then have the *energy* they need for learning more about it and making it a part of their lives. Without the energy for learning, nothing significant happens.

Learning How to Learn. In the course of their studies, students can also learn something about the process of learning itself. They may be learning how to be a better student, how to engage in a particular kind of inquiry (such as the scientific method), or how to become a self-directing learner. All these constitute important forms of learning how to learn.

Special value: This kind of learning enables students to *continue* learning in the future and to do so with *greater effectiveness.*

Interactive Nature of Significant Learning

One important feature of this taxonomy is that it is not hierarchical but rather relational and even interactive. The diagram in Figure 2.2 illustrates the interactive character of this taxonomy. This more dynamic diagram is intended to show that each kind of learning is related to the other kinds of learning and that achieving any one kind of learning simultaneously enhances the possibility of achieving the other kinds of learning as well. Why is this so important?

This interrelation matters to teachers because it means the various kinds of learning are synergistic. And this in turn means that *teaching is no longer a zero-sum game.* That is, teachers don't automatically have to give up one kind of learning to achieve another. Instead, when a teacher finds a way to help students achieve one kind of learning, this can in fact enhance, not decrease, student achievement in the other kinds of learning. For example, if a teacher finds a way to help students learn how to use the information and concepts in a course to solve certain kinds of problems effectively (application), this makes it easier for them to get excited about the value of the subject (caring). Or when students learn how to effectively relate this subject to other ideas and subjects (integration), this makes it easier for students to see the significance of the course material for themselves and for others (human dimension). When a course or learning experience is able to promote all six kinds of learning, one has had a learning experience that can truly be deemed significant.

FIGURE 2.2. THE INTERACTIVE NATURE OF SIGNIFICANT LEARNING.

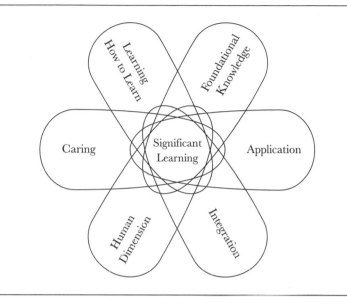

Formulating Course Goals Around Significant Learning

The taxonomy of significant learning has two major implications for teachers. The first is that the learning goals for a course should include but also go beyond content mastery. Including something besides foundational knowledge will make the learning experience inherently more worthwhile and at the same time make it more interesting for learners. The second is that if teachers use a combination of significant learning goals, it will be possible to create some interaction effects and synergy that greatly enhance the achievement of significant learning by students.

But to enjoy these benefits, teachers need to know how to formulate new course goals around the ideas of significant learning. How does one do that? Chapter Three contributes additional ideas to answering this question, but it's useful to start by looking at a general version of significant learning goals and then at a course-specific version.

General Version

Some teachers like to describe their course goals in general terms; others prefer more specifics. For those who prefer the former approach, Exhibit 2.1 shows a set of course goals that reflect the six kinds of significant learning. Most teachers

EXHIBIT 2.1. GENERAL COURSE GOALS FORMULATED IN TERMS OF SIGNIFICANT LEARNING.

By the end of this course, students will. . . .

Understand and remember key concepts, terms, relationships, and so on.

Know how to *use* the content.

Be able to *relate* this subject to other subjects.

Understand the *personal and social implications* of knowing about this subject.

Care about the subject (and about learning more on the subject).

Know *how to keep on learning* about this subject after the course is over.

would find these meaningful and would be delighted if students in their courses achieved these goals.

A generalized form of course goals, such as those in Exhibit 2.1, leaves open the question of what the specific concepts, terms, and relationships will be, what specific uses will be made of the content, and so forth. These will presumably become clear during the course as students work their way through the readings, lectures, application exercises, and other learning activities.

Developing Course-Specific Learning Goals

Other teachers prefer to describe their course goals, even initially, in more specific terms. What might the learning goals look like when formulated in terms of a specific course? To give a quick answer to this question, let me describe the learning goals for a course on world regional geography that I have taught, formulated around the six categories of significant learning.

"After this course is over, students will. . . ."

Foundational Knowledge

- Have a mental map of the world and be able to correctly locate major places—countries, mountain ranges, rivers, cities, oceans, and so on.
- Understand major geographic concepts—physical geography, human geography, scale, demographic transition, and so on.

Application

- Be able to find information on and analyze regional problems from a geographic perspective.
- Be able to use an atlas effectively and efficiently.

Integration

- Identify the interactions between geography and other realms of knowledge such as history, politics, economics, social structure, and so on.

Human Dimension

- Be able to identify ways in which one's personal life affects and is affected by interactions with other world regions.
- Be able to intelligently discuss world events with other people and the impact of geography on these events.

Caring

- Be interested in other places of the world and want to continue learning about those places via reading, TV, the Internet, and travel.

Learning How to Learn

- Be able to interpret the geographic significance of new information and ideas acquired in the future.
- Be familiar with a number of popular geography journals and other sources of knowledge about other parts of the world.
- Have some specific ideas about what else it would be desirable to know about other places in the world.

When different professors develop goals for their own courses, those goals will naturally look quite different from my sample. But this initial version nonetheless illustrates what significant learning goals for a specific course might look like. The next chapter, which addresses the initial steps in designing a course, will offer additional examples of how teachers create significant learning goals for specific courses.

Significant Learning and the Literature on College Teaching

One of the attractive features of a taxonomy as broad as this one is that it encompasses and integrates a wide range of literature on desirable kinds of learning. Familiar curricular goals come to life when viewed in relation to the taxonomy. In addition, the new taxonomy can organize and make sense of a broad range of published statements on what students can and should learn at the college level.

General Curricular Goals

The literature on college teaching contains numerous recommendations about what teachers should be teaching and students should be learning. By looking at these in the framework of significant learning, it becomes easier to see both what is distinctively valuable about each one and that none of them capture the whole of significant learning on their own.

Exhibit 2.2 contains a list of several educational goals that have been described in the literature of higher education as desirable for college courses and curricula. These have been sorted into groups, according to the kind of significant learning that each seems to best express.

The next step in understanding the value and meaning of this taxonomy is to relate it even more broadly to the literature on college teaching. People have written extensively about what students should learn and about how to teach so that students learn something significant. One of the tests of any taxonomy is how well it interprets and makes sense out of this literature.

To review this literature, I will start with the most familiar category, foundational knowledge, and work toward the more novel categories in the taxonomy.

First Kind of Significant Learning: Foundational Knowledge. The basic meaning of this kind of learning is *understanding and remembering.* Any sustained effort to learn about any topic, subject, or activity will almost inevitably require students to acquire a basic understanding of particular data, concepts, relationships, and perspectives, as well as the ability to recall this knowledge in the future.

However, some educators have offered important ideas to keep in mind, even when pursuing a basic understanding of a subject. Jerome Bruner is famous for many visionary ideas in education, and one of his important contributions is his belief that all subjects have a certain logic or conceptual structure associated with them (Bruner, 1960, 1966). Hence one of the responsibilities of teachers should be not just to teach factual knowledge about a given subject but also to help students gain a full understanding of that subject's underlying conceptual structure. Only then will students be in a good position to do something worthwhile with their new knowledge. Note that the second part of this argument, doing something with knowledge, refers to what the taxonomy of significant learning calls *application.* Bruner is correct, however, in arguing that a powerful grasp of foundational knowledge will require an in-depth understanding of the conceptual structure of a subject, something more than a large collection of poorly related facts and concepts.

During the last few decades, in part as a result of Bruner's influence but also as a result of rethinking educational ideas, practitioners in a number of disciplines have tried to articulate the key concepts and the conceptual structure of their disciplines.

EXHIBIT 2.2. MAJOR EDUCATIONAL GOALS AND SIGNIFICANT LEARNING.

This exhibit presents examples of the many types of significant learning described and advocated in the general literature on teaching and learning. The examples are categorized according to the specific type of learning they exemplify within the overarching framework of the taxonomy of significant learning.

Learning How to Learn:
How to be a better student: Learning how to engage in self-regulated learning or deep learning

How to inquire and construct knowledge: Learning how to engage in the scientific method, historical method, and other forms of inquiry

How to pursue self-directed or intentional learning: Developing a learning agenda and plan; becoming an intentional learner; becoming skilled in autodidaxy (the ability to direct one's own learning and life); being a reflective practitioner

Caring:
Wanting to be a good student: Wanting to have a high GPA or be an honors student

Becoming excited about a particular activity or subject: For example, developing a keen interest in bird watching, reading history, or listening to music

Developing a commitment to live right: For example, deciding to learn and follow Covey's seven habits of highly effective people

Human Dimension:
Leadership: Learning how to be an effective leader

Ethics, character building: Developing character and living by ethical principles

Self-authorship: Learning how to create and take responsibility for one's own life

Multicultural education: Becoming culturally sensitive in one's interactions with others

Working as a member of a team: Knowing how to contribute to a team

Citizenship: Being a responsible citizen of one's local community, nation state, and other political entity

Serving others (local, national, world). Contributing to the well-being of others at multiple levels of society

Environmental ethics: Having ethical principles in relation to the nonhuman world

Integration:
Interdisciplinary learning: Connecting different disciplines and perspectives

Learning communities: Connecting different people

Learning and living/working: Connecting different realms of life

Application:
Critical thinking: Analyzing and critiquing issues and situations

Practical thinking: Developing problem-solving and decision-making capabilities

Creativity: Creating new ideas, products, and perspectives

Managing complex projects: Being able to coordinate and sequence multiple tasks in a single project

Performance skills: Developing capabilities in such areas as foreign language, communication, operating technology, performing in the fine arts, sports

Foundational Knowledge:
Conceptual understanding: Developing a full understanding of the concepts associated with a subject to a degree that allows explanations, predictions, and so on.

One notable example of this is the recent effort in physics education by David Hestenes and his associates at Arizona State University to develop a clearer statement of the most fundamental concepts in physics (Hestenes, 1999). They have gone on to develop ways of helping students acquire a conceptual understanding of physics rather than just the ability to correctly perform the calculations involved in the usual exercise problems.

The central theme in all this is that almost all kinds of significant learning will be based on, and hence will require students to have, an in-depth understanding of some subject matter. And this is why it has been labeled here as *foundational knowledge*.

Second Kind of Significant Learning: Application. After foundational knowledge, application learning is probably the most common educational goal for many college teachers. They frequently talk about wanting their students to "learn how to *use* knowledge" in some way. However, knowledge can be used in multiple ways, which is why this category of significant learning has multiple meanings. As used here, *application* or using foundational knowledge includes developing particular skills, learning how to manage complex projects, and developing the ability to engage in various kinds of thinking.

Skills. When teachers say they want students to learn how to use some particular knowledge, they are sometimes referring to students' learning how to develop a skill of some kind, that is, the ability to engage in a particular kind of action. Sometimes this skill has a significant physical component associated with it. For example, anyone who learns how to play the piano must pick up a certain amount of foundational knowledge: notes, scales, harmonies, and so on. But at some point, new pianists must learn how to use their arms, hands, feet, and fingers to make this instrument create music. When they are learning how to do that, they are developing a skill, an ability to engage in a particular kind of action. Other familiar examples of skills include writing, oral communication, using computer programs, and operating laboratory equipment such as microscopes and burners.

Most skills have criteria associated with them that distinguish competent or expert-level performance of these skills from novice-level performance. The goal of any skill-focused learning is to move learners along a continuum in the direction of being able to perform an action at a higher level of competence.

Managing Complex Projects. Another kind of application is the ability to manage complex projects. Like the use of skill, this activity also has criteria associated with high-quality performance. But what distinguishes this activity from other forms of application learning is the complexity of the activity. This complexity requires students to learn how to organize and coordinate several tasks as part of one major project.

A good example of a complex project comes from a professor of regional and city planning at the University of Oklahoma who had a course that involved both undergraduate and graduate students. This professor had his students develop ideas on how the city of Los Angeles could beautify a river running through the city and then make an actual proposal to the city to implement the project. This required the students to learn about urban waterways, how to find information on Los Angeles and their particular river, how to use computers to build models and graphics, and then how to engage in the politics, marketing, and public relations required to sell their idea to the city. Part of what made this project distinctive is that the students had to learn how to organize and coordinate many different tasks to successfully complete the whole project.

A modest but perhaps more familiar example of learning to manage complex projects is when professors have students engage in a complex research project. Students have to learn how to organize and coordinate several subtasks to complete the whole project: learning how to focus the topic, finding relevant sources of information, extracting key information and ideas from the literature, analyzing and organizing these into a coherent paper or presentation, and the like. Completing such tasks helps students develop a general ability for managing complex projects.

The General Concept of Thinking. A third and very important kind of application is learning how to think. Few topics have received more attention in the literature on college teaching than this one. Almost every teacher who talks at length about educational goals will eventually say in one way or another, "I want my students to learn how to think." The scholarly literature on this topic is so voluminous that two authors have put together an annotated bibliography on the teaching of thinking (Cassel and Congleton, 1993). However, even a quick review of this literature makes it clear that teachers and writers are often referring to very different things when they use the term *thinking*. This has happened in part because of the complexity of the concept and in part because it is such an attractive term; people use it to describe their favorite kind of learning, whatever that is.

Regardless of which particular view of thinking a teacher holds, it will constitute a form of application learning. To cite one example that I have found particularly attractive, Robert Sternberg (1989) has what he calls the "triarchic" view of thinking, which he uses to help students learn to think more effectively. He sees *thinking* as a general concept and then identifies three distinct subcategories: critical thinking, creative thinking, and practical thinking. My own translation of this view makes the following distinction among these three kinds of thinking. *Critical thinking,* the term invoked most widely in higher education, has a specific meaning in Sternberg's triarchic view. Here it refers to the process of analyzing and evaluating something; hence criteria play an especially important role. *Creative thinking* occurs when one imagines and creates a new idea, design, or product; in these instances, novelty and "fit with the context" play a key role. *Practical thinking* occurs when a person is learning how to use and apply something, as when trying to solve a problem or make a decision. The product of this kind of thinking is a solution or a decision, and the effectiveness of the solution or decision is paramount. The use of case studies in business schools is a good example of promoting practical thinking; students are generally learning how to solve problems and make decisions.

To help teachers see the classroom meaning of this view of thinking, Sternberg created a list of questions that illustrates each of the three kinds of thinking, for six different kinds of courses. (See Exhibit 2.3.) Again, what this list shows is that, unlike many writers, Sternberg uses "thinking" rather than "critical thinking" as the appropriate label for the general concept; *critical thinking* is still important, but it is only one of three important kinds of thinking. I find this distinction helpful when visiting with teachers to talk about what it is they specifically want their students to learn. What are some familiar examples of course goals that reflect these three kinds of thinking?

Critical Thinking. When college teachers want their students to learn how to analyze and evaluate something, they have a critical thinking goal. Literature teachers want their students to "analyze and evaluate" when they ask students to interpret a novel. They want students to analyze the novel in terms of various concepts (plot development, the portrayal of characters, the creation of dramatic tension, and so on); whole-class discussions are then frequently used for students to learn how to assess different interpretations. Science teachers want their students to analyze when they ask them to use previously explained concepts (such as energy conservation or plate tectonics) to explain (or to predict) what is happening (or will happen) to certain phenomena under particular circumstances. Then they ask the students individually or collectively to assess those explanations and predictions.

In these and similar teaching situations, teachers are wanting their students to engage in and improve their ability to think critically. To do this, students need to have the relevant conceptual understanding, but they also need criteria for assessing the quality of interpretations, explanations, and predictions.

Creative Thinking. People who teach in the humanities are quite accustomed to encouraging their students to engage in creative thinking. In applied courses in the

EXHIBIT 2.3. QUESTIONS DESIGNED
TO PROMPT THREE KINDS OF THINKING.

Field	Critical Thinking	Creative Thinking	Practical Thinking
Psychology	Compare Freud's theory of dreaming to Crick's.	Design an experiment to test a theory of dreaming.	What are the implications of Freud's theory of dreaming for your own life?
Biology	Evaluate the validity of the bacterial theory of ulcers.	Design an experiment to test the bacterial theory of ulcers.	How would the bacterial theory of ulcers change conventional treatment regiments?
Literature	In what ways were Catherine Earnshaw and Daisy Miller similar?	Write an alternative ending to *Wuthering Heights,* uniting Catherine and Heathcliff in life.	Why are lovers sometimes cruel to each other and what can we do about it?
History	How did events in post WWI Germany lead to the rise of Nazism?	How might Truman have encouraged the surrender of Japan without A-bombing Hiroshima?	What lessons does Nazism hold for events in Bosnia today?
Mathematics	How is this mathematical proof flawed?	Prove [a given proposition] How might catastrophe theory be applied to psychology?	How is trigonometry applied to the construction of bridges?
Art	Compare and contrast how Rembrandt and Van Gogh used light in [specific paintings].	Draw a beam of light.	How could we reproduce the lighting in this painting in an actual room?

Source: Material supplied by Robert J. Sternberg, Psychology Department, Yale University. Used by permission.

humanities, teachers help their students find new forms and styles for expressing themselves in painting, writing, music, and other media. Even in nonapplied courses, teachers are often trying to get their students to find new interpretations of existing works. When this happens, they are encouraging their students to engage in creative thinking.

Creative thinking is also found in the social science and natural science areas. When teachers want their students to "think outside the box," to find new ways of answering questions, to develop new perspectives on the phenomena being studied, or to devise new solutions to old problems, they are urging their students to engage in creative thinking. The common element in creative thinking is helping students learn how to create new ideas, new ways of doing things.

Practical Thinking. A third kind of thinking is practical thinking, which means students are learning how to answer questions, make decisions, and solve problems. This is what we are doing when we ask students to engage in problem-solving or decision-making exercises. When teachers in business, engineering, or education, for example, say to their students, "Here is a problem. How would you solve it?" they are asking students to engage in practical thinking. When teachers say, "Here is a common situation where you have these choices. What choice or decision should you make?" they are again asking students to engage in practical thinking.

Whether we use hypothetical, simulated, or real problems and questions, we are asking students to learn how to engage in effective practical thinking, an ability that will have extensive value in their personal, social, and work life.

And that is the key value of all application learning. It provides students with a kind of learning that will be useful. Learning particular skills, learning how to manage complex projects, and learning how to engage in critical, creative, and practical thinking—these all allow students to take other kinds of learning and make them useful.

Third Kind of Significant Learning: Integration. The third realm of significant learning is integration. This is where students learn how to connect and relate various things to each other. Of the many examples that might be mentioned, I would like to note three major kinds of connections that many educators have emphasized.

Interdisciplinary Learning. Teachers have been interested for a long time in the goal of interdisciplinary learning. While recognizing the obvious need to continue learning about individual disciplines, a number of scholars have noted that most of the world's big problems are bigger than any single discipline (for example, see Davis, 1995). Therefore the world needs people who have learned how to look at problems from the perspectives of two or more disciplines and who can interact effectively with individuals who represent different perspectives and disciplines.

Sometimes interdisciplinary teaching is accomplished by one teacher in one course who presents the perspectives of two or more disciplines to the class. At other times, educators use team teaching, coordinated courses, interdisciplinary programs, or even the curriculum of a whole college to achieve interdisciplinary learning (Klein and Doty, 1994; Klein and Newell, 1996). Evergreen State University in Washington is one example of such a college; another is the College of Liberal Studies at the University of Oklahoma. The common element in all of these efforts is the goal of helping students learn how to connect and integrate different kinds of information, perspectives, and methods of inquiry and analysis—all in order to develop a more holistic understanding of a problem or issue.

Learning Communities. Another closely related activity that has gathered strong interest in the 1990s is the creation of learning communities. This activity also has the general goal of helping students learn how to integrate different perspectives but focuses on the strategy of connecting diverse people as well as diverse disciplines (Gabelnick and others, 1990; Shapiro and Levine, 1999).

These programs search for ways of creating new kinds of interactions between faculty, students, staff, and sometimes off-campus people. This is done in a variety of ways:

- Creating different residential arrangements
- Linking courses so that students take a set of courses together, often with team teaching as a corollary
- Bringing in outside people to do something with students on campus or sending students off-campus to work with people in other contexts and environments

Parker Palmer, in his enormously successful book *The Courage to Teach* (1998), also recommended and described another way of creating learning communities. Speaking partly allegorically and partly realistically, he urged educators to put the subject "in the center," and for the teacher and students to sit in a circle around the subject and try to learn about it together. The intent is to create a new kind of relationship between the teacher, the students, and the subject.

The theme that occurs repeatedly in the discussion of these ventures is the desirability of breaking down walls and overcoming the isolation of students and subjects from each other. That is, they are seeking to create hitherto absent connections and integration between different people and different ideas.

Connecting Academic Work with Other Areas of Life. A third closely related realm of educational effort has been in the direction of connecting what students learn in their academic work with other areas of their lives. These other areas often include students' work but also extend to students' personal and social lives.

When teachers have students interview older family members to learn via oral history, the students are learning how to gather information about history from a new source. But they are also developing a connection between the history they are studying in class and their own family life. When professors in pre-professional programs have students do internships or work in real-life settings while taking courses, the curriculum is intended to help students build connections between what they are learning in class and what they are or will be doing in the workplace. When professors create service learning opportunities, students are encouraged to find and create connections between what they are learning in class and the activities of the larger community in which they live. When teachers have students keep a journal, noting events in their personal lives that reflect whatever subject the students are studying, the teacher is trying to help students build connections between what they are learning in class and what is happening in other parts of their lives.

Fourth Kind of Significant Learning: Human Dimension. The fourth kind of significant learning addresses the important relationships and interactions we all have with ourselves and with others. When we learn how to fulfill these relationships in positive ways and how to honor and advance those relationships, we learn something very important. College students frequently report that learning about themselves and about others is among the most significant experiences they have during college. It is also clear that this is something very different from learning about "people out there," and the difference lies in the existence of a real relationship.

Learning About Self. When we learn about our Self, we might learn something that helps us understand who we are at the present time; this kind of learning changes or informs our self-image. At other times, we might learn something new about the person we want to become; this gives us a new self-ideal. Both are important and either may happen intentionally or as a by-product of the formal aspects of our education.

As an example of this kind of learning, imagine a new, first-generation college student taking a challenging chemistry or math class and thinking: "This material is difficult. But if I study smart and study hard, I find that I can do it. That is, I can understand challenging subjects and get good grades. I guess I am capable of doing college-level work." A student such as this can have doubts and uncertainty about being the kind of person who is capable of succeeding in college. But if the efforts go well, the student can develop a new self-image—as a new, more competent kind of person.

A student I interviewed some years ago told the story of how he was enrolled in a course on urban geography and how the teacher had the class working on an authentic project for the local city. One day the student was walking across campus with some maps under his arm and ran into a group of friends. They saw the maps, asked him what he was doing, and he told them he was working on a project to assess a new transportation system for the city. The friends were impressed. As a result of this exchange, this student felt he had become important in the eyes of his friends and therefore more worthwhile in his own eyes. But he also realized that he liked feeling this way, that is, feeling like a professional person. Consequently he decided that he wanted to become a professional city planner. What happened in this situation was that this person not only acquired a new self-image but also a new *self-ideal,* that is, a new image of the kind of person he wanted to become.

Journey Toward Self-Authorship. Marcia Baxter Magolda (1992, 1999, 2001) postulates an educational goal for all college teachers that is a powerful and valid example of this kind of significant learning: assisting students on their journey toward self-authorship. She is conducting a longitudinal study of a hundred students who began college in 1986 and has now followed these students into their early thirties. One of her conclusions is that it is possible for college teachers to do more than we are currently doing to assist students along on their journey toward being able to internally define their own beliefs, identity, and relationships, that is, toward self-authorship.

Underlying her recommendations are the beliefs that knowledge is complex and socially constructed and that Self is central to knowledge construction. Students must develop a strong sense of their own identity if they are going to take responsibility for constructing their own knowledge and the other aspects of their lives, that is, if they are going to engage in self-authorship.

Learning About Others. Sometimes our educational experiences enable us to better understand and interact with other people. For example, on my campus several professors are now using small groups with team-based learning in their classes. In one of these classes, a student team included an East Asian student. The group soon realized that this student was getting high scores on his individual tests but was often not volunteering his answers when they took the same test as a group. When they asked why he didn't speak up and share his answers more freely, he replied: "In my culture it is not polite to tell others they are wrong." After pondering this situation awhile, the rest of the group decided on a new strategy when it came time to take the group test. They would start their discussions by asking this student what his answer was and then go on to see what the rest of the group thought was correct. That way he wasn't forced into telling anyone they were wrong, yet the group was able to find out what his answer was. The students in this group learned a very important lesson about interacting with people from a different culture and specifically about people in cultures where saving face is very important.

A second example comes from a freshman orientation-to-college class I taught some years ago. That year I wanted to do something to counter the strong attitude of "me-ism" that I saw in that group of students. So I made arrangements for the class to do some community service. On this particular occasion we served lunch in a community kitchen called "Food for Friends." When the students later wrote about the experience, many commented on how they came to see poor people in a different light. They could see that these people were struggling hard to maintain their self-respect. And that experience in turn changed the way these students saw and interacted subsequently with other people in less fortunate circumstances than themselves.

In both these situations, students were acquiring a new understanding of and an ability to interact with others, that is, they were learning about the human dimension in learning and in life.

A Broader Concept of Others. Usually we are referring to other people when we speak of learning about Others. But sometimes *Others* extends to more than people.

I have been educated in very important ways by the writings and videotapes of Monty Roberts, the original "horse whisperer" (1997, 2001). As a young man he spent time observing wild horses in the open lands of Nevada and, as a result, developed an understanding of how they behaved and communicated with each other. Based on that, he created procedures for communicating and interacting with horses in a way that allows humans and horses to "join up" and do things together collaboratively rather than violently and forcefully. In this case, Monty Roberts (and other humans who have learned from him) has learned how to understand and interact with others, only in this case the Others are horses. In a similar vein, Native Americans sometimes speak of parts of nature as being significant Others in their lives.

Some people develop a similar, special kind of relationship with nonanimate Others, that is, with machines and technology. People who have read Charles Lindbergh's writings about his adventures with airplanes often conclude that he did not just operate airplanes, he "worked with them." Even the titles of his books reflect this relationship: *We* (1927) and *The Spirit of St. Louis* (1953). He had a relationship with this particular kind of technology, he understood it and cared for it deeply, and as a result seemed to be able to do things together with airplanes that others could not do. Today we often find people who have a similar kind of relationship with cars or computers. Again, these individuals have learned how to "understand and interact" with others, only in these cases the Other is a form of technology.

Human Dimension of Learning and Emotional Intelligence. The kind of learning I am referring to under the label of the human dimension of learning is similar to emotional intelligence as described by Daniel Goleman (1995, 1998). He has identified several different competences having to do with oneself (Personal Competence) and one's interactions with others (Social Competence):

Personal Competence:	*Social Competence:*
• *Self-Awareness:* Knowing one's internal states, preferences, resources, and intuitions	• *Empathy:* Awareness of other's feelings, needs, and concerns
• *Self-Regulation:* Managing one's internal states, impulses, and resources	• *Social Skills:* Adeptness at inducing desirable responses in others
• *Motivation:* Emotional tendencies that guide or facilitate reaching goals	

Source: Goleman, 1998, Table 1, pp. 26–27.

In essence Goleman is saying we must develop an understanding of ourselves and others, emotionally as well as intellectually; then we can learn how to direct our own activities and our interactions with others successfully. As he has documented so thoroughly, this kind of learning is extremely important for the quality of our personal lives as well as for our working lives.

Reciprocity of Learning About Self and Others. Once I started looking for examples of the human dimension in learning, I soon discovered a relationship that is extremely helpful to teachers: when one learns about one's Self, one almost inevitably learns about Others, and vice versa. This means that if teachers can work one kind of learning into their course, they will likely achieve both.

This relationship is found in several contexts. Teachers involved in minority cultural education have learned that students will learn about both their own ethnic group and other ethnic minorities at the same time, regardless of whether the course or curricular program primarily focuses on one or the other topic. Similarly, when students in a literature course read about characters in a novel, they often identify with and begin to relate to particular individuals in the story, thereby developing a fuller understanding of themselves while at the same time learning how to understand others.

One can also see this reciprocity in the list of major educational goals shown back in Exhibit 2.2: building character, learning how to interact with people different from oneself (multicultural insights), leadership, ethics (which may be personal, social, professional, or environmental), learning how to work effectively as a member of a team, citizenship, serving others, international awareness, and the rest. Some of these are focused primarily on learning about one's Self, others more on understanding Others. But essentially all of these involve learning about both, that is, developing a Self that is capable of interacting with Others in a more effective and productive way.

The lesson of this point is clear: Help students learn about Self and they will likely learn about Others, and vice versa.

Present in All Parts of the Curriculum? Some readers might wonder whether the human dimension aspect of significant learning is applicable to the natural sciences as well as the humanities and social sciences. To explore this question, I asked a physics teacher whether the human dimension kind of learning was relevant in his courses. After thinking a bit on the question, he decided that, yes, it was. He wants students to understand that the major figures in physics, as in all of science, are much like the students themselves. They all have very different personalities; some are noble, some are vain. Some gladly share their ideas and the results of their research with others; others are secretive and jealous of their work. Most have a strong passion, either about the awesome nature of the physical world or about research. This teacher's response suggests that this form of significant learning is applicable in all or almost all disciplines.

Fifth Kind of Significant Learning: Caring. The fifth kind of significant learning is caring. When I conduct workshops for faculty members on designing courses and significant learning, I often start by asking them to describe the most important things they would like students to get out of their courses. One of their most frequent answers is, "I want my students to get excited about. . . ." Sometimes the teachers want their students to get excited about the subject matter—"I want students to get excited about history." At other times the focus is on getting excited about learning as an activity—"I want students to be *curious*," or "I want them to be excited about doing research on [whatever]." Either way, what these teachers want is for their students to care more deeply about something, that is, to value something differently.

Caring as a Change in Feelings, Interests, or Values. When I talk with students about how they feel about a particular course (or subject) or with teachers about what kind of affective responses they would like to see in their students, they often respond with the following kinds of comments (phrased in terms of what students might say):

- I *enjoy* coming to this class. (Any course)
- I *like* looking through microscopes. (Biology)
- I find it *fascinating* to learn about why people do what they do. (Psychology, sociology)

Such statements indicate students have developed certain feelings associated with a particular subject or learning experiences (such as a course), that certain interests have emerged, and that various values have become important for them. Whenever any of these happen, students have come to care differently about something, and when students care, they have a different affective response.

The Focus of the Caring. When thinking about caring as an educational goal, it is important to remember that students can come to care about any of several possible foci for learning. As a result of their learning experiences, students might care more or differently about. . . .

- The *phenomena* studied: They may find a new interest in literature, history, birds, weather, rocks. . . .
- The *ideas* studied: They may become more curious about the perspectives through which geographers or historians study the world, the implications of the theory of relativity, the power of the theory of evolution to explain biological phenomena, the widespread insights offered by a feminist perspective on events. . . .
- Their own *Self:* "Maybe I have the potential for doing exciting things in life, more than I realized, or to become the kind of person I want to be."
- The *Others* they encounter in the class or the study: Students may find that people different from themselves—in terms of age, gender, ethnicity, religion, nationality, or whatever—are good people and that the process of understanding and interacting with them can be an exciting and enriching experience.
- The process of *learning* itself: When students start to care about learning and want to learn, either in general or about particular things, then truly powerful things can happen educationally. Then students not only care about phenomena, ideas, and the like, they also *care about learning about* them.

Sixth Kind of Significant Learning: Learning How to Learn. The sixth general kind of significant learning is that of helping students learn how to learn. This is an educational goal that has been attractive to teachers for a long time. Like valuing and thinking, this goal holds out the promise of being particularly effective in enabling other kinds of learning. If we can help people learn how to learn—both during the course and after the course is over—learners will be capable of continuing their learning for the rest of their lives, a truly attractive prospect.

Historical changes have also made this kind of learning particularly important. The twentieth century saw an explosion of knowledge in which the volume of ideas and information about virtually every topic and subject grew exponentially year after year, and that trend continues unabated. Students and teachers are both painfully aware of the educational implications of this explosion. Students buy textbooks that are larger and larger every year; teachers see more and more material they have to cover. As educators, the only strategy that offers any hope of dealing with this situation is to identify the fundamental knowledge for a given subject, make sure that students know that, and then teach them how to keep on learning after the course is over.

If one accepts this view, that learning how to learn is extremely important, what does this mean and how should we do it? Unfortunately the very popularity of the phrase "learning how to learn" has also led to a voluminous body of literature on this topic that can be confusing. This has happened because different people mean different things when they use this phrase. After reviewing the literature on this subject, I have concluded that scholars and teachers have three different sets of meanings for the idea of "learning how to learn":

- Learning how to be a better student
- Learning how to inquire and construct knowledge
- Learning how to be a self-directing learner

Each of these three meanings of learning how to learn is valid and distinct from the other two. And each one leads to different recommendations for teachers. Hence it is important to review the meaning of each of the three forms of "learning how to learn."

Learning How to Be a Better Student. A number of educational efforts have been initiated over the years, especially since the 1980s, aimed at helping students learn how to be more effective students.

The Freshman Year Experience started by John Gardner at the University of South Carolina in the early 1980s is a prime example of this. He and now others have written books (for example, Gardner and Jewler, 1999; Ellis, 2000) and sponsored programs intended to help beginning college students learn, among other things, how to read for better understanding, take notes in lectures, take tests, manage their time and attention, and handle a number of other life tasks during this major transition year. When successful, these programs allow students to learn what might be called the fundamentals of learning how to learn.

More recently several cognitive psychologists have developed the idea of "Self-Regulated Learning" (Pintrich, 1995; Schunk and Zimmerman, 1998; Zimmerman and Schunk, 1989). This is aimed at helping students learn how to regulate three dimensions of their learning: their observable *behavior,* their *motivation* and *affect,* and their *cognition* (Pintrich, 1995, p. 5). Although this is potentially applicable to the learning activities of people of any age and in any situation, the primary focus of the research and application effort has been with college students (Pintrich, 1994).

A similar effort has originated in Europe, starting with research in the late 1970s and becoming increasingly active and visible worldwide in the 1990s. It is concerned with "deep learning," which refers to students' orientation to learning (Marton, Hounsell, and Entwistle, 1997; Gibbs, 1992, 1993). After working with teachers who tried to promote more deep learning among their students, Gibbs has suggested that it is possible to move students toward a deeper approach to learning by doing the following (Gibbs, personal correspondence with the author, 1999):

- Develop their underlying concept of learning or of knowledge itself.
- Develop metacognitive *awareness,* so that they recognize that a deep approach is required, and metacognitive *control,* so that they can make appropriate "meaning making" moves.
- Provide the space and freedom to have time to explore personal interests.
- Make assessment demands explicit so that students understand that only full understanding will be acceptable as a learning outcome.
- Change teaching methods to make learning more active and interactive.

There is a feeling among this group (which is justified in my view) that simply training students in study skills will not have the same effect as changing their orientation to learning along the lines Gibbs lists.

Again, all three of these educational initiatives have the intent of helping college students learn what they need to learn in order to be more effective students. And this is one valid meaning of "learning how to learn."

Inquiring and Constructing Knowledge in Specific Ways. A second general meaning of "learning how to learn" is helping students learn how to add to their own knowledge in ways that are specific to particular domains of knowledge, such as science, history, literature, and so forth. The nature of knowledge in each of these domains is different, and therefore how one adds to that knowledge, whether publicly or personally, is also distinct. Educationally that means we need to help students learn what those differences are and how to at least continue adding to their own personal knowledge in each domain.

Science educators have supported the concepts of "inquiry teaching" and "inquiry learning" for some time. Much of this is based on the argument that science education should not only teach the results of other people's inquiry but should teach how scientific inquiry works (Schwab, 1962; Thelen, 1960). When teachers make a serious effort to respond to this challenge, they search for ways of helping students learn how to formulate questions and then how to seek information that will allow them to answer those questions.

In a more general form, this can lead into extended efforts to help students learn about canonical and innovative research procedures (for example, Barzun and Graff, 1992) in science (for example, Gower, 1997) and in other fields such as history with well-established research procedures (for example, Collingwood, 1993).

Novak and Gowin extended this form of learning how to learn beyond simply learning about research procedures to the construction of meaning and knowledge. In the preface of their book *Learning How to Learn,* they state that in their view the goal of education is not to produce a "change in behavior" but to produce a "change in the meaning of experience" (Novak and Gowin, 1984, p. xi). This led them to search for ways to help learners "reflect upon their experiences and to construct new, more powerful meanings." They offer two primary ways of doing this. The first is the "Vee" diagram (see Figure 2.3).

FIGURE 2.3. "KNOWLEDGE VEE" DIAGRAM.

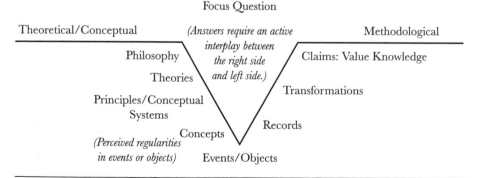

Source: Novak and Gowin, 1984, p. 3. Reprinted with permission of Cambridge University Press.

Based on the idea that any claim to knowledge has two dimensions, the theoretical (or conceptual) and the methodological, this diagram stresses the need to alternate back and forth between these two dimensions in an escalating search for "knowledge" or "knowledge claims." Novak and Gowin argue that when students learn how to construct knowledge on their own, their efforts lead to meaningful learning rather than rote learning (1984, pp. 7–9).

Their second way of helping students learn how to construct knowledge is by using "Concept Mapping" (Novak and Gowin, 1984, chapter 2; Novak, 1998). This is a technique in which teachers ask students to take the various concepts they have studied in a unit or course and then create a map or diagram showing the relationships among the concepts. Doing this prompts students to make sense of what they have learned, to see how other people might make a different sense of the same concepts, and to link new concepts to their preexisting understanding of the general topic.

Helping students learn how to ask and answer questions and then incorporate any resulting new knowledge into their existing knowledge is a second valid meaning of "learning how to learn."

Self-Directing Learners. The third meaning of learning how to learn involves helping students become "self-directing learners." (Note: The traditional term for this educational goal is "self-directed learning," but I prefer the more active and personal meaning implied by referring to the learners rather than the learning that takes place.)

In 1975 Malcolm Knowles laid the conceptual and theoretical groundwork for much of the research on this topic. In his view, learning how to learn involves two general steps: diagnosing one's own needs for learning and designing a learning plan (pp. 11–13).

Taking note of Allen Tough's research findings (1979) that adults learn on their own—all the time—Brookfield (1985) uses those observations to argue that teachers therefore need to be "facilitators of learning" rather than "transmitters of knowledge." In separate chapters in this same book, which is edited by Brookfield, he and Jack Mezirow (1985) both comment on the need for critical reflection by the learner. The adult, self-directing learner needs to consider multiple and alternative ways of understanding the meaning of each experience, and the key to this is *critical reflection.*

Phil Candy, in 1991, published what remains the most comprehensive review of self-directed learning to date. He notes the distinction between learning how to learn as a goal and as a method, and then takes this one step further by indicating how the two apply in life as well as in classroom learning. The relationships among these can be illustrated in the following way:

	Self-Directed Learning as a	
	Goal	*Method*
Use in life:	Personal autonomy	Autodidaxy
Use in the student role:	Self-managed learning	Learner-controlled activities

One of the reasons Candy emphasized these distinctions was that he wanted to note that "learner-controlled activities" were *not* the same thing as *autodidaxy,* which means knowing how to learn what one needs to learn in life. Many teachers give students an assignment to select a topic, do an independent study of it, and then report back to the class—in hopes that this will promote self-directed learning. And it does . . . but only in a limited way. According to Candy's analysis, this exercise only engages self-directed learning as a method of learning and only within the student role. Without the necessary accompaniment of critical reflection on the process, it does not serve as a major thrust toward the goal of "self-managed learning." And without linking this whole process to the larger process of engaging the student in the question—"What should I be learning beyond this topic, and why, and how?"—the learner-controlled activity does not lead to an enhanced capability to engage in autodidaxy for the purpose of enhancing personal autonomy in life. What can a teacher do to promote a stronger, fuller kind of self-directed learning? Candy offers the following suggestions (in chapter 11):

- Make use of learners' existing knowledge structure.
- Encourage deep-level learning.
- Increase questioning by the learners.
- Develop their critical thinking capabilities.
- Enhance their reading skills.
- Enhance their comprehensive monitoring (of their own learning).

For readers interested in further exploration of this important version of learning how to learn, I recommend three additional resources. Gerald Grow (1991) suggests that learners are often not ready initially for a mature kind of self-direction of their own learning; they may need to make progress toward this goal by going through a series of four stages: dependent, interested, involved, and self-directed. In each stage, the role of the teacher changes significantly. Maria Martinez (1998) labels this form of learning as "Intentional Learning." She uses this concept to develop ideas on what students have to learn to become intentional learners and describes four kinds of learners that will be recognizable to most teachers: resistant learners, conforming learners, performing learners, and intentional learners. And finally Donald Schön (1983, 1987) has persuasively argued that professional schools need to break down the separation between studying the principles of good practice and allowing students to apply them. In his view, good professionals are reflective practitioners, meaning they reflect on what they are doing *while* they are doing it, and college students in professional schools need a curriculum that allows and supports them in learning how to do both these tasks simultaneously.

Paradigm Shift

Now that I've described the multiple kinds of learning envisioned by this new taxonomy of learning, it's useful to step back and examine the implications of one very important feature. This taxonomy represents a major shift in the way we think about teaching and learning. In higher education most teachers still teach from what I would call a content-centered paradigm. In this paradigm, teachers respond to the question of what students should learn by describing the topics or content that will be included in the course:

Topics: A, B, C, D. . . .

In contrast, the taxonomy of significant learning is a learning-centered paradigm. In this paradigm, teachers respond to the question of what students should learn by describing different kinds of learning:

Learning How to Learn

Caring

Human Dimension

Integration

Application

Foundational Knowledge

These two paradigms operate in very different ways. Under the content-centered paradigm, teachers are always being challenged by the question of how much they can cover in the time available. The continuous publication of new research drives a felt need to cover more and more topics in more and more detail; this is clearly reflected in the ever-growing size of textbooks. This leaves the teacher feeling a need to not only cover the traditional topics—A, B, and C—but to add topics D, E, F, and even more if possible.

The learning-centered paradigm pushes teachers in a very different direction. As shown in Figure 2.4, it includes attention to important content but drives teachers to incorporate new kinds of learning (rather than new content):

FIGURE 2.4. THE EFFECTS OF TWO DIFFERENT PARADIGMS.

The learning-centered paradigm pushes teaching and learning in this direction, into multiple dimensions of learning.	Learning How to Learn
	Caring
	Human Dimension
	Integration
	Application
	Foundational Knowledge: Topics **A, B, C,** D, E, F, G, H, I . . .

The content-centered paradigm pushes teaching and learning in this direction, along one dimension of learning.

Now that it's clear there are in fact two different ways of looking at teaching and learning, on what grounds should we choose one over the other? To me, the learning-centered paradigm is the better choice. One reason relates to student learning, the other to faculty needs.

The Need for a Long-Term View of Learning. One of the concerns I often hear from teachers pertains to the ever-growing body of knowledge that characterizes essentially all fields of study. When I present this taxonomy, teachers frequently respond skeptically with: "But I can't cover all the content I need to cover now, and you are telling me I need to spend time on whole new kinds of learning as well??!!"

I respond to this issue by asking teachers to face the facts. Are they currently covering everything that students will ever need to know about the subject of their courses? They always answer, "Of course not." No one can, and the situation is getting worse. What then are our options in dealing with this dilemma? One option is talk faster and faster each year; this is clearly a simplistic response that is neither effective nor attractive. Furthermore, the research described in Chapter One suggests that cramming more and more material into a course does not lead to learning that lasts. What else can we do?

My own belief is that the only viable option is to take a long-term view of learning. This means we need to identify the most important topics in our courses and then simultaneously promote multiple kinds of learning as a way of increasing the likelihood that students will keep on learning after the course is over.

Consider the two options. If we include lots of content but students end up neither caring about the subject nor learning how to keep on learning, what are the chances that students will either retain what they have learned or make the effort to keep on learning? The evidence from research and from the widespread faculty observation that students do not currently retain what they learn—even from one course to another—suggests that this is not the option we want.

On the other hand, if students learn how to apply the content, can see how it connects with other knowledge, understand the human implications of what they have learned, and come to care about the subject and about learning how to keep on learning, it seems much likelier that they will both retain what they have learned and continue to enlarge their knowledge after the course is over. Hence, if we take a long-term view of student learning, attending to significant kinds of learning seems like the right choice to make.

Significant Learning and Faculty Dreams. The second reason for choosing the learning-centered paradigm relates to teachers. In Chapter One I describe the responses of faculty when I ask them to dream about what they would really like for students to get out of their courses. They have consistently responded by describing exciting kinds of learning. Do these dreams reflect the content-centered or the learning-centered paradigm? Exhibit 2.4 shows the relationship between faculty dreams and the taxonomy of significant learning. This list takes all of the faculty dreams for student learning described in Chapter One and indicates the kind(s) of significant learning each one exemplifies.

My conclusion—drawn from the close relationship between the taxonomy of significant learning and the list of faculty dreams—is that choosing the learning-centered paradigm will allow faculty to come much closer to realizing their own deep dreams for student learning than will the content-centered paradigm.

Does the Learning-Centered Paradigm Abandon Content? Sometimes faculty feel a shock at having to think about student learning in such a different way. This shock prompts them to wonder whether we have abandoned their original goal of communicating the content of a course in the process of widening the scope of the course to include other desirable kinds of student learning.

My answer to this is, "No, we have not abandoned course content." We have simply given it a new name, foundational knowledge, and then wrapped several other important kinds of learning around it. The other kinds of significant learning still require students to acquire new information and ideas about the subject being studied. But rather than being the sole purpose of the course, "acquiring new knowledge of the content" becomes the basis for achieving several other kinds of learning—learning how to use the content and how to integrate it with other realms of knowledge, understanding its personal and social implications, and so forth.

EXHIBIT 2.4. FACULTY DREAMS AND SIGNIFICANT LEARNING.

"My dream is that students in my courses will. . . ."

- Be ready to engage in life-long learning.

- Value continuous improvement.

} = Learning how to learn

- Develop a deep curiosity.

- Experience the joy of learning.

} = Caring

- See the connections between themselves and their own beliefs, values, and actions, and those of others.

- Think about problems and issues in integrated ways, rather than in separated and compartmentalized ways. Students will see connections between multiple perspectives.

} = Integration

- Take pride in what they have done and can accomplish in whatever discipline or line of work they choose.

- See the importance of community building, both at work and in their personal lives.

- Learn how to stay positive, despite the setbacks and challenges of life and work.

- Mentor others.

} = Human dimension

- Be able to apply and use what they learn in real-life situations.

- Find ways to make the world better, be able to make a difference.

- Be creative problem solvers.

- Develop key skills in life, such as communication skills.

- Become critical thinkers.

} = Application

- Think holistically rather than in compartments. See the big picture.

} = Foundational knowledge

- See the need for change in the world and be a change agent. (Application/thinking and human dimension/self)

- Dissect problems, reconstruct them into new solutions, and connect the solutions to personal life and lives of other people. (Application/thinking and human dimension/self and others).

} = A Combination

How Do We Achieve Significant Learning?

If one accepts the value of the learning-centered paradigm, the next question is likely to be: How do we achieve more significant kinds of learning for our students? Simply defining one's teaching goals in terms of the taxonomy of significant learning does not, by itself, improve the quality of student learning. To do that, we must find ways of designing and creating a special kind of learning experience for our courses. Only then is there any likelihood that these more exciting kinds of learning will be realized.

And that is the purpose of the next three chapters in this book. Chapters Three and Four introduce the model of integrated course design as a way of creating more powerful learning experiences for students. Chapter Five provides specific ideas on how to change the way we teach so that significant learning happens more frequently for more students.

CHAPTER THREE

DESIGNING SIGNIFICANT LEARNING EXPERIENCES I: GETTING STARTED

The first two chapters of this book have presented two key ideas: all teaching should strive to create significant learning experiences, and it is useful to have a taxonomy—a language and set of concepts—for identifying what constitutes such experiences. If one accepts the associated premise that higher education is and ought to be moving toward a learning-centered approach, then the question arises, How can teachers do a better job of creating significant learning experiences for students?

The answers to this question obviously have several important components, but it is clear that if professors want to create courses in which students have significant learning experiences, they must learn how to *design that quality into their courses*. Unless a course is designed properly, all the other components of effective teaching will have only limited impact.

This chapter and the following one will present ideas on how to design courses that will generate powerful learning experiences for students and fulfill those deep dreams that faculty have for their teaching (as described in Chapter One). The present chapter will lay out some general ideas about designing courses, introduce a new model of the course design process, and then walk readers through the first three steps of the process. Chapter Four will examine the remaining steps, in which the classroom events that actually shape the learning experience are created.

Two Basic Ways of Putting a Course Together

When professors face the task of putting together a course, they use one of two distinct approaches. The first, which I call the "list of topics" approach, is especially widespread among new professors who have had no training for this task, but it is also common among experienced professors. Here's how it works: The teacher looks at the subject, creates a list of eight to twelve topics on it, and then proceeds to work up lectures on each topic. With the addition of a midterm exam or two plus a final, the course is ready to go. The list of topics may come from the teacher's own understanding of the subject or from the table of contents of a good textbook. In extreme cases, teachers use the "two textbook" version of this process: they select one text for the students to read, usually one that is easy to grasp, and a second, more sophisticated text as a resource for their own lectures. In my own early days of teaching a course on world regional geography, for example, my course design—if I can call it that—consisted of nothing more than laying out the sequence of regions (following the order provided by the text) and adding a few exams. In a matter of minutes, I had the course design finished.

The attractive feature of this approach is that it is extremely quick and easy to do. Creating the week-to-week outline of topics rarely takes more than thirty to forty-five minutes. The downside, on the other hand, is that it focuses on the organization of the information and pays little or no attention to how that information will be learned, and therefore typically supports only the learning of foundational knowledge. Unfortunately, as research indicates, this kind of learning by itself has a relatively short half life and, more significantly, does not meet the educational needs of students and society today.

The alternative to this traditional, subject-centered approach is to take a learning-centered approach and put the course together systematically, in a process I call "integrated course design." In this approach, the teacher takes responsibility for deciding what would constitute high-quality learning in a given situation and then designing that quality into the course and into the learning experience. What would this approach look like? That is the subject of this and the following chapter.

Integrated Course Design: A New Model

There is a sizable body of literature on the subject of instructional design, most of which is aimed at public school teachers. But some notable books do focus on higher education (Diamond, 1998; Bergquist, Gould, and Greenberg, 1981).

In each of these models, the design process includes a number of common elements—identify the educational goals and objectives and then look at the learning activities, resources, assessment, and so on—but the models differ in how they lay out the various steps, which steps they break into separate parts and which they lump together, and similar matters.

The model of integrated course design that I will introduce here has some of these same characteristics. It includes the same key components but lays them out in a distinctive fashion. The key difference is that it is a relational model, not a linear model—hence the term *integrated*. In addition, this particular formulation of the design process has a number of attractive features. It is

- *Simple:* It is relatively easy for teachers to remember the basic model.
- *Holistic:* It unpacks and reveals the complexity that exists in effective course design.
- *Practical:* It identifies what one needs to do in the course design process.
- *Integrative:* It shows the interactive relationships among the key components of a course.
- *Normative:* It provides specific criteria for determining whether a given course design is good or not.

The basic features of integrated course design are shown in Figure 3.1. The box at the bottom ("Situational Factors") refers to information that needs to be gathered; the three circles refer to decisions that need to be made. The arrows coming up from the box indicate that this information should be used in the process of

FIGURE 3.1. KEY COMPONENTS OF INTEGRATED COURSE DESIGN.

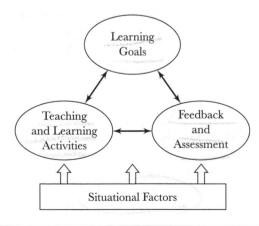

making the three key sets of decisions. The arrows connecting the three circles indicate that the components need to be connected to and support each other.

This basic outline leads to a series of key questions that need to be answered when designing any learning experience:

1. What are the important *situational factors* in a particular course and learning situation?
2. What should our full set of *learning goals* be?
3. What kinds of *feedback and assessment* should we provide?
4. What kinds of *teaching and learning activities* will suffice, in terms of achieving the full set of learning goals we set?
5. Are all the components *connected and integrated,* that is, are they consistent with and supportive of each other?

Backward Design

Careful readers may note that in the sequence of questions, the one on "feedback and assessment" comes before the one on "teaching and learning activities." For many people, this is counterintuitive. However, after many years of working with professors on designing and redesigning their courses, I have noticed that if we deal with feedback and assessment first, it greatly enhances our ability to identify what teaching and learning activities are needed.

Grant Wiggins (1998) has given this sequence the wonderfully descriptive label of *backward design.* As implied by the label, the designer starts the process by imagining a time when the course is over, say one or two years later, and then asking: "What is it I hope that students will have learned, that will still be there and have value, several years after the course is over?" The answer to this question forms the basis of the learning goals. Then the designer moves backward in time to the end of the course and asks the feedback and assessment question: "What would the students have to do to convince me that they had achieved those learning goals?" The process of working out the answer to that question clarifies the real meaning of the learning goals. And then it's time to move back in time once more, to the time of the course itself, and ask: "What would the students need to do *during* the course to be able to do well on these assessment activities?"

One can successfully design a course either way, by doing the teaching and learning activities first or the feedback and assessment activities first. But experience suggests that backward design, that is, doing the feedback and assessment first, greatly clarifies and facilitates answers to the question of what the teaching and learning activities need to be. Hence this is the sequence that I will present here.

A Key Feature: Integrated Components

One very important feature of this model of course design is the proposition that the three initial decisions need to be integrated: the learning goals, the teaching and learning activities, and the feedback and assessment must all reflect and support each other. To illustrate how critically important this is, let me describe a hypothetical course that lacks integration.

Imagine yourself talking to a professor who is teaching a very bad course, one that violates all the known principles of good teaching. He has come to you asking for help in analyzing the course and figuring out what needs to be changed. First, you ask the professor what he wants students to get out of the course. His response: "I want to cover all the important content in world regional geography." After pointing out that "covering the content" is what the teacher does, not what the students do, you repeat your request for a statement about *learning* goals. So he converts his statement to a learning goal: "I want the students to master all the important information and ideas about the different world regions." So you note that one of his learning goals is for students to fully understand and remember important content. But you press a bit more with this question: "Is there not anything else you would like students to learn in this course?" After some reflection, he replies, "Well, it would probably be nice if they could also learn how to think critically about world geography." Now he has a learning goal that is a bit more significant: critical thinking. You could press for more significant learning goals, but you have two you can work with—foundational knowledge and a critical thinking version of application learning.

Now you turn to the question of the teaching and learning activities used in the course and find that the course is a straight lecture course: fifteen weeks of lectures, interrupted only long enough to administer a midterm and final exam. Each week the teacher lectures on a new region and has students read the relevant chapter on that region. Here is the first problem: a disconnect or lack of integration between the learning goals and the teaching and learning activities. Assuming for the moment that the teacher is effective as a lecturer, that he has a good textbook, and that the students are good note-takers and readers, there is a moderate possibility that they will succeed in learning the content. But they are getting no practice and feedback that will support learning how to think critically about the subject. In terms of our basic diagram of the course design process, this means the course has the disconnect shown in Figure 3.2 between the learning goals and the teaching and learning activities.

But the problem gets worse. When it comes time to create the midterm (or final) exam, this professor has a problem: What kinds of questions should he write

FIGURE 3.2. COURSE INTEGRATION PROBLEM.

for the exams? He can write content-related questions, and—with a little luck—the students may do acceptably well on these questions. But the dilemma he faces is whether to include questions that call for students to engage in critical thinking about world geography problems. If he does include thinking questions, the exam will accurately reflect his learning goals, but the students will probably do poorly because the teaching and learning activities did not give the students any practice in critical thinking. In terms of the course design model, this means there is now a second disconnect in the course, between the teaching and learning activities and the feedback and assessment activities, as shown in Figure 3.3.

On the other hand, the professor could opt *not* to include thinking questions on the exams because he knows that including them would not be fair, given the way he taught the course. In this case, the assessment would properly reflect the teaching and learning activities but would not be supportive of the learning goals. Again, this solution produces a disconnect in the course, but now it is in a different part of the model, as shown in Figure 3.4.

Notice the dilemma this teacher faces: No matter what he does with the exam, two of the three needed connections in the course are broken. And this points to a key relationship that is true with all courses. Any teacher who breaks one of the three connections will inevitably have to break a second connection! This means that two out of three important connections will be broken. And a course with two broken connections is a broken course. It will not work and cannot work effectively because it is not integrated. This is why it is so important for any course design to make sure that all three components are integrated, that is, that they reflect and support each other.

FIGURE 3.3. SOLUTION #1: MATCH ASSESSMENT WITH GOALS.

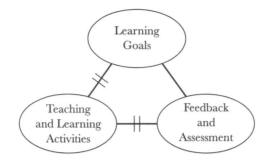

FIGURE 3.4. SOLUTION #2: MATCH ASSESSMENT WITH LEARNING ACTIVITIES.

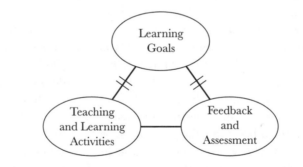

Getting Started with Designing a Course

This model for designing a course includes three phases, each of which involves a number of substeps, as shown in Exhibit 3.1 (and as elaborated somewhat more fully in Appendix A). The remainder of this chapter will describe how this process gets started and will include comments on the first three steps of the initial phase. Chapter Four will address the remaining steps, these shape the activities that students will actually experience, plus the other two phases of the process.

It is my own belief that this process works best if teachers work on each step one at a time and in this sequence. This is important because each step forms the

EXHIBIT 3.1. THE TWELVE STEPS OF INTEGRATED COURSE DESIGN.

If professors want to create courses in which students have significant learning experiences, they need to design that quality into their courses. How do they do that? By following the twelve steps of the instructional design process, as laid out here.

Initial Phase: BUILD STRONG PRIMARY COMPONENTS.
1. Identify important *situational factors.*
2. Identify important *learning goals.*
3. Formulate appropriate *feedback and assessment procedures.*
4. Select effective *teaching and learning activities.*
5. Make sure the primary components are *integrated.*

Intermediate Phase: ASSEMBLE THE COMPONENTS INTO A COHERENT WHOLE.
6. Create a thematic *structure for the course.*
7. Select or create a *teaching strategy.*
8. Integrate the course structure and the instructional strategy to create an *overall scheme of learning activities.*

Final Phase: FINISH IMPORTANT REMAINING TASKS.
9. Develop the *grading system.*
10. Debug the *possible problems.*
11. Write the course *syllabus.*
12. Plan an *evaluation* of the course and of your teaching.

basis for subsequent steps, that is, they build on each other. Therefore it is important to finish the early steps and do them properly before one attempts to complete the later steps.

Initial Phase: Build Strong Primary Components

The initial phase of the design process calls for the teacher to build strong primary components—the learning goals, feedback and assessment measures, and teaching and learning activities shown earlier in Figure 3.1. These components must be built properly because they form the basis for the rest of the design process. And this initial phase begins by examining various situational factors and determining which of them may be significant in a particular course.

Step #1: Identify Important Situational Factors

When designing a new course or redesigning an old one, the first step needs to be a careful review of situational factors that may affect the three key decisions. If you skip over this step or do a superficial job, you increase the chances of ending up with a course that doesn't work for the students involved, doesn't meet the needs of the curriculum, doesn't fit the teacher, or otherwise misses the mark. Hence it is important to take the time necessary to carefully review a number of potentially important factors and determine which of them need to be kept in mind during the rest of the design process.

Drawing from the literature on instructional design and my own experience in working with faculty, I have put together the checklist of potentially significant factors in Exhibit 3.2. I have tried to make the list as comprehensive as possible by including questions about the specific context, the general context, the subject matter, and the characteristics of the learner and of the teacher.

Steps in Integrated Course Design

Initial Phase: Building Components Parts
1. **Situational Factors**
2. Learning Goals
3. Feedback & Assessment
4. Teaching & Learning Activities
5. Integrate the Component Parts

Intermediate Phase: Coherent Whole
6. Course Structure
7. Teaching Strategy
8. Overall Set of Learning Activities

Final Phase: Four Remaining Tasks
9. Grading System
10. Possible Problems
11. Write Syllabus
12. Evaluation of Course and Teaching

The assumption is that for any given course, some of these factors will be important and others will not be. But if you systematically go through the whole list, you should be able to identify all the major factors for any particular course.

Specific Context. This set of questions is always important. Knowing whether there are twenty students or a hundred, whether the course is a freshman introductory course or a graduate seminar, whether the class meets M-W-F for fifty minutes or once a week for three hours, whether the course is going to be conducted live in a classroom or delivered totally online—such information will always be important when making key course design decisions.

Expectations of External Groups. Groups external to the course frequently have expectations about what students should learn, and the teacher needs to take these expectations into account. For example, *society* wants graduates of college courses in U.S. government and U.S. history to have a basic knowledge of this aspect of our country and perhaps a commitment to the ideals and activities of civic-minded citizens in a democracy. Hence those courses need to give consideration to

EXHIBIT 3.2. IMPORTANT SITUATIONAL FACTORS.

Specific Context of the Teaching and Learning Situation
- How many students are in the class?
- Is the course lower division, upper division, or graduate level?
- How long and frequent are the class meetings?
- How will the course be delivered: via live classroom instruction, interactive TV, as an online course, or some combination?

Expectations of External Groups
- What does society at large need and expect, in terms of the education of these students, in general or with regard to this particular subject?
- Does the state or related professional societies have professional accreditation requirements that affect the goals of this learning experience?
- What curricular goals does the institution or department have that affect this course or program?

Nature of the Subject
- Is this subject matter convergent (working toward a single right answer) or divergent (working toward multiple, equally valid interpretations)?
- Is this subject primarily cognitive, or does it include the learning of significant physical skills as well?
- Is this field of study relatively stable, in a period of rapid change, or in a situation where competing paradigms are challenging each other?

Characteristics of the Learners
- What is the life situation of the students at the moment: full-time student, part-time working student, family responsibilities, work responsibilities, and the like?
- What life or professional goals do they have that relate to this learning experience?
- What are their reasons for enrolling?
- What prior experiences, knowledge, skills, and attitudes do the students have regarding the *subject*?
- What are the students' *learning styles*?

Characteristics of the Teacher
- What prior experiences, knowledge, skills, and attitudes does this teacher have in terms of the *subject* of this course?
- Has the teacher taught this subject before, or is this the first time?
- Will this teacher teach this course again in the future, or is this the last time?
- Does the teacher have a high level of competence and confidence in this subject, or is this on the margins of the teacher's zone of competence?
- What prior experiences, knowledge, skills, and attitudes does this teacher have in terms of the *process of teaching*? (That is, how much does this teacher know about effective teaching?)

Special Pedagogical Challenge
- What is the special situation in this course that challenges the students and the teacher in the desire to make this a meaningful and important learning experience?

those learning goals. Sometimes the *college or university* wants particular courses to contribute to the institution's writing-across-the-curriculum agenda. Sometimes *departments* have courses designated to attract majors (if they want more majors) or, at other times, to separate the wheat from the chaff (if they want to limit the number of majors). In other instances *professional societies* have licensing exams, and the department designates certain courses to prepare students for these exams (or for specific parts of the exams).

Nature of the Subject. There are significant differences in the nature of different subjects taught in higher education, and these differences need to be reflected in the course design. Some courses deal with subject matter that is primarily theoretical; the general purpose here is for students to understand the differences between various theories and the implications of these differences. Other courses deal with subject matter that is very practical in nature, meaning the direct goal is for students to learn how to do something.

Another important difference among courses concerns whether the subject is convergent or divergent. Many science, mathematics, and engineering courses are *convergent* in that the intellectual effort is aimed at problems that have a single correct answer. Other courses, especially in the humanities and sometimes in the social sciences, are more *divergent*, meaning the goal is often to search for multiple interpretations of a given phenomenon or to understand multiple perspectives on a problem. These characteristics need to be reflected in the way the course is designed.

And one other feature is sometimes characteristic of a subject. At times a given discipline undergoes a major change in the way research is done or in its reigning paradigm. At such times, there may be controversy within the discipline about the relative merit or value of old and new paradigms. When I was in graduate school, for example, the discipline of geography was debating the proper place of quantitative analysis. When there are changes or controversies such as this within a field of study, some of the courses in a department's curriculum need to inform students about this situation and assist them in developing a thoughtful response of their own to the issues involved.

Characteristics of the Learners. Every educational situation has a set of students involved, and these students differ from course to course and even from student to student within a given course. Different students bring different life or professional goals, even to the same course. They are in different working or family situations. A teacher would need to plan differently for a class that consists primarily of single nineteen-year-olds living on campus than for a class with a high percentage of students who are parents, perhaps married, twenty-five to forty years old, and working full or part time.

In addition to demographic differences, students also bring different feelings, relevant experiences, and prior knowledge to different courses. Students often bring a high level of fear or anxiety to courses on some subjects, such as math or statistics. In other courses, they may come with anticipation or excitement. For example, in my region of the country, a course titled "Geography of Sports" will always create enthusiastic interest.

This is also the place in the design process to consider the topic of students' varied learning styles. Some learners prefer visual ways of learning, others verbal or kinesthetic or a combination. Students also vary in the level of education, maturity, or sophistication they bring with them. Some are ready to engage in "deep learning" while others are only accustomed to superficial learning.

With the growing interest in online and distance education, teachers and researchers are discovering that some kinds of students work well in this mode but others don't. This information can be used to advise students on whether to take an online course, but it can also be used in the course design to decide how much student support needs to be built in.

If teachers know or can gather information about the characteristics of the students likely to sign up, this can be very helpful in making decisions about how their courses will and should operate.

Characteristics of the Teacher. Although it may seem obvious, it is easy to forget about the other party always present in an educational event: the teacher (or, in some cases, a set of teachers). It is important to take time to review your own characteristics when designing your courses.

While college teachers are generally competent in their discipline, there are times when people teach courses that are on the edge of their area of expertise. This may affect not only the time required to generate problems and exercises but also the level of risk they are ready to take when choosing a teaching strategy.

It is also wise to honestly assess your current level of teaching skills. That is, how developed are your interaction skills with students, your course management skills, your course design skills, and so on? If your realistic assessment is that these are still fairly basic, you may want to keep the course design close to your comfort zone. If your teaching skills are well developed, you can feel free to take on more challenging goals and more powerful teaching strategies.

Related to teaching skills, but one step more fundamental, is the philosophy of teaching, that is, the teacher's underlying values and beliefs. We all have tacit beliefs about how learning really occurs and our own values concerning what constitutes good learning and good teaching. On a long-term basis, these are variables that it's useful to examine and revise. But in the short term, when designing a given course, it's essential to take them as given and shape the course design decisions accordingly.

At the most fundamental level, we all have a particular attitude toward our subject and our students. How much do we care about our students, really? To what degree and in what ways do we perceive our subject to be exciting and important? I have met teachers who did and did not in fact care about their students, individually or collectively, and teachers who did and did not see their subject as interesting. All these personal factors need to be taken into account in the course design process.

The Special Pedagogical Challenge. After a teacher has reviewed each of these situational factors and decided which are relevant to a given course, I often find it useful to pose a concluding question as a way of integrating and focusing this information: "What is the special pedagogical challenge of this course?" That is, what is the special situation in this course that challenges both students and teacher to make this a meaningful and important learning experience? If the teacher can find a way to successfully meet that challenge, the chances of the course being a success for the students are high. Let me give some examples to illustrate different kinds of challenges.

One outstanding teacher of statistics on my campus sees the specific pedagogical challenge of his course as students' fear of statistics. Students, in his view, often see statistics as a complex, mysterious process that "only the gods can understand." If he can find a way to demystify this perception of statistics and get students to see this subject as just a systematic way of doing the same kind of calculations that they all do every day, then he has an excellent chance to move them along to a more sophisticated level of understanding and ability to use statistics.

In contrast, teachers in psychology sometimes say their special pedagogical challenge as just the opposite. Students often come into their courses believing that psychology is just everyday common sense, and therefore they "already know all this stuff." The challenge in this case is to get students to see that there are some unexpected phenomena out there, that theories, experiments, and research give us insights that are contrary to many popular beliefs, and that we therefore need to study others and ourselves carefully to really understand why people do what they do.

One of the more surprising responses to this question came from a teacher of modern German history. When asked what the special pedagogical challenge of that course was, she thought awhile and finally said, "Hitler." Her explanation was that today's students have been so filled with stories of World War II, the Holocaust, and the rise and fall of Hitler and the Nazis, that they think that is the whole focus of all German history. So her special challenge is to help students see that that as only one chapter, a dreadful chapter to be sure, but only one aspect of German history, and that there are other aspects that are equally important and fascinating, and as positive as Hitler was negative.

A Resource for Analyzing Situational Factors. Anyone who wants additional ideas and examples on how to collect information about important situational factors would do well to read chapter 6 of Robert Diamond's book on designing courses (1998, pp. 59–78). Diamond believes that a careful analysis of these factors is extremely important to any design and describes the thorough processes he has used in his work with course and curriculum design at Syracuse University and elsewhere. His examples show how to collect information with survey questionnaires and achievement tests as well as with informal discussions to clarify situations where assumptions tend to fly in the face of real understanding, and how to use this information to identify specific needs and desired outcomes for the course or curriculum at hand.

Summary of the First Step. The key point to remember about this first step in the course design process is that it is important to do a careful, in-depth job of collecting and analyzing information about various situational factors. Skipping this step or doing a cursory job will result in bad decisions later on. On the other hand, a thorough, in-depth analysis here positions one to see important needs and contextual factors and will often even suggest answers to the design questions that need to be considered next—important learning goals, meaningful forms of feedback and assessment, and appropriate teaching and learning activities.

Step #2: Formulate Significant Learning Goals

Steps in Integrated Course Design

Initial Phase: Building Components Parts
1. Situational Factors
2. **Learning Goals**
3. Feedback & Assessment
4. Teaching & Learning Activities
5. Integrate the Component Parts

Intermediate Phase: Coherent Whole
6. Course Structure
7. Teaching Strategy
8. Overall Set of Learning Activities

Final Phase: Four Remaining Tasks
9. Grading System
10. Possible Problems
11. Write Syllabus
12. Evaluation of Course and Teaching

The natural inclination of most faculty, given their training and disciplinary socialization, is to take a content-centered approach to learning goals. That is, they say, in one way or another: "I want students to learn about (or to master) topics X, Y, and Z." This is an understandable response, but it is not the best place to use one's content expertise. That will come later, when it comes to creating a structure for the course and setting up learning activities within that structure. But creating a list of topics won't give you what you need to create more significant learning experiences for students.

Instead of making a list of topics, use a learning-centered approach and identify what students should get out of the course. This is where the taxonomy of significant learning described in Chapter Two will be of value. This taxonomy, in essence, suggests that any course has the potential to support multiple kinds of significant learning:

- *Foundational knowledge:* knowledge about the phenomena associated with the subject and the conceptual ideas associated with those phenomena
- *Application:* an ability to use and think about the new knowledge in multiple ways, as well as the opportunity to develop important skills
- *Integration:* the ability to connect one body of knowledge with other ideas and bodies of knowledge
- *Human dimension:* discovering how to interact more effectively with oneself and with others
- *Caring:* the development of new interests, feelings, and values
- *Learning how to learn:* developing the knowledge, skills, and strategies for continuing one's learning after the course is over

If you can use this taxonomy (or any other formulation of significant kinds of learning) to describe what you want students to learn in your course, then and only then will you be able to select the kinds of teaching and learning activities and the feedback and assessment activities needed to support this kind of learning.

Formulating Significant Learning Goals. The basic procedure for formulating learning goals is to ask a series of questions about each kind of learning that is potentially relevant. Using the taxonomy of significant learning, this would involve asking what each kind of learning would mean in the context of the specific course. Exhibit 3.3 contains a list of questions focused on the six kinds of learning in this taxonomy. The suggestion is that you answer each question, or at least the most important question within each set, for the course you are working on.

To illustrate what the answers might look like, I have shared the responses of three professors—in art history, psychology, and microbiology—I interviewed concerning their learning goals. Their answers are shown in Exhibit 3.4. Notice the lead-in question for this exhibit. By framing the question in terms of what you want to be true about students a year or so after the course is over, you focus on the lasting impact of the course on students. Asking the question this way keeps you from describing what are in fact learning activities to be used during the course rather than the desired outcomes of these activities.

The other important feature of the learning goals shown in Exhibit 3.4 is the verb that begins each statement. It is important to formulate goals that start with verbs, to indicate what it is you actually want students to do in the future. But it is also important for these verbs to be as concrete and as specific as possible. Pushing yourself to find and use such verbs will clarify for you and your students what it is

EXHIBIT 3.3. QUESTIONS FOR
FORMULATING SIGNIFICANT LEARNING GOALS.

What impact do I want this course experience to have on students, that will still be there a year or more after the course is over?

FOUNDATIONAL KNOWLEDGE
- What key *information* (facts, terms, formula, concepts, relationships. . . .) is important for students to *understand and remember* in the future?
- What key *ideas* or perspectives are important for students to understand in this course?

APPLICATION
- What kinds of *thinking* are important for students to learn here:
    Critical thinking, in which students analyze and evaluate?
    Creative thinking, in which students imagine and create?
    Practical thinking, in which students solve problems and make decisions?
- What important *skills* do students need to learn?
- What *complex projects* do students need to learn how to manage?

INTEGRATION
- What *connections* (similarities and interactions) should students recognize and make. . .
    Among ideas *within* this course?
    Between the information, ideas, and perspectives in this course and those in other courses or areas?
    Between material in this course and the students' own personal, social, and work life?

HUMAN DIMENSION
- What can or should students learn about *themselves*?
- What can or should students learn about understanding and interacting with *others*?

CARING
- What changes would you like to see, in what students *care* about, that is, any changes in their. . .
    Feelings?
    Interests?
    Values?

LEARNING HOW TO LEARN
- What would you like for students to learn about. . .
    How to be a good student in a course like this?
    How to engage in inquiry and construct knowledge with this subject matter?
    How to become a self-directing learner relative to this subject? That is, have a *learning agenda* of what else they need and want to learn and a *plan* for learning it.

EXHIBIT 3.4. SIGNIFICANT LEARNING GOALS FOR THREE COURSES.

A year after this course is over, I want and hope that students will . . .

Kinds of Learning	Microbiology	Art History	Psychology (Statistics)
Foundational knowledge	. . . remember the terms associated with microbial anatomy, biochemistry, and disease. . . . understand *orders of magnitude*, that is, what exists at different levels or scales, in relation to other objects. . . . remember the primary categories of organisms.	. . . remember some of the main stylistic categories (for example, prehistoric, medieval), artists, times and chronology, and locations of major works of art in world civilization. . . . be able to identify the key elements of design in any work of art.	. . . remember the meaning of terms related to population and parameter, sample and statistics. . . . understand the meaning of two key concepts: variance and correlation; and remember the formula for calculating variance. . . . understand that relations inside numerical systems mean things, that is, map into the real world.
Application	. . . be able to critically evaluate bodies of literature in academic and popular outlets. (Critical thinking.) . . . be able to mathematically calculate the rate and extent of microbial growth. (Skill.)	. . . be able to do a formal analysis of pictures when they visit an exhibition in an art museum in terms of the main elements of design. (Analytical thinking.) . . . identify the era or style (and likely artist) when encountering a new picture for the first time and interpret the likely symbolic meaning of the content. (Analytic thinking.)	. . . be able to look at a graph and see relationships in the real world that are being described. (Skill) . . . be able to engage in quantitative reasoning, that is, construct a distribution of quantitative information. (Creative thinking) . . . become critically sensitive to the size of things, that is, able to evaluate the significance of the size of something in terms of appropriate contextual information. (Critical thinking)
Integration	. . . integrate ideas about energy from chemistry and microbiology. . . . relate ideas about microbial biology to processes in higher organizations, for example, metabolism, disease.	. . . identify particular ways in which the art forms of various times and places in history reflect the milieu (social, religious, economic, political, and so on) of those times and places.	. . . connect numerical systems of statistics with the widespread use of numbers in the students' everyday personal and public life. . . . relate statistical procedures to quantitative reasoning that goes on

	in all other courses, including the humanities (for example, visual perspective in art). ... identify the differences and relationship between the two central concepts of variance and correlation (for example, I can measure the variance of IQ within this class, and then I can measure the correlation between IQ and course grades).	... identify some of the similarities between the styles of different art forms (for example, painting, sculpture, architecture, and so on) in a given time and place ... identify some of the similarities between the art forms of different places at the same time.	
Human dimension	... come to see themselves as people who are more educated about microbiology than the average layperson. ... be able to inform and educate other intelligent citizens about the role of microbiology in personal and public life, for example, educate their roommates about proper ways of cooking hamburger.	... become more sensitive to and aware of how a learner's day-to-day aesthetic environment reflects various artistic styles and periods and how these different environments affect the learner. ... become more aware of how different people (from various cultures, places, and times) create different kinds of aesthetic environments and the reasons for that. ... become more aware of and interact with the efforts of others as they try to make residential, work, and public places more aesthetic.	... become more confident about their ability to learn this material and be less intimidated by it. (Self) ... come to see themselves as having their own special way of learning, use that to their advantage, and not have to worry about whether they are better or worse than other learners. (Self and Others)
Caring	... be excited about microbiology as a broad, complex, multifaceted field of study, that is, a subject that is concerned with more about organisms than just their role as causes of human diseases. ... value the importance of precise language in this field of work, as part of professionalism.	... be more interested in attending art exhibits. ... consider collecting some nice works of art for their own homes. ... be interested in searching out how different countries and different people create urban environments and how they decorate their environments.	... find that learning about quantitative reasoning is fun. ... be anxious to critically evaluate the quantitative material that they encounter regularly in the public media.

EXHIBIT 3.4. SIGNIFICANT LEARNING GOALS FOR THREE COURSES, Cont'd.

A year after this course is over, I want and hope that students will . .

Kinds of Learning	Microbiology	Art History	Psychology (Statistics)
Caring (continued)		. . . take time to try to understand what prompts various art styles and periods, whether they intuitively like it or not.	
Learning How to Learn	. . . be able to know how to read assigned material responsibly. (Being an effective student.) . . . know how the scientific method works, especially the importance of identifying and testing the hypothesis. (A method of learning that is particular to this subject matter.) . . . be able to identify important resources for their own subsequent learning. (Being a self-directing learner.)	. . . know how to continue building a fuller understanding of the art of a particular style or period. . . . be able to identify some of the major locations of artworks and exhibits in the local community and region. . . . be able to identify several resources (movies, TV, books, magazines, computer programs) available to help them continue learning about art in different times and places. . . . have a fairly clear sense of what they would like to learn next about art and art history.	. . . have learned about their own preferred learning style and use it in the future. . . . understand the need for multiple exposures to material in order to develop a solid understanding of it, for example, listen to lecture, review notes, read text. . . . continue to be proactive with data collecting and data analysis in their own lives, for example, able to calculate mortgage rates to determine whether to refinance a mortgage or make early payments.

you really want in terms of student learning. To help with this process, Exhibit 3.5 lists some verbs that would be appropriate for each type of significant learning.

As you formulate your learning goals, consider these tips on how to approach each kind of significant learning:

Foundational Knowledge. The key here is to limit yourself to identifying only what is really important for students to have in long-term memory one to three years later. Of course, we would all like all our students to remember everything. In reality, however, "everything" is not extremely important—but some things are. Notice

EXHIBIT 3.5. VERBS FOR SIGNIFICANT LEARNING GOALS.

Foundational Knowledge:

Remember	Understand	Identify

Application:

Use	Judge	Calculate
Critique	Do [skill]	Create
Manage	Imagine	Coordinate
Solve	Analyze	Make decisions about . . .
Assess		

Integration:

Connect	Relate	Integrate
Identify the interaction between . . .	Compare	Identify the similarities between . . .

Human Dimension:

Come to see themselves as . . .	Understand others in terms of . . .	Decide to become . . .
Interact with others regarding . . .		

Caring:

Get excited about . . .	Be more interested in . . .	Value . . .
Be ready to . . .		

Learning How to Learn:

Read and study effectively . . .	Identify sources of information on . . .	Frame useful questions
Set a learning agenda	Be able to construct knowledge about . . .	Create a learning plan . . .

how the microbiology professor, after thinking about it, limited the list to *certain* terms, the *concept* of orders of magnitude, and the *primary* categories of organisms, not all categories and subcategories. The course may well introduce all categories, but the professor would be satisfied if some years later the students at least remember the primary categories.

Application. This is where thinking skills and other skills come in. Ask yourself: What is it you want students to be able to *do* in relation to this subject, one to three years after the course is over? What situations are students likely to be in, where the learning from this course will be relevant? In those situations, what would you like them to be able to do: critically evaluate something, analyze something, or create, design, or calculate something?

Integration. The main point with integration is to think about what kind of connections you want students to make. Do you want them to connect the course material to their everyday life (like the psychology professor did), to other realms of study (like the art history professor), or to other closely related subjects of study (like the microbiology professor)? These are all valid forms of integration, but each teacher has to decide what kinds of integration are important when studying a given subject.

Human Dimension. This kind of learning has two closely related components: learning about oneself and about others. For the first component, ask yourself whether you would like the students to see themselves in some new way. For example, you might want students to see themselves as being more educated about an important topic and hence carrying a new responsibility for social leadership on that topic. For the second component, ask whether you want your students to gain a new understanding of how to interact with other people in relationship to this subject. They can interact, for example, with other students, experts in the field, future colleagues, or whatever. When a teacher accepts this kind of learning goal, it means students will do more than learn *about* the theory and content of a field; they will learn how the theories and content can affect their own lives and their interactions with others.

Caring. Most professors want their students to gain an increased appreciation for the subject being studied, that is, to value it more highly than before. To the degree that this is true, this should be one of the explicit goals for the course. Sometimes subjects entail additional specific values that are desirable to promote, such as valuing the importance of precise language (like the microbiology course) or attending art exhibits (like the art history course).

Learning How to Learn. This kind of learning is more complex because it has three distinct forms: becoming a better student, learning how to inquire about this particular subject matter, and becoming a self-directing learner. If one is selective and focused, it is possible to imagine a course addressing all three in one way or another, as the statements by the microbiology professor imply. The other two examples, though, also show some of the varied and rich forms this kind of learning can take.

Two Tips for Selecting Learning Goals.
In addition to using the language of significant learning to shape your learning goals, I would offer two other suggestions.

Include As Many Kinds of Significant Learning As Possible. In Chapter Two I mentioned that the taxonomy of significant learning was interactive in nature. One implication of this is that the more of the six kinds of significant learning you can include as goals for your course and really support, the better each kind of learning will happen. If you can design five or six such goals into the course, each of those will happen more fully and more effectively for your students than if you only include one or two.

That may sound like magic or hocus pocus, but it is not. Excellent teachers are already demonstrating this principle in their teaching. The secret is learning how to be creative in developing and incorporating powerful learning activities that allow students to become more aware of what they are learning and how it all relates. I'll say more in Chapter Five about specific teaching and learning activities and feedback and assessment procedures that result in a powerful learning experience for students. But for the moment, I am only making the point that "more is better" when it comes to formulating learning goals.

Link Your Learning Goals to Your Own Dreams. In the first chapter of this book I noted that essentially all faculty have rich and exciting dreams for their teaching, even though these dreams are sometimes buried deep beneath the challenges and difficulties of everyday teaching. However, when you formulate the learning goals for your courses, this is a good time to put yourself in touch with your own deep dreams and to let these inform and shape the goals for your courses. If you want students to learn how to "make a difference in the world," "fight for social justice," "become creative writers," or "find a lifelong joy in continued learning" about your subject, you need to translate those dreams into explicit goals for the courses you teach. The language of significant learning is capable of helping you do that in a controlled and focused way, but also in a way that enables you to dream as fully and as richly as you possibly can.

Step #3: Formulate Feedback and Assessment Procedures

The third component of a course that a teacher must design is feedback and assessment. For many teachers, this has meant little more than giving the traditional "two midterms and a final." And that involves the one task that many teachers find to be the most distasteful part of teaching: grading. Teachers often lament: "If I could only teach and not have to grade, it would be so much more fun." Similarly, students often feel the same way: "Taking a course isn't so bad, but gearing up for those exams is a real pain."

Steps in Integrated Course Design

Initial Phase: Building Components Parts
1. Situational Factors
2. Learning Goals
3. **Feedback & Assessment**
4. Teaching & Learning Activities
5. Integrate the Component Parts

Intermediate Phase: Coherent Whole
6. Course Structure
7. Teaching Strategy
8. Overall Set of Learning Activities

Final Phase: Four Remaining Tasks
9. Grading System
10. Possible Problems
11. Write Syllabus
12. Evaluation of Course and Teaching

What is the reason for this? Can anything be done about it? And what does this have to do with instructional design? There are several reasons why the taking and grading of exams is so onerous for both parties, but one of the main reasons is that many teachers have a very limited view of the nature of feedback and assessment. Much as teachers need to expand their view of learning goals to include more significant learning, they also need to expand their view of feedback and assessment to include more *educative* assessment.

Much of what follows is similar to the general message of two publications that have much to offer on this topic: *Effective Grading* (Walvoord and Anderson, 1998), and *Educative Assessment* (Wiggins, 1998). I have made my own interpretation of their ideas, but their ideas and mine are all aimed at the same goal: formulating grading and assessment procedures that support learning rather than hinder it.

"Audit-ive" Versus Educative Assessment. Grant Wiggins (1998) has generated a concept that is extremely important here. He distinguishes between "audit-ive" and educative assessment (see Figure 3.5 for my illustration of the meaning of these two concepts). Teachers whose only feedback and assessment procedures are two midterms and a final exemplify the perspective of audit-ive assessment. When this is the only feedback and assessment that occurs in a course, it serves only one function: to audit student learning as a basis for the grade turned in. This approach to feedback and assessment is typically based on backward-looking assessment, with exams that look back on what was covered during the last several weeks and aim simply at determining whether the students got it or not.

FIGURE 3.5. AUDIT-IVE AND EDUCATIVE ASSESSMENT.

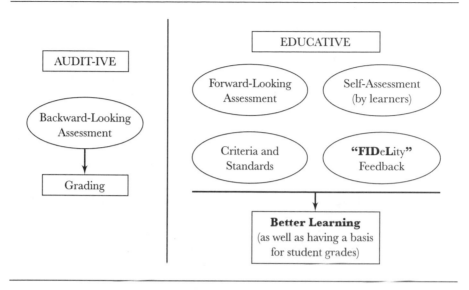

In contrast, the primary purpose of educative assessment is to help students learn better. As long as society requires grades, teachers will need a valid and fair basis for their grades. The problem is that teachers do not know how to go beyond grading to being able to provide the kind of feedback and assessment that will enhance the learning process itself, that is, to do more than simply record the results of the learning process. Teachers need to learn what educative assessment is and how to incorporate it into their teaching.

As indicated in Figure 3.5, educative assessment has four primary components: forward-looking assessment, criteria and standards, self-assessment, and "FIDeLity" feedback. ("FIDeLity" feedback is my own addition to the concept of educative assessment. This acronym refers to feedback that is Frequent, Immediate, and Discriminating (based on clear criteria and standards), and delivered Lovingly. (This kind of feedback is described more thoroughly later in this chapter.) If teachers can learn how to develop procedures for each of these four components, they will give themselves and their students a much clearer understanding of the degree to which the students are learning something correctly. That in turn will enable students to start the process of monitoring and evaluating their own learning, a key step if they are ever to become self-directing learners.

Looking at how these four components operate in and beyond a course will help indicate both their relationship to each other and their significance for high-quality student learning. An expanded model of educative assessment is shown in

Figure 3.6. The top box indicates what happens during a course, and the bottom box indicates what happens after a student has finished the course and is engaging in whatever activity the course was intended to support and enhance.

During the course (top box), learners engage in some kind of learning activity in an effort to learn how to do something: read and interpret novels, design scientific experiments, use sociological theories to explain aspects of human behavior, or whatever. While the students are learning how to engage in the relevant activity, they should each be getting feedback to help them understand whether they are doing it well or not. This feedback usually comes from the teacher, but

FIGURE 3.6. EDUCATIVE ASSESSMENT (EXPANDED MODEL).

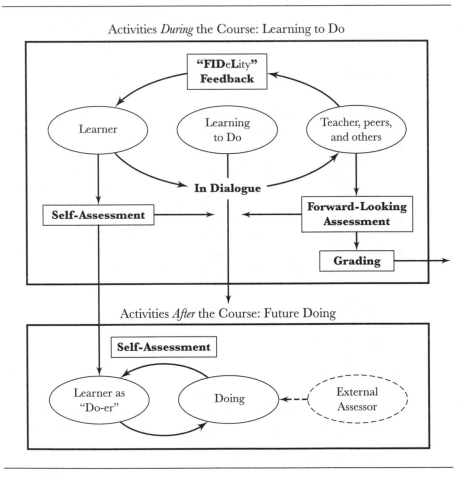

good teachers find ways to generate feedback from other students and occasionally even from an outside expert brought in for that purpose.

The diagram indicates that feedback needs to be done in dialogue. Whereas the results of *assessment* can simply be announced, the intended purpose of *feedback* requires a back-and-forth dialogue between those giving the feedback and those receiving it. When I tell a student, for example, that an experimental design needs some "control variables" added to it, I need some response from the student in order to know whether my message has made sense. That is why feedback needs to be done in dialogue.

After the students have practiced learning to do something for a while, their individual ability to perform high-quality work will need to be assessed. The teacher, or sometimes an outside expert, will need to conduct some form of assessment. This is also necessary to provide a basis for the grades that most institutions require for purposes external to the course. But in addition, the learners also need to engage in self-assessment. This too will take practice because the criteria and standards relevant to this particular activity will be new to the students, who will need time and practice to learn how to apply these standards to their own work.

Why is it so important for students to learn how to assess their own work and activities? Because after the course is over (bottom box of Figure 3.6), the teacher will no longer be present, and the learners will henceforth be the ones primarily responsible for determining whether they are doing a worthwhile job and, if not, looking for ways to improve. In some situations, especially in work settings, there may be a supervisor who in essence becomes an external assessor. But the people doing the activity will always be the ones who must be able to assess the results of their own work. And they will have difficulty engaging in self-assessment effectively at this time unless they have had practice and have learned how to do it back in the course.

Although the other component of educative assessment, criteria and standards, does not appear on this diagram, it is essential throughout the whole process. Feedback, forward looking assessment, and self-assessment (both during and after the course)—none of these can be done properly without clear and appropriate criteria and standards.

The next few sections offer some explanation on how to implement each of the four features of educative assessment.

First Feature: Forward-Looking Assessment. When a teacher creates any of the various assessment procedures that are typically used in a semester-long course (assignments, tests, and the individual questions involved), one perspective that can be very helpful is to strive for forward-looking assessment rather than backward-looking assessment. Teachers using backward-looking assessment look back on what has been covered during the last four weeks, for example, and in essence say to the students: "We have covered topics X, Y, and Z. Did you get it?" In forward-looking assessment, teachers look ahead to what they expect or want students to be able to *do* in the future as the result of having learned about X, Y, and Z. The relevant question becomes: "Imagine yourself in a situation where people are actually using this knowledge. Can you use your knowledge of X, Y, and Z to do [this]?"

Wiggins, when writing about what is necessary to ensure authentic performance (1998, chapter 2), identifies two key elements: authentic tasks and performer-friendly feedback. These are essentially the same as what I am calling here forward-looking assessment and FIDeLity feedback respectively. He describes very convincingly why authentic tasks are so important, if we want to create testing situations that will teach and improve student learning, not just measure it. "Assessment must be anchored in and focused on authentic tasks because they supply valid direction, intellectual coherence, and motivation for the day-in and day-out work of knowledge and skill development. . . . Assessment is authentic when we anchor testing in the kind of work people do, rather than merely eliciting easy-to-score responses to simple questions" (1998, p. 21).

To create forward-looking or authentic assessment, Wiggins (1998, pp. 22, 24) recommends that teachers create questions, problems, tests, and assignments that

- *Are realistic.* The task or tasks replicate the ways in which a person's knowledge and abilities are tested in real-world situations.
- *Require judgment and innovation.* The student has to use knowledge and skills wisely and effectively to solve unstructured problems, such as when a plan must be designed, and the solution involves more than following a set routine or procedure or plugging in knowledge.
- *Ask the student to do the subject.* Instead of reciting, restating, or replicating course content and prior knowledge through demonstration, the student has to carry out exploration and work within the discipline of science, history, or any other subject.
- *Replicate or simulate the contexts in which adults are tested in the workplace, in civic life, and in personal life.* Contexts involve specific situations that have particular constraints, purposes, and audiences. Typical school tests are contextless. Students need to experience what it is like to do tasks in workplace and other real-life contexts, which tend to be messy and murky. In other words, genuine tasks require good judgment. Authentic tasks undo the ultimately harmful secrecy, silence, and absence of resources and feedback that mark excessive school testing.
- *Assess the student's ability to use a repertoire of knowledge and skill efficiently and effectively to negotiate a complex task.* Most conventional test items are isolated elements of performance—similar to sideline drills in athletics rather than to the integrated

use of skills that a game requires. Good judgment is required here, too. Although there is, of course, a place for drill tests, performance is always more than the sum of the drills.

- *Allow appropriate opportunities for students to rehearse, practice, consult resources, and get feedback on and refine performances and products.* Although there is a role for the conventional secure test that keeps questions secret and keeps resource materials from students until during the test, that testing must coexist with educative assessment if students are to improve performance.

The idea is to focus student learning on realistic and meaningful tasks through cycles of *performance-feedback-revision-new performance.* This is essential to help them learn to use information, resources, and notes in order to perform effectively in context. Rather than create questions and problems with no context, the teacher should strive to create a problem or question that has a meaningful, real, authentic context that the students might well face in the future and that allows the students to actually use recently acquired knowledge and skills.

Changing Backward-Looking Assessment to Forward-Looking Assessment. Some examples may help teachers understand how to transform backward-looking assessment activities into forward-looking assessment.

The first example comes from my own course on world geography. We studied a different world region each week and periodically had an exam either on one region or several regions. After studying a given region, an easy backward-looking option for assessment was to give students one of the following two assignments. "List three distinctive characteristics of each country in this region" or, in a multiple-choice format, "Which of the following features most accurately characterizes country 'X' in this region?" This is a content-centered approach to assessment: present some content, and then ask, in essence: "Do you understand it, and can you remember it?"

Here's a better and more forward-looking option, which I worked up after a few years of teaching this course:

Imagine that you are working for an international company that wants to establish a commercial presence in this region. The company sells a product that requires a modest per capita income for people to purchase it. The corporate executives understand that they will not realize significant income during the first five years or so. But they want to establish a foothold in the region with hopes of financial success in the not-too-distant future.

The key to success is being in a country that will have enough political stability to allow economic growth and sufficient other factors to support at least moderately high earning power among the general population.

The company has asked you to serve on an advisory board that will recommend the country in which the company should open a new branch operation.

Given what you have learned about the countries in this region, what country would you recommend as best meeting the needs of this company?

This simulation problem requires students to review the information they have studied. But the information they need was not presented in this form in the text or in class. Therefore they have to think about what kinds of information are related to political stability, economic growth, GNP, and so on. And then they have to compare information from several countries and make a "best choice" recommendation. When I used this assignment and watched the students working on it, I was impressed with the kind of thinking that occurred and with the quality of their answers. They also worked on this task in groups, and the discussion that followed when we compared answers across groups was quite stimulating. They had to learn to articulate the reasoning behind their answers in order to defend it against different recommendations from other groups.

Wiggins (1998, pp. 26–27) also presents some examples related to assessing student knowledge of basic mathematical calculations. A typical approach, which I regard as backward-looking assessment, contains a series of simple out-of-context problems, with the usual: "Here is a shape, calculate the surface area or volume." As an alternative, which I see as forward-looking assessment, Wiggins suggests asking students to imagine that they are in charge of gift wrapping in a large department store. The students are given some data about volume of sales and so on. But they need to generate some key data for themselves. The task is to identify the box shape that will require the least amount of wrapping paper and then recommend to the supervisor how many boxes and the total amount of wrapping paper that will be needed for the coming year. The assignment also provides specific criteria, another key component of educative assessment.

Exercising Versus Forward-Looking Assessment. As we strive to formulate forward-looking assessment, it is important to understand the difference between this and what can be described as *exercising.* When we introduce a particular protocol for working on a specific kind of problem, we then often give students homework problems in which they perform this protocol several times, with slightly different parameters to the problem. This kind of exercise characterizes many end-of-chapter problems. Exercising is good in that it provides practice and familiarity with how a particular mental activity works and hence is valuable in the early stages of learning. But exercising is not the same thing as forward-looking assessment. Eventually students will find more intellectual excitement and motivation if they are challenged to use their new knowledge on realistic tasks that they can relate to more effectively.

An important key to developing forward-looking assessment is for the teacher to think, "What am I trying to prepare students to do? What is it I am trying to determine that students are ready or not ready to do?" An example of an institution that has widely accepted the idea of forward-looking assessment (without calling it that) is Alverno College. Because it has an outcomes-based curriculum, it also has sophisticated assessment procedures. As a result, its student assessment procedures are typically framed in the following way: "As the result of having studied and learned about X, is the student ready to do Y?" In the Alverno Department of Education, for example, students put together a learning portfolio that is assessed by a teacher and a school principal. The whole point of the learning portfolio is to allow the assessors to answer the question, "Is this student ready to teach?" That is the proper way to conduct forward-looking assessment.

Second Feature: Criteria and Standards.

All assessment is an attempt to measure the quality of something and therefore, by definition, requires an appropriate yardstick. Hence an extremely important aspect of the assessment component of course design is to have clear and appropriate criteria and standards for use in both forward-looking assessment and self-assessment. The term *rubric* is commonly used these days to describe the combination of criteria and standards for either a project or a whole course. It is extremely important for a course to have a clear and appropriate rubric because students need to know what constitutes high-quality performance in whatever activity they are trying to learn.

Although the need for clear criteria and standards would seem rather obvious, empirical studies indicate that faculty members frequently overlook this aspect of their teaching. Michael Flanigan (2000) conducted a longitudinal study of writing assignments that started with a sample of more than a hundred freshmen at a large state university. He collected every writing assignment and every returned paper they received during their next four years in college. One of the biggest problems he discovered was that, in the majority of the assignments given and in the evaluations returned to the students, the criteria and standards by which the writing was evaluated were not clear, even to Flanigan. In a separate study, Richard Paul and his associates (1997) interviewed 140 college teachers about their efforts to promote critical thinking. He found, among other things, that only a very small percentage of the teachers (8 percent) were able to identify the key criteria and standards by which they evaluate the quality of their students' thinking.

How can professors do a better job of clarifying the criteria and standards for student work? In *Effective Grading* (1998), Walvoord and Anderson examine grading as a "tool for learning and assessment." One impressive feature of this book is that it addresses a number of course design issues while starting with a focus on the topic of feedback and assessment.

One of the major contributions of these two authors is their insistence on the importance of having clear criteria and standards. In their fifth chapter, they describe a well-developed method called Primary Trait Analysis (PTA) that can be used to give students a better understanding of what the teacher wants and to help the teacher generate more meaningful feedback and assessment.

To construct a PTA scale for an individual assignment, a teacher should:

- Make sure you are clear about your objectives for the assignment.
- Identify the *criteria* or "traits" that will count in the evaluation.
- For each trait, construct a two- to five-point scale by creating descriptive statements of good and poor versions of this trait (this constitutes the *standards* for the assessment).
- Try out the scale with a sample of students or with colleagues, and revise as necessary [Walvoord and Anderson, 1998, p. 69].

To give this a more concrete meaning, the authors offered two examples. One is concerned with criteria one might find in science and the other in the humanities (pp. 81–82):

An Example from Science:
- *Criteria or Desired Trait: Hypothesis Construction*
- *Standards:*
   3 = *Correct* statement of problem with accompanying null and alternative hypothesis. *Good* choice of alpha level.

   2 = *Correct* statement of problem but does not include alternative hypothesis or alpha level.

   1 = Statement of problem is vague or missing, or hypothesis is *incorrect*.

An Example from the Humanities:
- *Criteria or Desired Trait: Elegance of Argument*
- *Standards:*
   5 = Original and clearly stated thesis; persuasive, well-organized, imaginative use of source material.

   4 = Clearly stated thesis, good use of sources, well organized.

   3 = Facts straight with a reasonable explanation of the subject under consideration.

   2 = Poorly stated thesis, inadequate survey of available sources, poor organization.

   1 = No awareness of argument or complexity.

Example of a Full Set of Criteria and Standards. To provide an example of how criteria and standards can be developed in relation to major course goals, I will describe an example of one professor I worked with in physics. He had a lab course on electronics. We spent some time identifying the main learning goals for the course and eventually formulated the following statement that focused on application learning:

BY THE END OF THIS COURSE, STUDENTS SHOULD
BE ABLE TO *DESIGN, CONSTRUCT,* AND *ASSESS* ELECTRONIC
APPARATUS TO MEASURE PHYSICAL PROPERTIES.

Once these three key areas of student performance had been identified, he was then able to proceed to construct the important *criteria* related to each goal, as shown in Exhibit 3.6.

Then for each of the criteria, he developed a set of four-point standards. These described different levels of quality performance for each criterion. The high (++) and low (−−) ends of his *standards* for three of the criteria are shown in Exhibit 3.7.

The process of clarifying his learning goals and then developing a clear statement of the associated criteria and standards had a powerful impact for this professor. It gave him the clarity and tools he needed for a variety of assessment tasks.

EXHIBIT 3.6. CRITERIA FOR AN ELECTRONICS LAB COURSE.

I. Design: To "design" well, students should be able to . . .
  A. Conceptualize problem
  B. Use a computer program to design
    1. Effectively
    2. Efficiently
  C. Identify the accuracy and precision needed for the measurement and available from the experiment.
II. Construct electronic measure equipment that is. . .
  A. Effective (measures properly, accurately, and only the intended property)
  B. Efficient
    1. Few wires
    2. Small amount of time to construct
  C. Robust (durable)
  D. Reliable
  E. Useful in the future
III. Analyze and Assess
  A. Determine how well the apparatus works.
  B. Determine how it can be improved.

EXHIBIT 3.7. STANDARDS FOR
THREE CRITERIA IN AN ELECTRONICS LAB COURSE.

Learning Goals:
 I. Design:
   Criterion A: *Conceptualize the problem.*
   ++ Considers errors, accuracy, and precision first. Still focused on the
      immediate but considers improvements as an afterthought.
   −− Cannot start or continue, even with a few hints. Needs everything laid out.
 II. Construct:
   Criterion C: *Construct a robust (durable) instrument.*
   ++ Reliability and durability questions are considered as part of planning
      process and are incorporated at each step.
   −− Reliability and durability are completely beyond thinking and
      understanding.
 III. Assess:
   Criterion A: *Determine how well the apparatus works.*
   ++ Thinks of what is necessary for a given measurement and makes sure that
      data is obtained to definitely answer the question at hand if possible.
   −− Does not understand or give consideration to this question.

With these tools, the students could engage in self-assessment with more focus and clarity. As for the teacher, he was able to assess student performance with more confidence and more focus.

The basic idea here is fairly straightforward. If we want assessment procedures that are good, we as teachers must make clear for ourselves and for our students what criteria we are going to use to measure student performance and what standards we have for each criterion.

Third Feature: Self-Assessment. In addition to developing forward-looking assessment procedures and clarifying our criteria and standards, a third change toward creating educative assessment is to create multiple opportunities for students to engage in self-assessment of their performance.

At some point, to be powerful performers in life as well as self-directed learners, students must learn how to assess the quality of their own work. This is important for psychological reasons, but it is also a skill that students simply have to develop. It does not happen automatically. What can a teacher do to assist students in developing their ability to assess their own performance? I see three related activities that teachers can use to support self-assessment.

Identify Relevant Criteria. First, the students need to acquire or develop an initial understanding of the relevant criteria and standards for assessing a particular kind of activity. What distinguishes high-quality from mediocre work in this area? Most of the time, students do not begin courses knowing the answer to this question, nor is it generally self-evident to a novice learner. One option is for the teacher to simply tell the students what the relevant criteria and standards are. But a better option, when it is possible, is to give students an opportunity to develop these criteria and standards themselves. This process can be initiated by having students brainstorm a list of criteria that they think might be relevant and appropriate. Then they can refine this list and develop their ability to use the criteria, first, by assessing the work of other students and then their own work.

Practice Using the Criteria on Other Students' Work. After students acquire or develop a preliminary list of relevant criteria, the next step in developing their ability to apply these criteria is to practice using them in the process of giving feedback to other students on their work. Some teachers, for example, have students read copies of other students' draft papers and give feedback. To do this, students have to have some sense of what constitutes a good paper and then apply those criteria to new papers, in this case, the papers of other students.

Practice Using the Criteria on One's Own Work. A third phase in this process occurs when students are able to apply performance criteria to their own work and make improvements based on that assessment. For this to happen, students need to perform some challenging task (for example, write an essay, give a speech, think critically about a problem) and then use relevant criteria to assess their own performance. When students can do this effectively, they have succeeded in learning how to engage in honest self-assessment. If all college graduates could do this in all or nearly all the areas they study, it would be an enormous enhancement of their adult life activities.

Three Examples of Self-Assessment Activities. One interesting example of students giving feedback to each other occurs with Post-it notes.

In one business course, several student teams are asked to be consultants for a rapidly growing day-care center that has outgrown its paper-based record-keeping system and needs a new, computer-based system for keeping records of children, attendance, payments, and so on. The teams are all instructed to make recommendations for hardware, software, and operating procedures. After working on the problem for a few class sessions, the teams put their recommendations on a large sheet of paper and then tape the sheets to the wall. After the recommendations have been posted, the teams all go around the room reading, analyzing, and assessing the relative quality of each set of recommendations. At the end of the assessment time, each team puts a *blue* Post-it note by the set they think is best and a *yellow* Post-it note on the one about which they have a significant question. They also write the nature of their question or concern on the yellow note. After the responses have all been made, each team whose recommendations have received any yellow Post-it notes is given a chance to answer or address the questions posed by their peers. The level of attention and energy at the time the Post-it notes are posted is quite high.

In this assignment, the student teams learn how to assess one another's work quite closely. They see how different people can come up with different solutions to the same problem, and they have to ask themselves: "Which of these plans would work best? Why do I think some would be better than others?" This leads to the tacit development of criteria, which then become explicit when they write comments on the Post-it notes. The discussion that ensues when each team responds to concerns identified by other teams stimulates in-depth thinking and analysis, in this case, of what the differences are between the various hardware and software options, and how important these are for the problem at hand.

A second example comes from a teacher in one of my workshops and illustrates a way to have students assess their own work. In her course, students are asked to write a substantial end-of-semester paper that incorporates much of the subject for the semester—a standard sort of assignment. When the assignment is made, students are also given the criteria by which the papers will be evaluated, which is less common but not unheard of. But the teacher then tells the students to use those criteria to assess their own papers. When the students turn in their papers, they also indicate what grade they think their own paper deserves and why.

The teacher still reads the papers and does her own preliminary evaluation. If the student's self-declared grade is within one level of the grade the teacher would give (on a plus-minus scale), the student's grade is the one that goes in the grade book. If the difference is more than one level, the student must come in for an appointment and talk with the teacher about why the self-declared grade was as high or as low as it was. At this time the teacher shares her view of the paper. The student then goes home, reassesses the paper, and turns in a new grade and justification; sometimes this is a higher grade and sometimes a lower grade.

This is a good example of students' going beyond the assessment of other students' work to being able to apply such criteria to their own work. This is what eventually needs to happen if they are to become self-assessing people in their adult life.

The third example is a particularly ingenious approach to self-assessment that involves the development of critical thinking.

Richard Paul (1996), who offers national and regional workshops on how to teach critical thinking, also teaches his own course titled "Critical Thinking." As a final project in that course, he has students write a statement assessing how well they have learned to engage in critical thinking by the end of the course. He notes the pressure this creates for doing an honest self-assessment. A well-thought-out paper in which the student argues "I only did a mediocre job of learning to think critically" will receive a high grade and therefore will probably raise the student's course grade. On the other hand, a paper that tries to argue "I did a great job of learning to think critically" but is unable to provide persuasive evidence for that point will receive a low grade and therefore will probably lower the student's course grade. Paul has created an assessment situation in which it very clearly pays for the student to do a good job of critical self-assessment and to be absolutely honest.

Fourth Feature: "FIDeLity" Feedback. Feedback occurs whenever teachers, fellow students, or even people from outside the course look at a student's performance and give the student an evaluation of it. Like assessment, feedback is inherently evaluative; that is, it presents information about what is good about the work and what could be improved, but it also helps the learner find ways to improve it. In this sense, it puts the feedback provider in the role of a coach.

There are two important differences, though, between feedback and assessment. The first is that feedback does not become part of the course grade; only assessment does that. Second, feedback is done in dialogue with the learner, whereas assessment is announced to the learner. The result of the assessment, for example, might be: "You got a 75." (Or a "C," depending on the symbols being used). To provide feedback, the teacher needs to share an evaluation of the student's work, find out what the student thought of the work and what criteria the student was using, share information about the teacher's criteria and how they were applied, and so on. This dialogue is important because it allows the teacher to be sure the student understands the criteria and how they apply, and it starts the process of helping the student learn how to engage in self-assessment.

One way of characterizing the traits of high-quality feedback is with the acronym of FIDeLity. As noted earlier, this simply means that good feedback is

- *F*requent
- *I*mmediate
- *D*iscriminating (based on criteria and standards)
- Done *L*ovingly (or, supportively)

Frequent feedback occurs in every class if possible or at least every week. The students are doing something about which they get feedback, usually from either the teacher or fellow learners. The widespread practice of giving feedback only in the form of two midterms and a final is simply insufficiently frequent for high-quality learning.

Immediate feedback occurs very close in time to the learning activity itself, if possible during the same class. The problem with delayed feedback is that students cease to care about why their answer or activity was good or not. When the feedback comes a week or more after the learning activity, they just want to know, "Wha'd I get?"

Discriminating feedback distinguishes between good and poor performance in a way that is clear to the students. Just writing "OK" on a paper or project is neither informative nor discriminating. To be properly discriminating, the feedback needs to be based on clear criteria and standards, the same kind of criteria and standards that are involved in assessment. Students need to know, for example, that the criteria for a particular kind of essay include clear organization and the proper use of evidence and reasoning. Knowing that their organization was good but their use of evidence and reasoning was poor provides more discriminating and useful feedback than either "OK" or a "B" grade.

Lovingly delivered feedback is essential to get the message through. Why is this? When feedback is not done in the context of a loving, caring relationship, students are not likely to hear the desired message. Instead, they will filter the message for bare facts and think, "I need to do what this teacher is telling me, so I can get the grade I need and get out of here," rather than, "This teacher is providing me with the information I need if I want to learn and improve my ability to engage in this kind of activity, now and in the future." When there is empathy, personal understanding, and love, students are more likely to open up and internalize the multiple meanings of feedback in a fuller way. This principle is based on the psychology of feedback and assessment.

Feedback that has all these characteristics may sound attractive, but how can it be done? I will suggest some possible ways, first by looking at what we can learn from the psychology of feedback and assessment and then by examining two specific examples.

The Psychology of Feedback and Assessment

One key idea in educative assessment is that this process has multiple goals. In addition to needing procedures that give the students and teacher valid information about student performance, courses need procedures that support the student's ability and desire to continue learning. This means teachers need to attend to the psychological effects of different ways of providing feedback and assessment. I have two suggestions on this topic.

The Need for a Scoreboard and for Applause. As a sports fan and occasional coach for my son's sports activities, I have noted the impressive motivation that sporting activities generate in people, despite the painful and universal experience that even the best teams have when they lose. What accounts for the players' continuing motivation to get better? After looking at this phenomenon and at teaching and learning situations, I have come to believe that situations with a scoreboard and applause have the elements necessary to powerfully stimulate high performance, whether that be in sports or in educational settings.

In sports, players have a scoreboard that gives them quick, reliable feedback on the quality of their performance. Basketball players know immediately whether that jump shot they have been practicing was successful this time or not. In education, this is the function of feedback based on clear criteria, frequently and fairly applied. Whether students are learning how to think critically or how to interpret a novel, they need prompt feedback and clear criteria for knowing whether they did it well or not this time.

The other important psychological factor in sports is the applause of the audience. As any coach knows, the support of a friendly audience for every successful play is very motivating and is the main reason it is a lot easier to win at home than it is on the road. In education, this is the function that can be fulfilled by other students, the teacher, or even an external assessor. When other students, the teacher, or external assessors compliment learners on their success in learning, they provide a powerful incentive to continue learning and to continue improving.

Examples of Successful Use of Scoreboards and Applause. One example of successful use of a scoreboard and applause is a music education professor who prepares students to be band directors. He described for me what he considers to be a key observation in his teaching. He set up the following learning sequence that is repeated several times during the course:

- Each student transcribes a piece of band music.
- That student then has to teach the new piece of music to an ad hoc band composed of fellow students in a series of ten-minute periods once a week.
- Each teaching session is videotaped.
- Immediately following the teaching episode, the student teacher receives verbal and written feedback from peers, TAs, and the college teacher.

- Following the videotape the student teacher also writes a self-analysis of the session in a journal: personal feelings that occurred while teaching and after watching the videotape, how well the class seemed to respond or perform, and so on.
- Before the next teaching session, the student teacher meets with the college professor for a coaching session, using the videotape and the student's self-analysis, and trying new ways of leading the rehearsal and other possible behaviors.

This professor noted a typical pattern of change in the students during this process. During the first several weeks, the student teachers try to teach their impromptu band and dutifully follow the professor's instructions. If he tells them to make their instructions to the players more succinct, they work on that. If he tells them to do some advance planning for the rehearsal session, they do that. But they only act in response to the teacher.

Then, at some point, the student teacher gets it and moves to a different level of operation. All the pieces come together—the planning, talking, directing, and the rest—and the student teacher has a noticeably more successful practice session. The feeling of success leads to a feeling of pride. Fellow students respond with comments such as, "Hey, that was a great session you did today." The college teacher acknowledges and compliments the student on the quality of the session. The success, based on clear criteria (like points on the scoreboard) plus the positive feedback from fellow students and the teacher (like applause) lead to a key change in the students: They start to care about the whole action of whatever it is they are learning to do (in this case, directing a group of band students).

From that point on, the professor reports, student teachers approach the rehearsal sessions very differently. They are composed and relaxed; they are ready to accept the role of teacher and be in charge; they start to become self-directing learners who are searching for ways to get better.

This teacher also added some interesting information about what happens to students who go through this procedure and then go on to actual school teaching situations. His observation is that, when placed in new situations, the new teachers often take one or two steps backward in their performance while they are dealing with the many unknowns in their new situation. But generally this only lasts for a short while. After this initial adjustment stage, the new teachers progress and quickly reach a level of performance that is even higher than that displayed in the preparatory phase of their development.

Another example of the effective use of a scoreboard and applause also comes from the field of music, this time from a trumpet professor. For years he had been following the usual pattern in studio lessons with individual students: listening to them play and then telling them what they need to do to get better. At one point he realized that his students had in fact learned a lot from their high school band teachers (as well as others) and that both he and the students needed to acknowledge that. So he developed the simple but powerful idea of writing a "tribute letter." The students would each identify one or more people who had helped them learn some valuable skill, for example, good fingering, good tone, and good practice habits. Together they would then compose a letter from the college professor, thanking that person for the contributions to this student's music development.

In addition to creating extremely good public relations between the university and the public at large, this simple device had an unusual impact on both the students and the teacher. For the teacher, it shifted his focus from "What is not good in this student's playing that needs to be improved" to "What is good that can be commended?" This in turn resulted in a much more positive general relationship with the student. For the students, it developed a more positive view of themselves. The more positive tone of the interaction with the professor led them to think things like: "I have a good base of learning, and from that, I can continue to build toward an even better level of performance." This in turn created an appreciation of the people who had contributed to their own learning and—as a result of the preceding—a more positive attitude toward continued learning.

This whole cycle of a more positive interaction began with the professor looking for ways to give "applause," that is, positive feedback and not just critical feedback.

The Importance of Empathy in Feedback. Wiggins (1998), when discussing "Educative Assessment," identifies two key elements as being fundamental in generating assessment as truly educative. The first is "authentic tasks," or what I have labeled forward-looking assessment, as noted earlier. But the second key element is providing "performer-friendly feedback" (p. 21). He notes that when teachers do in fact give students challenging and authentic tasks to learn, and on which they will be assessed, students generally do not do well initially because the "bar has been set high." At this point in their learning, it is critical that they receive encouragement to do well. Then, with time, the teacher can "raise the bar" and begin to call for greater expectations. Hence an attractive sequence of feedback is to initially emphasize encouragement (that is, "performer-friendly feedback"); then as time goes on, the assessment can gradually move toward the still necessary goal of "honoring excellence," that is, still provide a valid scoreboard of high-quality performance.

Summary of Suggestions for Feedback and Assessment

This concludes our discussion of step #3 in the initial phase of designing a course: formulating good procedures for feedback and assessment. In this section I have suggested using the principles of educative assessment, that is, feedback and assessment procedures that enhance the quality of the learning process itself, that go well beyond simply giving the teacher a basis for issuing a grade to students.

To do this, teachers need to work on the four basic components of educative assessment:

- Create *forward-looking assessment* questions and problems.
- Develop clear and appropriate *criteria and standards* for evaluating student performance.
- Create opportunities for students to engage in *self-assessment.*
- Provide *FIDeLity feedback:* feedback that is frequent, immediate, discriminating, and done lovingly.

Figure 3.7 provides a visible summary of these components and their interrelationships.

FIGURE 3.7. FOUR BASIC COMPONENTS OF EDUCATIVE ASSESSMENT.

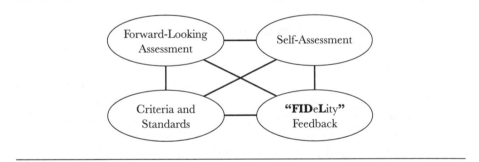

Review of the Course Design Process Thus Far

In this chapter I have introduced a new model of the course design process, *integrative course design,* and started the task of showing how it can help teachers design more powerful learning experiences for students. This began with the first step of analyzing the situational factors in the teaching situation, which must be done thoroughly and carefully because the results of this analysis will affect the three key decisions that have to be made. The second step focuses on the question of what the teacher wants students to get out of the course, that is, the learning goals for the course. My recommendations are that this task be done in a way that is learning-centered rather than content-centered and that the taxonomy of significant learning be used to formulate a powerful set of learning goals. The third step is to formulate good feedback and assessment procedures. My recommendation here is to use a set of procedures known collectively as *educative assessment.* These procedures are capable of supporting and furthering the learning process itself while still providing the teacher and the learner with information about how well the student is learning.

The next step in the course design process is to develop the actual teaching and learning activities that will determine the character of the learning experience for students. And that is the beginning topic of the next chapter.

CHAPTER FOUR

DESIGNING SIGNIFICANT LEARNING EXPERIENCES II: SHAPING THE LEARNING EXPERIENCE

This chapter continues the process of designing significant learning experiences for students. Once you have carefully analyzed the situational factors, identified significant learning goals, and formulated educative feedback and assessment procedures, you have the basic components in place. But you still have some essential work left to do in the initial phase of the design process: you need to decide what teaching and learning activities to use and to make sure the main component parts of your course are properly integrated.

The second half of this chapter addresses the intermediate and final phases of the design process shown back in Exhibit 3.1 (p. 67). The intermediate phase covers the tasks of developing a differentiated course structure, selecting an effective instructional strategy, and then combining these into an overall scheme of learning activities for the whole course. The final phase completes the design process by setting up the grading system, debugging the design, writing the course syllabus, and planning an evaluation of the course.

Initial Phase, Continued

The remaining efforts in the initial phase are particularly important. To a major extent, they shape the nature and quality of the students' learning experience, so it's necessary to give them as much attention as was given to the preceding components of the course.

Step #4: Generate Teaching and Learning Activities

This fourth step is both crucial and challenging. If the preceding steps have been done well, though, you will at least be in a good position to respond to this challenge. After carefully analyzing the teaching and learning situation, identifying the learning goals, and formulating feedback and assessment procedures, you now face two questions: What will the students actually do (the learning activities) and what will you do (the teaching activities) to make significant kinds of learning happen?

For many decades or even centuries, teachers have followed a tradition in which their teaching activity consists primarily of presenting an organized summary of their understanding of the subject (that is, lecturing) and leading occasional whole-class discussions of the subject (sometimes euphemistically called Socratic dialogue), using questions intended to both intrigue the students and reveal new aspects of the subject. This tradition creates the kind of learning experience for students that primarily consists of listening to and taking notes on lectures and participating in class discussions with one's own thoughts and very occasionally an original question.

> *Steps in Integrated Course Design*
>
> **Initial Phase: Building Components Parts**
> 1. Situational Factors
> 2. Learning Goals
> 3. Feedback & Assessment
> **4. Teaching & Learning Activities**
> 5. Integrate the Component Parts
>
> **Intermediate Phase: Coherent Whole**
> 6. Course Structure
> 7. Teaching Strategy
> 8. Overall Set of Learning Activities
>
> **Final Phase: Four Remaining Tasks**
> 9. Grading System
> 10. Possible Problems
> 11. Write Syllabus
> 12. Evaluation of Course and Teaching

In the last decade or so this tradition has been seriously challenged by the concept of active learning. The research literature on college teaching has raised serious questions about the effectiveness and adequacy of the lecture-discussion tradition and has suggested that students will learn more and will retain that learning longer if more active methods of teaching and learning are used (Bonwell and Eison, 1991; Bonwell, 1992–93; Meyers and Jones, 1993; Bean, 1996; Sutherland and Bonwell, 1996).

What do we mean by the concept of active learning? In the publication that crystallized this concept, Bonwell and Eison offered a straightforward definition of *active learning* as "anything that involves students in doing things and thinking about the things they are doing" (1991, p. 2). While that definition still seems on target, I would like to expand it slightly and conceptually reorganize it in a way that will allow teachers to do four important tasks:

- Analyze what is valuable in both traditional and contemporary ideas about teaching.

- Identify the key activities that allow effective teachers to be effective.
- Generate appropriate teaching and learning activities for a given subject that are consistent with the principles of active learning.
- Reveal the synergistic interdependence among the three components of active learning.

As teachers search for ways of moving beyond the lecture-discussion tradition, what ideas are available to guide this effort? Figure 4.1 shows a basic model of passive and active learning. This diagram is based somewhat on the definition of active learning given by Bonwell and Eison, but it also expands that definition somewhat. What they call "doing things" is referred to here as "experiences," and I simply note the importance of recognizing two basic kinds of experience: doing and observing. What they describe as having students "thinking about the things they are doing" is here termed "reflection."

Explanation of the Components. I will comment briefly on each of the three components of Figure 4.1 and then begin the process of expanding and reorganizing the idea of active learning.

Receiving Information and Ideas. Passive learning refers to what happens for students when they listen to a lecture or read a book: they receive information and ideas. This is an important part of learning, but by itself, it is very limited and limiting. When teachers see their job as being primarily to cover the material, this results in students' spending many hours of class time listening to "teacher talk." Although it is true that intellectually mature students can and will do their own reflection and make connections, this is an optional activity, not one the teacher has built into

FIGURE 4.1. PASSIVE AND ACTIVE LEARNING.

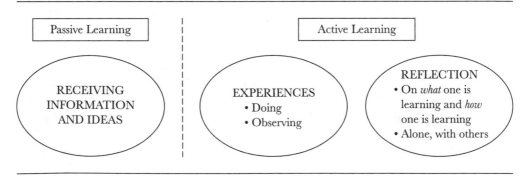

the learning experience. To get beyond "teacher talk" and add more power to the learning experience, we need to incorporate more active modes of learning into the design of the course experience.

"Doing" Experiences. "Doing" refers to any learning activity where the learners actually do that which we want them to learn how to do: design a reservoir dam (engineering), conduct a high school band (music education), design and conduct an experiment (natural and social sciences), critique an argument or piece of writing (the humanities), investigate local historical resources (history), make an oral presentation (communication), and so on. When you think about the goals for your course, think about what it is that you want students to do with this subject after the course is over: design something, read articles critically, write essays about the subject. Whatever it is that you want students to learn how to do, that is what they need to be doing during the course.

"Observing" Experiences. "Observing" occurs whenever a learner watches or listens to someone else doing something related to what they are learning. This might be observing a teacher demonstrate something ("This is how I critique a novel"), listening to other professionals perform (musicians), or observing the phenomena being studied (natural, social, or cultural).

Observing gives learners a chance to experience the reality of the phenomena they are studying. Providing this opportunity can sometimes be challenging for a teacher, but creative teachers are always searching for effective ways to do this.

One good example of an opportunity for students to observe comes from a professor who teaches a class titled "Native American Music" for non–music majors. She takes her students on a weekend trip to observe an authentic Pow Wow. She could have taken the easy route and just played recordings or even showed video clips. But she found that when she has students go to a Pow Wow and experience it firsthand, they typically make two discoveries. First, they discover that the subject they have been studying is something real and significant. Second, they discover that the content of the course (the analytical tools, the information, and so on) allows them to meaningfully interpret and understand what they experience at the Pow Wow, that is, to make sense out of it. Hence, including a strong, direct observing experience allows students to discover the reality of the subject and the value of what they have been learning about the subject.

Reflection and the Making of Meaning. Reflection, the second major component of active learning, was part of the original definition, but Bonwell and Eison did not develop it as fully as their experiential component. When the act of reflection is linked to the human need to make meaning, the enormous significance of this activity becomes clear.

People are meaning-making beings. We make meaning based on our experiences and on the information and ideas we encounter. However, this is where a potential problem crops up. Whenever someone has a new experience or encounters a new idea, those events automatically have an initial meaning. But this initial meaning may remain buried at the unconscious or subconscious level. When this happens, the meaning may be limited, distorted, or even destructive. As humans, we have the capacity to change the meaning of our ideas and experiences—but only when we pull our original meanings up to the conscious level and reflect on what new meaning we want those ideas or experiences to have. Only then do we become *meaning-making* beings, rather than simply meaning-receiving beings. One goal in teaching is to help students to become more adept at meaning making, and that means they need to spend time reflecting on the meaning of the experiences and new ideas they acquire.

Reflection: Alone or with Others? Some portion of the meaning-making process will always need to be done by individuals who spend time reflecting alone. But most people find that making meaning entirely by themselves is not the most effective way of accomplishing this task. When we engage in dialogue with others, the possibility of finding new and richer meanings increases dramatically. In addition, when people collaboratively search for the meaning of experiences, information, and ideas, they also create the foundation for *community*. Creating a sense of community is a concept that can greatly enhance the quality of a learning experience at the level of an individual course and at the level of the whole college experience.

A Holistic View of Active Learning. These three components of active learning combine to form an enlarged and more holistic view of the topic—one that includes "getting information and ideas" as well as "experiences" and "reflection." We need a more holistic view to create the kinds of learning activities capable of achieving significant learning. Figure 4.2 illustrates this new conceptualization of active learning, one that makes all three modes of learning an integral part of a more complete set of learning activities.

This new view of active learning suggests that two principles should guide the choice of learning activities. First, an effective set of learning activities is one that includes activities from each of the three components of active learning: information and ideas, experiences, and reflection. Second, direct ways of providing these three forms of learning are preferable whenever possible. Indirect, or vicarious, forms may be necessary at times. But teachers who can find direct ways of providing active learning enhance the quality of student learning.

FIGURE 4.2. A HOLISTIC VIEW OF ACTIVE LEARNING.

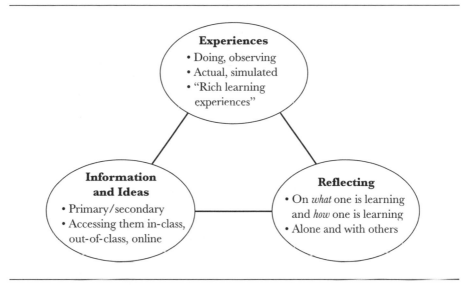

Specific Activities That Promote Active Learning. Exhibit 4.1 identifies a number of specific learning activities, categorized in terms of which component of active learning they support. As indicated there, some activities engage students directly in a particular aspect of learning while others do so indirectly. This exhibit also includes ideas on how active learning might be accomplished with online instruction.

Getting Information and Ideas. It's easiest to start with the most familiar component. When a teacher has students read a textbook or listen to a series of lectures, what is happening for students? They are getting information and ideas, and they are doing this indirectly; that is, the information and ideas have been organized and interpreted by an intermediary—the textbook writer or the lecturer. Some teachers move student learning up to a direct mode of getting information and ideas by having them read original sources and examine original data, that is, ideas and data that have not yet been fully analyzed and interpreted by others.

"Doing" Experiences. As noted earlier, there are "doing" experiences and "observing" experiences, both of which are valuable. A *direct "doing" experience* consists of students' engaging in a real action in an authentic setting. For example, if a teacher wants to prepare music students to be public school band teachers, then providing

EXHIBIT 4.1. ACTIVITIES THAT PROMOTE ACTIVE LEARNING.

	Getting Information and Ideas	Experiencing		Reflecting (on *what* one is learning and *how* one is learning)
		Doing	Observing	
Direct	• Original data • Original sources	• Real doing, in authentic settings	• Direct observation of phenomena	• Classroom discussions • Term papers • In-depth reflective dialogue and writing on the learning process
Indirect, Vicarious	• Secondary data and sources • Lectures, textbooks	• Case studies • Simulations • Role-play	• Stories (can be accessed via film, literature, oral history)	
Distance Learning (online courses, interactive video, correspondence courses)	• Course Web site • Internet • Video lectures • Printed materials	• Teacher can assign students to "directly experience" . . . • Students can engage in indirect kinds of experience, at distant sites or online.		• Students can record their reflections, and then, if they choose, share their reflections with others in writing, via TV, or online.

them with an opportunity to go into a real school setting and lead the band students there, even if only for a short time, would be providing them with a direct "doing" experience. Or a teacher who wants to prepare students to use their knowledge of biology to shape public policy could have them attend and participate in a community or regional discussion of environmental issues.

Sometimes teachers are unable to provide students with direct "doing" experiences and therefore need to find or create an *indirect or vicarious "doing" experience*. Case studies, gaming, simulations, and role-playing—all are forms of learning that provide students with a vicarious form of doing. When medical schools and business schools give their students case studies, the students are practicing the doing of problem solving and decision making. When small groups work in class to solve problems in chemistry or answer questions in history, they are practicing the doing of those disciplines. When students in education or the humanities engage in role-playing, they are also translating ideas into human actions and thereby are engaging in another form of doing that is related to those fields. In each case, these indirect or vicarious forms of doing allow students the advantage of actually engaging in the kind of activity that the course is preparing them to engage in after the course is over. And the vicarious form allows them to do this without the risks and consequences that might be associated with making a learning mistake in a real situation. For example, if a business class makes a bad decision about how a company should market a new product while doing a simulation, the only result is an opportunity to learn; in real life, the consequences would be costly.

"Observing" Experiences. As with doing, students can directly observe relevant phenomena in some cases, but in other cases they may need to seek indirect observations. Some familiar examples of *direct observation* might include the following:

- Students in an art class go to a painter's studio and observe how a professional (or at least a high-quality) painter goes about the task of creating a picture.
- Students in a sociology class observe and make notes on human behavior in a crowded public place or in a family setting.
- Students in an astronomy class make nightly or weekly notes on their observation of the positions of the moon and stars.

In these situations, students are directly observing the phenomena they are trying to learn about. What they observe may be some kind of object (a painting, a human behavior, a star), or it may be the people interacting with these objects (a painter, a would-be leader in a social group, an astronomer), depending on what the teacher is trying to get students to learn about. But in either case, the students directly observe the phenomenon itself.

In other cases, students will *indirectly observe* some phenomena, generally by getting stories about the topic under study. This has the disadvantage of being indirect and thereby less full or authentic, but it also has the important advantage of significantly broadening the range of phenomena to which students have access. For example, in one of the case studies presented in the next chapter, students in a nursing class were trying to learn about cultural issues involved in childbearing. The teacher showed them a film about childbearing women in a variety of cultures, for example, Native American, Asian, and so on. These students would never have been able to directly observe and interview such women in so many different cultures. But viewing the film allowed them to acquire, indirectly—via the eyes of the filmmaker and the women who were interviewed—a wide-ranging and valuable set of observations on the meaning of childbearing in different cultures. Even as films and videotapes are able to provide students with indirect observations, literature and oral histories about the subject of a course can also provide students with stories that allow them to indirectly observe people and events (real or imagined) in times and places to which they might never have direct access.

Reflection. After students have encountered new information and ideas and had new "doing" or "observing" experiences, they need time to reflect in order to decide what meaning to give these other learning activities. Without this reflection, they have learned something but they have not made that learning fully meaningful to themselves.

Teachers commonly use two activities that encourage students to *reflect on the subject of the course:* participating in classroom discussions and writing term papers. When teachers lead a whole-class discussion about something the students have read, students are engaging in reflective dialogue about the topic at hand and what a full and proper understanding of it is. The same thing happens when a class debriefs a simulation or problem-solving activity. They have just had an experiential form of learning, and now they are reflecting on what new understanding of the subject this has given them.

A rarer but potentially even more important form of learning occurs when teachers ask students to *reflect on the learning process* itself. A teacher can ask students to keep a journal for a course or to develop a learning portfolio. In either case, students write about what they are learning, how they are learning, what role this knowledge or learning plays in their own life, and how it makes them feel. Brookfield (1995, chapter 6) has suggested that teachers have students write about critical incidents in a class and their reactions to these incidents. This is a recommendation to have students reflect on the learning process.

Three Strategies for Implementing Powerful Forms of Active Learning. To incorporate active learning into your courses in an effective way, you need to build learning activities that include all three components of active learning. You also need to make sure that each of the three components is implemented as powerfully as possible. What are some ways of doing this?

Strategy #1: Create Rich Learning Experiences. Probably the single most powerful change most teachers can make in their courses is to expand the experiential dimension of student learning. What can students do or observe that will allow them to experience the subject in a meaningful way? The best experiences are those that will support the several kinds of significant learning goals established in Step #2 of the course design process. As a result, I find the concept of *rich learning experiences* to be useful here. These are learning experiences in which students are able to simultaneously achieve multiple kinds of significant learning.

Exhibit 4.2 lists some examples of rich learning experiences that have the potential for enabling students to acquire multiple kinds of significant learning simultaneously. This means, for example, that they can learn or review the content of the course (foundational knowledge), learn how to apply and use the knowledge (application knowledge), explore the personal and social meaning of the subject (the human dimension), combine one kind of knowledge with other kinds of knowledge (integration), and so on—all at the same time.

EXHIBIT 4.2. RICH LEARNING EXPERIENCES.

What are they?
  Learning experiences in which students are able to simultaneously achieve multiple kinds of significant learning.

What are some examples?
  In class:
  - Debates
  - Role-playing
  - Simulations
  - Dramatizations

  Outside of class:
  - Service learning
  - Situational observations
  - Authentic projects

My own campus has three courses or programs that offer good examples of rich learning experiences. These come from engineering, business, and regional and city planning courses.

Sooner City—a simulated engineering project. An exciting curricular innovation in the engineering college is a multiyear project focused on promoting students' design skills (Kolar and others, 2000; http://www.ou.edu/idp/newsletters/archive/recent-apr00.html). Believing that engineering students need to go beyond the "plug-and-chug" experiences of learning how to calculate specific, prestructured problems, the Division of Civil Engineering and Environmental Science developed a project called "Sooner City" (using the nickname for our sports teams). Starting with freshman courses and continuing through courses in their senior year, students work on projects that add to and eventually create a place called Sooner City. In a freshman class, for example, students may design a fire station and traffic corridor, meeting specific criteria provided by the professor. Later they build a power plant, add office buildings, survey the city to lay out a street system, and so on. Each new component that is added must be integrated with what is already in place; hence the project as a whole steadily becomes more complex and more interdisciplinary.

Although the first set of students to start this project is still enrolled, it is already clear that this curricular innovation is providing students with a rich learning experience. Each of these course projects requires students to gain additional design and computer competencies, learn how to work on major projects with deadlines, how to work together in teams and make public presentations about their project proposals, how to integrate different kinds of knowledge, and so forth.

Starting and running a real business. A small group of professors in the business college also started a curricular innovation in 1995 that has been winning national awards and creating some impressive results (http://www.ou.edu/idp/newsletters/archive/recent-may.html). Called the "Integrated Business Core" (IBC), this program is a set of four courses that students take in their first semester as majors in the business college, usually as second-semester sophomores or first-semester juniors. This program includes three fundamental courses (management, marketing, and legal issues) plus a practicum course in which new companies of thirty-five students each have to start and run a real business for one semester. Within a period of sixteen weeks, the student companies have to do the following:

1. *Get started:* Decide on a product or service to provide, obtain real start-up funding, get organized, and so on.
2. *Run the business:* Actually market and sell the product.
3. *Close out the business:* At the end of the semester, the company must stop sales, close out accounts, make a report of expenses and profits, and so on.

In addition, each company must select a local community service organization with which to work. Each company employee averages more than ten hours of service with the designated community organization, and all company profits are donated to this organization at the end of the semester.

After six years and twenty-four different companies, no company yet has gone bankrupt. In the first two years, most companies realized a net profit after sixteen weeks of between $1,000 and $2,000. The later companies have obviously been learning from the experiences of earlier companies because the average net profits in the last few years have been in the $10,000–$20,000 range. In the fall of 2001, two companies set new IBC records with net profits of $35,000 and $50,000.

Student comments indicate that participants have learned many different kinds of things from this integrated package of courses. They now know *why* they need subsequent courses in the curriculum; they have learned a lot about themselves in terms of their strengths and limitations as business personnel; they have learned about the relationship between business organizations and other community institutions (banks, service organizations); and they have learned from experience about the intricacies of getting organized and keeping a focus on the delivery of a quality product or service.

Recent data from graduating seniors indicate that over 50 percent of the seniors who went through the IBC program select this as the most significant learning experience they had during their entire time in the business college. Students have to use ideas at the same time they are learning about them; hence they clearly see the relationship between theory and practice. They have to engage with ideas as well as with other students, and they are required to engage in an activity they have never done before but can recognize that they will be doing in the future. This is powerful testimony to the impact of a well-coordinated, rich "doing" experience; it works year after year, even though the students in it have had no prior formal instruction in running a business.

Redesigning the Los Angeles River. One enterprising teacher of landscape architecture had a course where he gave his class—a combination of several undergraduates and a few graduate students—the opportunity to work on a major national project (James Sipes, personal communication).

In conjunction with professional teams from other parts of the country who were working on different aspects of the project, the students had to develop and propose a plan for enhancing the river that runs through the city of Los Angeles. In Phase I of the project, they learned how to use the Internet and other resources to obtain extensive information about Los Angeles, the river in its current form and use (or nonuse), and the like. In Phase II, they worked in teams to develop a proposal for what the city *could* do to enhance the beauty, use, and value of the river, in essence making it a river parkway. This included creating a computerized but realistic fly-over model of what the river would be like if such changes were made. In Phase III, these students actually went to Los Angeles for the first time and presented their proposal to the City Council. Their level of commitment became quite apparent when their whole computer program crashed the night before their meeting. They had to work until 4 A.M. to get it back up and running in time for a morning presentation to the City Council.

They did make their presentation successfully and the council bought the idea. In the fall of 1996, the citizens of Los Angeles approved a $319 million bond to fund the improvements proposed by the class!

These students, who were not a group of computer wizards before the project began, obviously learned a large amount of factual and conceptual information about urban planning. But they also learned numerous other things, all more or less simultaneously: how to apply conceptual ideas to specific problems, how to use computers to find information and to create models, how to work intensely with others, and how to meet deadlines, develop confidence in themselves, experience the exhilaration of seeing a major project through to completion (successful completion in this case), as well as how to interact effectively with new and different kinds of people (such as the L.A. City Council). This, in my view, is a classic example of a rich learning experience.

The main point of reviewing these three examples is to show that good teachers manage to find different ways of creating rich learning experiences. Some do it with real projects (IBC), others with simulated projects (Sooner City). Some use projects that are done on campus; others connect with places at some distance (the Los Angeles River Project). The common theme in these diverse examples is recognizing the need to provide students with a complex, challenging, context-rich "doing" experience that generates several kinds of learning simultaneously. The challenge this presents to all teachers is: What can I have my students do that will present them with a complex, challenging, context-rich learning experience?

Strategy #2: Find New Ways to Introduce Students to Information and Ideas. The second component of active learning pertains to the information and ideas that students need in order to understand a subject. This is basically synonymous with what teachers traditionally call the *content* of a course. At the present time the content is typically delivered by lectures and assigned textbooks. While this is a convenient method of delivery, it also has a significant limitation and a serious drawback in terms of student learning.

The limitation is that lectures and textbooks primarily expose students to secondary sources and secondary data. New learners will always need help from a teacher or book to create a context for understanding why a particular author or subject is important. But the more frequently students can experience original authors themselves and encounter primary data about a subject, the sooner they will learn how to make sense out of and use primary sources in their own lives.

The drawback to lectures as a means of delivering content is that they consume an inordinate amount of a scarce and expensive resource: class time. Relying on lectures requires the university to provide a room and utilities as well as make arrangements for a content expert and all the students to come together at the same time in the same place for several successive weeks. This is a costly undertaking. If teachers can find other, less expensive ways to introduce students to the important ideas and information in a course, the expensive resource of class time can be used for rich learning experiences, activities that cannot easily be undertaken elsewhere. What are some alternative ways of doing this?

The traditional option, having students read the material, is still valid—but we need to find ways to get this done both *outside* of class and *before* class. Many teachers will quickly object that when they assign material now, students do not read it. And this is true. But when I talk to students about why this is so, many say they do not even bother to buy the text for many of their courses because they don't need it: the teacher covers the same material in class.

What we have here is a double-feedback loop. The teachers do not believe the students will read the book, so they cover the material in lectures. When the students see that the teacher is going to cover the material in class, they decide not to do the reading. Getting out of this cycle requires a three-part response by the teacher. If you make a reading assignment, do not lecture on the same material in class. Instead, do something that lets students know you will hold them accountable for the assignment—say, give a quiz—but then also set up an in-class activity in which students will be able to use the information and ideas they have read. This will give them an intrinsic reason for doing the reading. Creating a sequence of activities like this will be described in more detail later in this chapter under the topic of setting up an "instructional strategy."

A second way of introducing students to information and ideas outside of class comes via the computer. The amount of original text material and specific kinds of data available on Web sites is increasing exponentially. Many teachers are finding this to be an important source of information and ideas for their students. One zoology professor who teaches physiology has found great value in a Web site containing numerous pictures of the human liver: healthy livers, diseased livers, with photographs taken from multiple angles. In his view, this Web site gives students better visual information on this topic than they could obtain from any textbook or even from working with livers in a laboratory setting. Similarly teachers in classics departments now have access to Web sites with documents in their original language (Latin, Greek, French, Chinese), with multiple versions available to compare different editions, different translations, and so on. These represent a valuable resource for both text material and data that students can access and read—outside of class.

If you are successful in finding ways to introduce rich learning experiences into your course (Strategy #1) and novel ways to enable students to learn the important information and ideas (Strategy #2), they will need some way to sort out all this learning and make sense of it. This is the function of the third strategy.

Strategy #3: Promote In-Depth Reflective Writing on the Learning Process. The third strategy for making teaching more powerful is related to the third component of active learning, reflection, and is focused on the special value of writing about the learning process itself.

This recommendation is based on two beliefs. The first is that writing, when viewed as a process and when done properly, has a unique ability to develop the interior life of the writer. The second belief is that the act of focusing students' attention on the learning process will make them more aware of themselves as learners and will thereby begin the process of developing their ability to create meaning in their lives. Exhibit 4.3 outlines some basic ideas about reflective writing.

I am making a distinction here between what I call substantive writing and reflective writing. By *substantive writing,* I am referring to writing that is focused on

---

EXHIBIT 4.3. IN-DEPTH WRITING TO FURTHER LEARNING.

For Whom?
  Oneself (journaling, learning portfolios)
  Others (teacher, other students, people outside class)

About What?
  Substantive Writing: about the subject of the course
    • What is a correct and full understanding of this concept or topic?

  Reflective Writing: about the learning process
    • What am I learning?
    • Of what value is this?
    • How did I learn best, most comfortably, with difficulty?
    • What else do I need to learn?

What Forms of Reflective Writing?
  One-minute papers
  Weekly journal writing
  Learning portfolios (end-of-course, end-of-program)

---

a topic and that attempts to present an organized statement about the information and ideas the writer has about that topic. The familiar practice of assigning term papers and essays has been used for centuries to engage students in substantive writing. *Reflective writing,* on the other hand, focuses on the writer's learning experience itself and attempts to identify the significance and meaning of a given learning experience, primarily for the writer. Hence it is quite acceptable in this kind of writing to address more personal issues, such as: What am I learning? Of what value is this, to me? How did I learn best, most comfortably, with difficulty? What else do I need to learn?

Both kinds of writing are valuable but for different reasons. Substantive writing allows and prompts writers to thoroughly think through their own ideas on a topic; hence the process of substantive writing itself often deepens the writer's understanding of the topic. Reflective writing has a different value, that of helping the writer become more self-conscious about learning. Becoming more aware of themselves as learners starts the process of allowing students to become self-directing and meaning-making learners.

Three forms of reflective writing are being used more and more by teachers who want to promote reflective learning. These are one-minute papers, regular journal writing, and learning portfolios.

A brief form of reflective writing: one-minute papers. Several writers (Angelo and Cross, 1993; Bean, 1996) have suggested the use of one-minute papers as a way of quickly and easily getting students to reflect on their learning and to do so in a way that is easily shared with the teacher. At the end of an individual class session or at the last class of a weekly sequence, the teacher asks students to take a piece of paper and write a short answer to a question. The question can vary but is often one of the following:

- What was the muddiest point in today's lecture?
- What was the most important idea you encountered in class this week?
- In your own words, how would you describe the relationship between topic X and Y?
- What important questions remain unanswered for you?

Students cannot respond to this assignment without in some way grappling with the question of: Well, what *was* the main point (or the muddiest point)? And to do that, they have to mentally review the whole lesson, a powerful learning activity. Initially students often give a wide range of answers in response to what the teacher thinks is a clear and straightforward question. One of the reasons for this is that students are not accustomed to doing this kind of reflective thinking nor to receiving feedback on the accuracy of their sense-making effort. But most professors also find that if they continue asking for and responding to one-minute papers, students get much better at giving valid responses. This suggests that, with practice and appropriate feedback, students can become effective at engaging in reflective dialogue with themselves about the nature and meaning of their learning experience.

An intermediate form of reflective writing: journals, diaries, and learning logs. A more extended kind of writing comes in the form of journals, diaries, and learning logs. In general, these call for students to keep a running commentary during a whole course (or some other extended learning experience). Usually the teacher collects these periodically, reads them, makes comments on them, and returns them. Again, this kind of writing prompts students to reflect on the meaning of their learning experience. The main difference between this and the one-minute papers is that course-long journal writing allows students more opportunity to connect and build on their interpretation of the whole learning experience.

An extended form of reflective writing: learning portfolios. The concept of having students create learning portfolios is a natural extension of the idea of reflective writing. In my view, the concept of learning portfolios is one of the more powerful educational ideas to emerge in recent times. Its unusual power derives from the fact that it simultaneously integrates and promotes all three of the main components of instructional design: significant learning goals, active learning activities, and educative feedback and assessment (see Figure 4.3).

The central idea of learning portfolios is for students to reflect on a selected learning experience—which may be a single course, all the courses in their major, or their whole college experience. Then, at the end of the course or program, students put together a document that describes and illustrates the meaning of the whole learning experience. Generally the portfolio consists of two parts: a narrative statement and an appendix with various kinds of material that illustrate and support the comments in the narrative. Zubizarreta (2003) gives more detailed guidelines on what learning portfolios are and how teachers can use them.

The main point to note here is that learning portfolios can be a powerful addition to the set of learning activities in a course. They can be used alone, but they work even better when used in conjunction with the previously mentioned forms of reflective writing. If students are periodically prompted throughout the course to write one-minute papers and weekly journals, they will gradually become more comfortable with—and capable of reflecting on and writing about—the quality of their learning experience. If they do this frequently during the course, they will have a substantial collection of ideas that can be extended and organized into the form of a learning portfolio at the end of the course.

Knowing that they will be doing a learning portfolio encourages students to reflect along the way on what they can and should be learning from a particular experience, how well they are achieving the learning goals set by the institution

FIGURE 4.3. THE EDUCATIONAL VALUE OF LEARNING PORTFOLIOS.

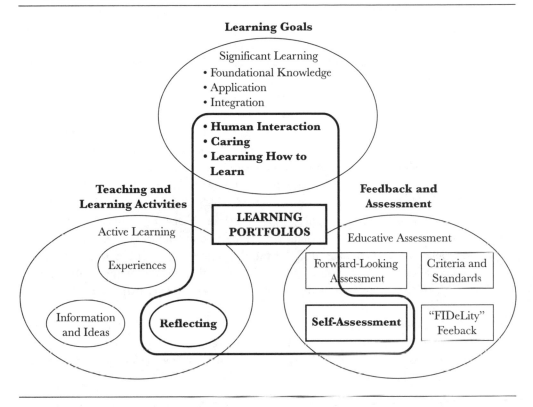

or by themselves, and what else they need to be learning. The final product also allows students to communicate with others what they have learned and, when appropriate, can become a tool that can be used for self-assessment and institutional assessment.

Different Ways of Using Learning Portfolios. Several individuals have written about using learning portfolios in the context of a single course. Annis and Jones (1995, p. 185) describe how Jones asked students in a communication course to include two types of information in the learning portfolio:

1. A well-written statement about your ability to communicate . . .; this may take several double-spaced pages.
2. An appendix of communication samples. These should be identified by page number and referred to in the introductory statement.

The portfolios she received ranged in size from ten to fifty pages. She reports that this assignment gave credibility to the other course assignments because students continuously looked for connections to their future work and for materials to include in their portfolio. Later, she notes, "They interacted more with the subject matter, with each other, and with me. . . . The more the students saw the relationship between their course work and their career objectives, the more enthused they became about the portfolio" (p. 189).

Brookfield has written about his use of "Participant Learning Portfolios" (1995, pp. 102–106). He viewed these as a "cumulative record of a student's experience as a learner in a particular course," adding that they worked best when "students have had the opportunity to practice weekly reflection on their learning." He was careful not to grade the quality of the reported experience, only the care with which it was documented. He also had students share their portfolio entries with each other in small groups so they could see the similarities and differences in how they had experienced learning in that course. His instructions to the students were more extended than in the preceding example, but he basically asked students to look at the "critical incidents" that he had them write about each week. Then, at the end of the semester, their task was to summarize both what they learned and how they learned.

Wlodkowski (1999, pp. 260–263) has labeled what he uses a "process folio." He sees this as a powerful tool for enhancing motivation and allowing him as a teacher to respond to the interests and concerns of diverse learners. He asks students to reflect on and write about three primary considerations:

1. The *content* of the learning: What have you learned about the subject (that is, about the content of the learning experience)?
2. The *context* of the learning: How does your learning fit into the larger context of your individual life, your social/organizational life, and/or your work life?
3. The *learning process:* What have you learned about how you do learn (or how you could learn) more effectively?

This allows students to document and reflect on challenges and understandings that emerge over time.

The Taxonomy of Significant Learning as a Structuring Device. When students write in a learning portfolio about *what* they have learned in a course or program, the taxonomy of significant learning works well as a structuring device. It offers a set of questions and concepts that points students to several possible meanings that their learning experience may have for them.

One professor in a business course on my campus used this taxonomy to guide students in the development of an end-of-semester learning portfolio. To do this, he gave students the following questions to guide their reflection:

1. What *key ideas or information* have you learned about the subject of this course?
2. What have you learned about *how to use or apply* the content of the course?
3. What parts of your knowledge, thinking, or actions have you been able to *integrate* or connect within or external to this learning experience?
4. What have you learned about the *human dimension* of this subject? That is, how have *you* changed in some important way, and have you changed in your ability to interact with *others?*
5. Have any of your interests, feelings, or *values* changed as a result of this learning experience?
6. What have you learned about *how to learn?*

This framework generated a high level of awareness for the students, both about what they were learning and how they were learning it.

Effective Use of Portfolios at the College Level. Alverno College in Milwaukee, Wisconsin, has all students work on a learning portfolio throughout their entire time as undergraduates there (Alverno College Faculty, 1994). Students collect information about their own learning in reference to the eight central abilities that guide the curriculum at Alverno:

- Communication
- Analysis
- Problem solving
- Valuing in decision making
- Social interaction
- Global perspective
- Effective citizenship
- Aesthetic response

To graduate, students must, among other requirements, be able to document a certain level of proficiency on all eight abilities. Teachers, administrators, and assessors at Alverno feel that the process of creating portfolios is a very important part of their effort to create an ability-based learning experience for students and a central part of the institution's effort to monitor how well the educational program is succeeding.

Online and Distance Learning: Are They as Good as a Live Classroom? Another question about active learning relates to online and distance learning. One of the more significant changes occurring in higher education, in the United States and in a number of other countries, is the rapidly growing use of information technology. The traditional mode of distance education—correspondence courses—has been augmented by interactive TV and especially by computer-mediated forms of teaching and learning: use of the Internet as source of course-related information, course-specific Web sites, two-way e-mail and general e-mail discussion groups for a class, and so forth.

These three forms of distance education each have their unique characteristics. Correspondence courses have a long-standing tradition and are less expensive to offer, at least as compared to the other two forms. Interactive TV adds a visual dimension to teacher-student interactions. But it is the computer-mediated form of distance education, which I see as a special form of online learning incorporating both synchronous and asynchronous interactions, that is attracting the most attention while also raising the most questions.

If one accepts active learning as a valuable principle for shaping the learning experiences of students, many people are led to ask: Can online learning be as good as learning in a live classroom? Can students really learn what they need to learn when a course is delivered completely or even partially online?

A quick but incomplete answer is that good online learning is definitely superior to poor classroom learning. But the real question is whether high-quality online learning is as good as high-quality classroom learning. In my view, the holistic model of active learning introduced in this chapter provides a conceptual framework that can be used to answer this question.

If we focus on the three components of active learning shown in Exhibit 4.1 (p. 108) and ask whether each of these can be fulfilled in a satisfactory manner with online learning, we will have a meaningful basis for deciding whether this form of learning has the potential to be a high-quality form of learning.

Access to Information and Ideas. In terms of giving students access to information and ideas, online learning is at least equal to and possibly superior to classroom teaching and learning. Anything that can be put into a textbook or even into a lecture can be put on a Web site (or CD-ROM). And simply as sources of information, Web sites have some significant advantages. They can be updated more easily and more quickly than textbooks, and they can provide high-quality text and rich illustrations—including sound as well as both still and moving pictures—available to anyone, anytime, anywhere.

Reflection. It is also relatively easy for online learning to support opportunities for student reflection. Students can record their private reflections in a file on their own computer, and they can interact electronically with other students and the professor via e-mail, discussion groups, bulletin boards, and chat rooms. Current software makes electronic dialogue a little slower and more cumbersome than live dialogue, but this is likely to improve as communication programs continue to improve. And some teachers have noted important advantages in electronic dialogue among students: students who tend to hold back in a live discussion feel freer to contribute online, and all students have more time to compose their thoughts in an online discussion.

Experiences. The biggest challenge to online learning, in my view, will be in providing a meaningful form of course-related experiences for students. However, with a little imagination, creative teachers may be able to come up with one or both of two kinds of responses. They can assign students to engage in a *direct,* authentic "doing" or "observing" experience, outside of class, even as teachers in a live classroom currently do. Or they can find ways for students to work online with *indirect* forms of experience such as working on case studies, simulations, accessing stories, and the like. At the present time, with current levels of hardware and software, this is possible but not easy to do. However, as the quality of computer hardware and software become more sophisticated—and if enterprising teachers can find creative ways of accomplishing this component—significant progress is likely to be made.

Conclusion. Briefly, my overall assessment of online learning is that it is strong in providing information and ideas and adequate for reflective dialogue. The weak link currently is the limited ability of online learning to provide significant forms of "doing" and "observing" experiences. If and when teachers find ways to do this effectively, good online learning will clearly be comparable with learning in good classroom courses (meaning classroom courses that also provide all three components of active learning).

This assessment of the relative strength and limits of online learning is reflected in the current operation of many hybrid courses, ones that continue to meet live but for fewer hours per week while conducting a significant portion of the coursework online. These courses frequently use the online component of the course to provide students with access to the information and ideas (that is, the content) and for online discussions. Live class time is then reserved for various kinds of experiential learning, for example, working on case studies, simulations, and so forth.

Summary of Active Learning. This discussion of generating effective teaching and learning activities for a course has focused on the task of expanding the set of learning activities in use. The learning activities that have traditionally been employed in higher education are lectures, whole-class discussion, and assigned readings. To make their courses more learning centered and more powerful, teachers will need to identify and use learning activities that incorporate all three components in the holistic view of active learning, as shown in Figure 4.2.

The single biggest improvement most teachers can make is to give students more "doing" and "observing" experiences related to the subject of the course. Direct experiences are the most powerful. But when these are not feasible, indirect and vicarious forms of doing and observing are still very valuable. Teachers can use the concept of rich learning experiences to guide their search for experiences that will support multiple kinds of learning simultaneously.

A second major area for attention is ensuring that students have significant opportunities to reflect on the learning process. In addition to thinking and writing about the subject, students also need frequent opportunities to step back from the other activities in the course and reflect on the learning process itself. Adding one-minute papers, weekly journals, and an end-of-term learning portfolio would be a strong combination for in-depth reflective writing.

Students will always need ways to acquire information and ideas relevant to the subject of the course, and there will always be value in lectures and secondary sources as a basis for students' study of a given topic. But teachers can facilitate the whole course design process if they can make two changes with this component of active learning. If they can find ways to move students' initial exposure to the content to *outside-of-class* learning activities, that will free up in-class time for things like rich learning experiences. And teachers need to continue searching for ways to introduce students to original authors and primary data. This will give students direct contact in their courses with the information and ideas we would like for them to be able to handle after the course is over.

If you can do all this, you will have completed Step #4 in the design process by creating a powerful set of learning activities, ones that reflect the principles of active learning.

Step #5: Integrate the Primary Components

Steps in Integrated Course Design

Initial Phase: Building Components Parts
1. Situational Factors
2. Learning Goals
3. Feedback & Assessment
4. Teaching & Learning Activities
5. **Integrate the Component Parts**

Intermediate Phase: Coherent Whole
6. Course Structure
7. Teaching Strategy
8. Overall Set of Learning Activities

Final Phase: Four Remaining Tasks
9. Grading System
10. Possible Problems
11. Write Syllabus
12. Evaluation of Course and Teaching

The final step in this initial phase of the course design process is to make sure the main components are properly integrated. This means you need to check the four components to be sure that they support and reflect each other. This is essentially a "check and change as necessary" operation. To do this, you examine each of the important connections between components.

Integrating Information About Situational Factors with the Course Decisions. The first step in the whole course design process was to gather information about the salient situational factors and then use that information while making the three major sets of course decisions. The question here is: Are the decisions consistent with the information gathered about the situational factors?

Some sample problems that can be detected and changed at the integration stage include the following:

- Are there presumptions of student knowledge or attitude that are not valid?
- Is the structure of the course consistent with the teacher's beliefs and values about teaching?
- Are there any conflicts between student goals and the teacher's goals?

If there are problems of inconsistency here, something needs to be changed.

Integrating the Three Components. The other part of the integration process involves the three components. The learning goals, the teaching and learning activities, and the feedback and assessment procedures all need to support each other.

One easy way to ensure integration of these components is to use the worksheet shown in Exhibit 4.4. First, write in all the primary learning goals for your course. If possible, include one for each kind of significant learning. In the first

EXHIBIT 4.4. WORKSHEET FOR CREATING INTEGRATED COMPONENTS.

Learning Goals for Course:	Procedures for Assessing Student Learning:	Learning Activities:
1. Understand and remember key concepts, terms, relationships, and the like.	?	?
2. Know how to use the content.	?	?
3. Be able to relate this subject to other subjects.	?	?
4. Understand the personal and social implications of knowing about this subject.	?	?
5. Care about the subject (and about learning more on the subject).	?	?
6. Know how to keep on learning about this subject after the course is over.	?	?

column of the worksheet, I have listed the general version of the six kinds of significant learning, to show what this might look like; you would translate these general statements into specifics for your course. Second, for each goal, identify the assessment procedures that will tell you whether students have achieved that kind of learning. For some learning, these may be the familiar paper-and-pencil tests. For other kinds of learning, you will probably need to find new and more innovative forms of assessment. Third, for each goal, identify specifically what students will need to do (that is, the learning activities) necessary to achieve that kind of learning. Some activities may be out-of-class reading, reflective writing, or other homework. In-class activities might be case studies, role-playing, whole-class discussions, small group problem solving, and the like (see Chapter Five).

An important benefit of using such a worksheet is that it helps the course designer avoid the easy trap of giving lip service to important learning goals but then going about teaching in a way that does not really support those learning goals.

Once teachers have designed strong primary components for the course and checked these components to be sure they reflect and support each other, they are ready to connect these activities in a way that allows the activities to build on and support each other.

Assessment of the Initial Phase

A major benefit of the model of integrated course design is that it provides specific criteria for assessing the quality of a course design. The highlighted areas in Figure 4.4. illustrate the primary components of this assessment.

These criteria indicate that the initial phase of the course design is good if it includes all the following elements:

- *An in-depth analysis of situational factors:* It is based on a systematic review that has identified all the major situational constraints and opportunities of the course.
- *Significant learning goals:* It includes learning goals focused on several kinds of significant learning, not just the understand-and-remember variety.
- *Educative feedback and assessment:* It includes the components of educative assessment—forward-looking assessment, opportunities for students to engage in self-assessment, clear criteria and standards, and "FIDeLity" feedback. These allow the feedback and assessment to go beyond audit-ive assessment.
- *Active teaching and learning activities:* It includes learning activities that engage students in active learning by incorporating powerful forms of experiential and reflective learning, as well as ways of getting basic information and ideas.
- *Integration and alignment:* All the major components of the course are integrated. That is, the situational factors, learning goals, feedback and assessment, and

FIGURE 4.4. CRITERIA FOR ASSESSING
THE INITIAL PHASE OF A COURSE DESIGN.

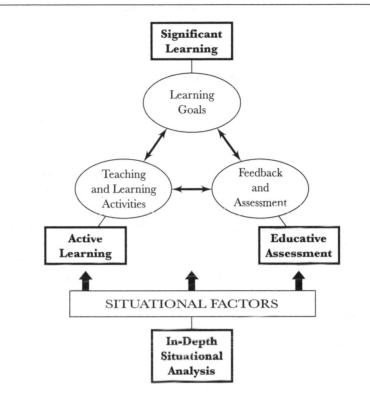

teaching and learning activities are all aligned so they reflect and support each other (as indicated by the arrows in Figure 4.4).

If the course design rates "High" on each of these five criteria, then the basic components of good design are in place.

Intermediate Phase: Assemble the Primary Components into a Coherent Whole

Once you have strong primary components for your course, you need to assemble those components into a powerful, dynamic whole. The two key steps in this process are creating a *course structure* and selecting an effective *instructional strategy.*

Then these two items have to be merged into an *overall scheme of learning activities.* You have the option of either creating the course structure first or the instructional strategy first; either way will work. I suggest starting with the course structure first simply because most people find that easier to do.

Step #6: Creating a Course Structure

Steps in Integrated Course Design
Initial Phase: Building Components Parts
1. Situational Factors
2. Learning Goals
3. Feedback & Assessment
4. Teaching & Learning Activities
5. Integrate the Component Parts
Intermediate Phase: Coherent Whole
6. Course Structure
7. Teaching Strategy
8. Overall Set of Learning Activities
Final Phase: Four Remaining Tasks
9. Grading System
10. Possible Problems
11. Write Syllabus
12. Evaluation of Course and Teaching

To create a thematic course structure, you need to look at the whole subject of the course and identify the most important concepts, issues, topics, or themes that constitute the subject of the course—usually at least four and no more than seven. These topics then need to be arranged in some kind of sequence. The topics might be arranged chronologically, or from simple to complex, or from fundamental topics to ones that emerge from the fundamentals, or possibly in some other pattern. The goal is to sequence the topics so that they build on one another in a way that allows students to integrate each new idea, topic, or theme with the preceding ones as the course proceeds. Creating a good structure also enables the teacher to identify problems or assignments for students to work on that gradually become more complex and challenging (see Figure 4.5).

For example, a professor teaching a course titled "Organizational Behavior" might select the following topics for the course:

- Organizational effectiveness
- Organizational design
- Motivation
- Communication and decision making
- Groups, teams, and leadership
- Organizational culture and change

Likewise, a chemistry professor might identify these topics for a first-semester physical chemistry course:

FIGURE 4.5. COURSE STRUCTURE FOR A HYPOTHETICAL COURSE.

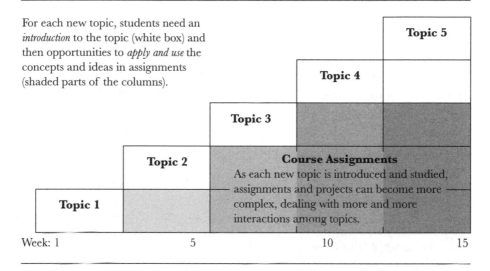

For each new topic, students need an *introduction* to the topic (white box) and then opportunities to *apply and use* the concepts and ideas in assignments (shaded parts of the columns).

Topic 5

Topic 4

Topic 3

Topic 2

Course Assignments
As each new topic is introduced and studied, assignments and projects can become more complex, dealing with more and more interactions among topics.

Topic 1

Week: 1   5   10   15

- First law of thermodynamics
- Second law of thermodynamics
- Equilibrium
- Kinetic-molecular theory of gases
- Ideal solutions

In each case, the teacher has in essence said that, if students can focus on and gain a good understanding of each of these concepts or topics, they will have a good grasp of the essential content of the subject and a good foundation for future learning. Each topic may have important subtopics under it, but these topics encompass the primary dimensions of the course.

Once the main topics have been identified, the teacher can decide on the sequence in which they will be studied and how many weeks will be devoted to each topic. They may all have the same amount of time, or some may need more time than others. Figure 4.5 shows how a course with five topics might be graphed out in a fifteen-week semester. Doing this clarifies opportunities for designing problems and assignments that involve all the topics studied to date. As the students go along, they should be able to work on more complex problems and on issues involving interactions among topics.

Step #7: Selecting an Effective Teaching Strategy

In the initial phase of the design process, teachers identify specific learning activities that will be effective enough to accomplish significant learning goals. What needs to be done now is to arrange these individual learning activities into an effective teaching strategy. This very important step requires a clear understanding of the distinction between a "teaching technique" and a "teaching strategy."

A *teaching technique* is a specific teaching activity. Lecturing is a technique; leading a class discussion is a technique, as is lab work, using small groups, assigning essays, covering case studies, and so on. These are all discrete, individual activities. A *teaching strategy*, on the other hand, is *a particular combination of learning activities in a particular sequence.* The goal is to find a combination and sequence of learning activities that work together synergistically and build a high level of student energy that can be applied to the task of learning.

Steps in Integrated Course Design
Initial Phase: Building Components Parts
1. Situational Factors
2. Learning Goals
3. Feedback & Assessment
4. Teaching & Learning Activities
5. Integrate the Component Parts
Intermediate Phase: Coherent Whole
6. Course Structure
7. Teaching Strategy
8. Overall Set of Learning Activities
Final Phase: Four Remaining Tasks
9. Grading System
10. Possible Problems
11. Write Syllabus
12. Evaluation of Course and Teaching

To understand the difference between techniques and strategies, and to lay the foundation for learning how to create a strategy, I would like to introduce an analytic exercise developed by Barbara Walvoord (personal communication in a workshop; see also Walvoord 1998, pp. 53–55). She postulates that all teachers face two common tasks. Teachers want and need their students to

- Master the content of the course.
- Learn how to use that content in some way.

In a general sense, the first task, introducing students to the content, is primarily valuable as a means to a more important end—the second task: learning how to use that content and identifying its value or significance.

What tools do teachers have to accomplish these tasks? They have a variety of different learning activities (which I call teaching techniques) that can be sorted into in-class activities and out-of-class activities, as in the diagram shown in Figure 4.6.

The problem, as Walvoord sees it (and I agree), is that most of us end up with very little time for the second task. Why is this? Because we spend so much class time trying to accomplish the first task (covering the content) that we have very lit-

FIGURE 4.6. TEACHING ACTIVITIES.

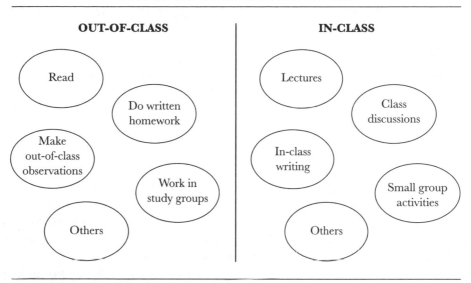

Source: Walvoord, workshop handout.

tle time left for the second one (helping students learn how to use the content). What is the solution to this problem? Finding some way to move the initial learning of the content to out of-class activities, leaving more in-class time for learning how to use it.

This analysis, while very helpful, needs to go one step further. To do this, I take Walvoord's diagram, rotate it 90 degrees counterclockwise, and create the template shown in Figure 4.7.

In this diagram, each box of in-class activities represents a class session and each box of out-of-class activities represents the time between class sessions when students can do out-of-class work. This template provides a framework for identifying the combination and sequence of activities, in- and out-of-class, that you want to use. It also highlights the planned sequence so you can see whether it is likely to synergistically build energy as it unfolds.

Examples of Three Teaching Strategies. To make this template more concrete, let me describe three teaching strategies from the literature on college teaching and show how each one fills in this template.

Team-Based Learning. Since the early 1990s, many teachers have begun to use small groups in their teaching. They have found that this is a relatively easy way to

FIGURE 4.7. THE "CASTLE TOP" DIAGRAM:
A GENERAL TEMPLATE FOR CREATING A TEACHING STRATEGY.

In-Class Activities:	Class Session		Class Session						
Out-of-Class Activities:		Between Classes		Between Classes					

incorporate active learning into their course and that it can make a dramatic difference in the quality of the learning experience. However, many teachers use
small groups as a teaching technique rather than as a strategy. In this case, small
groups are used as an independent activity, inserted here or there into a preexisting and basically unchanged course structure.

Team-based learning, on the other hand, is a sophisticated version of teaching with small groups that works at the level of a teaching strategy (Michaelsen,
Knight, and Fink, 2002; http://www.teambasedlearning.org/). This teaching strategy uses small groups extensively but sets up a particular sequence of activities that
transforms groups into teams and then uses the extraordinary capabilities of teams
to accomplish a high level of content and application learning (see Figure 4.8).

In this teaching strategy, students read the related material on their own, then
come to class and take a test on that material both individually and as a group.
This sequence, called the "Readiness Assurance Process," brings nearly all students up to a moderate level of content understanding quickly and effectively.
Then the students are able to spend a significant amount of time working in class
in small groups, learning how to apply that content through a series of practice
application exercises. Eventually students take a test that measures both their content understanding and their ability to use that content. Then the cycle starts over,
focused on the next major topic in the course.

By working through this sequence and getting frequent, immediate feedback
on their performance, the small groups gradually evolve into and become something quite different: "learning teams." Once these newly formed groups have
jelled and become cohesive teams, the members become very committed to the
work of their teams and the teams become capable of accomplishing some very
challenging learning tasks.

In terms of the holistic model of active learning recapped in Figure 4.9, the
team-based learning cycle begins with students' acquiring information and ideas

FIGURE 4.8. SEQUENCE OF ACTIVITIES IN TEAM-BASED LEARNING.

- Covering Two to Three Weeks
- Covering One Major Topic Within the Course

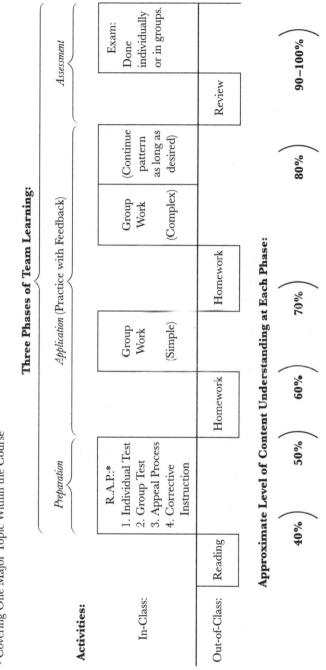

Three Phases of Team Learning:

| *Preparation* | *Application* (Practice with Feedback) | *Assessment* |

Activities:

In-Class:

R.A.P.:*
1. Individual Test
2. Group Test
3. Appeal Process
4. Corrective Instruction

Group Work (Simple)

Group Work (Complex)

(Continue pattern as long as desired)

Exam: Done individually or in groups.

Out-of-Class:

Reading   Homework   Homework   Homework   Review

Approximate Level of Content Understanding at Each Phase:

40%   50%   60%   70%   80%   90–100%

*R.A.P. refers to "Readiness Assurance Process"; the steps needed to make sure that students are ready to proceed to learning how to use the content.

Source: Michaelsen, Knight, and Fink, 2002. Used with permission.

FIGURE 4.9. SEQUENCE OF EVENTS IN TEAM-BASED LEARNING.

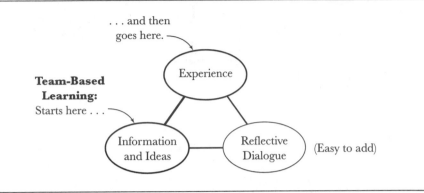

in the Readiness Assurance Process. Then the process gives students a powerful opportunity to gain some kind of "doing" experience, usually in the form of case problems or simulations.

Reflective dialogue, although not originally included in the team-based learning model, is a relatively easy component to add. In fact, the originator of this approach to teaching, Larry Michaelsen, has added periodic journals and learning portfolios in his team-based learning courses with good effect.

Problem-Based Learning. Problem-based learning (PBL) has also grown in popularity as an instructional strategy during the last three decades (Duch, Groh, and Allen, 2001; Wilkerson and Gijselaers, 1996; Boud and Feletti, 1998; http://www.udel.edu/pbl/; http://www.samford.edu/pbl/; see also http://edweb.sdsu.edu/clrit/PBL_WebQuest.html). In the 1970s professors at medical schools in New Mexico and at McMaster University in Canada developed the basic idea of PBL. The results were impressive enough that other medical schools adopted this approach in the 1980s, including a number of high-profile institutions like Harvard, Michigan State, and Maastrict (in the Netherlands). Some individuals, such as Donald Woods, a professor of chemical engineering at McMaster University (http://chemeng.mcmaster.ca/pbl), have adapted it to other realms of learning. It would seem to have the potential for effective use in a variety of subjects, but especially in any professional school.

What is PBL? The best short answer to this question is that in PBL, the problem comes first. In practice, this means that the first thing students are given is not a lot of information about a subject but a realistic problem in the form of a case study. This ideally is a problem that students might actually encounter later in their personal or professional work. In medical schools, this reverses the long tradition of having students study only content information during the whole first two years of their curriculum and waiting until their third year before they start working on the kinds of problems they will encounter in clinical practice.

Once students have their problem, they begin working, usually in groups, to answer some key questions such as the following:

- What systems or topics seem to be involved here?
- What do we already know about these systems or topics?
- What do we not know? (This is very important because it allows students to identify the learning issues they need to work on.)
- How can I learn about that system or subsystem (say, the heart or the liver)?
- How can I use my understanding of the general system and of this particular situation to analyze and diagnose the problem?
- What solution or therapy seems appropriate?

Tutors are frequently but not always employed to help students learn how to engage these questions. Learning how to work through the right questions in the right sequence is a very important part of the learning process. And these are all questions or skills that professional practitioners continually confront in their work. Using the Castle Top diagram, the basic sequence of events is shown in Figure 4.10.

FIGURE 4.10. SEQUENCE OF ACTIVITIES IN PROBLEM-BASED LEARNING.

In-Class Activities:	Groups presented with a problem; decide what information and ideas are needed.		Groups collect and apply new information and ideas to original problem.		Groups present solutions to teacher and rest of class.
Out-of-Class Activities:		Individual students seek new information and ideas.		Students review solutions.	

Although this description is somewhat simplified, the basic idea in problem-based learning is to start the sequence by presenting the students with a realistic case situation or problem. Each group then has to analyze the case and decide what the learning issues are and what information and ideas are needed. Students individually or in subgroups then proceed to find information on and consolidate their understanding of the related learning issues. After this has happened, the new knowledge is examined to see if it adequately addresses the issues at hand. Eventually each group presents its solution to the teacher and the rest of the class.

What is happening in PBL, in terms of the holistic model of active learning? The sequence starts with a realistic case problem that is, in essence, a simulated "doing" experience, as shown in Figure 4.11. Then students work back and forth through the other two components: reflective dialogue about the subject and the learning process, and finding new information and ideas about the subject. Eventually students return to the original situation and try to analyze and solve the problem. If the process includes a full review of the learning process at the end, it will contain all three major components of active learning.

Accelerated Learning. This is a relatively new approach to teaching that nonetheless clearly qualifies as an instructional strategy. Using findings from recent brain research and ideas on multiple intelligences, Colin Rose and Malcolm Nicholl (1997) have created a six-step "MASTER Plan" for accelerated learning:

FIGURE 4.11. BEGINNING OF PROBLEM-BASED LEARNING.

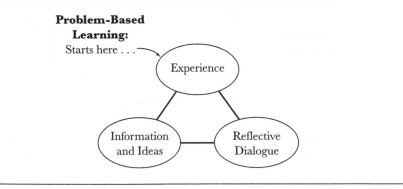

1. *M*otivate your mind.
    - Don't worry about mistakes; create high self-confidence.
    - Find the point of it all—for you.
2. *A*cquire the necessary information.
    - In the right way for you: visual, auditory, kinesthetic.
3. *S*earch out the meaning.
    - This involves "meaning making" rather than fact finding or remembering.
    - This is necessary in order to get the learning into long-term memory.
    - Use as many of your eight intelligences as possible.
4. *T*rigger the memory.
    - Use different memory strategies: association, categorizing, stories—whatever works for you.
5. *E*xhibit what you know.
    - This provides elaborative rehearsal.
    - Share it with someone else; adds a social dimension.
6. *R*eflect on your learning experience.
    - *What* did you learn?
    - *How* did you learn?
    - How could you have learned *better?*
    - *Why* is this *important* for you?

It is not easy to identify specific in-class and out-of-class activities from the MASTER list description and translate it into the Castle Top diagram, although that presumably could be done. It is easier to relate the sequence of events in this teaching strategy to the model of active learning, as shown in Figure 4.12.

The sequence begins with students' engaging in some personal reflection to get into the right frame of mind. Then they work on acquiring the necessary information and ideas, using an appropriate learning style. This is followed by activities aimed at meaning making by engaging in various kinds of experiences, depending on which of the various multiple intelligences are available and appropriate. The meaning is then linked with various memory strategies to get the learning into long-term memory. Once this has been accomplished, students exhibit what they know, which is a form of reflective dialogue with others. The final recommended procedure is for students to individually reflect on what they have learned, which is in essence "reflective dialogue with self."

This strategy does not have an extensive track record in higher education yet. But it has been used in public schools (Rose and Nicholl, 1997, chapters 16 and 17) and in corporate training (chapter 19), both with significant success.

FIGURE 4.12. SEQUENCE OF EVENTS IN ACCELERATED LEARNING.

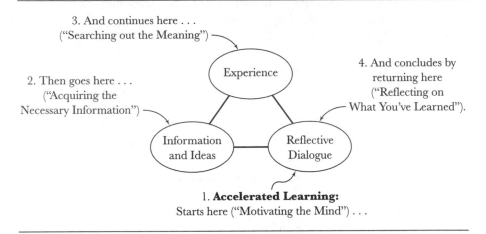

Strategy Versus Technique: A Recap. These three examples of instructional strategies point up the difference between an instructional strategy and a teaching technique and show why a strategy is by far the more important. Teachers still need to be effective and proficient with whatever techniques they use. But it is the particular way those techniques and learning activities are combined and sequenced that determines whether a course creates synergy among its component parts. It is the strategy that creates the energy necessary for significant learning, not the techniques themselves.

Hence, for teachers who want a truly powerful course, my admonition is: Don't think *technique*—think *strategy*.

Steps in Integrated Course Design

Initial Phase: Building Components Parts
1. Situational Factors
2. Learning Goals
3. Feedback & Assessment
4. Teaching & Learning Activities
5. Integrate the Component Parts

Intermediate Phase: Coherent Whole
6. Course Structure
7. Teaching Strategy
8. Overall Set of Learning Activities

Final Phase: Four Remaining Tasks
9. Grading System
10. Possible Problems
11. Write Syllabus
12. Evaluation of Course and Teaching

Step #8: Creating the Overall Scheme of Learning Activities

The final step in the intermediate phase of the course design process is to integrate the *course structure* and the *instructional strategy* into an *overall scheme of learning activities*. In doing this, it can be helpful to create a diagram that combines the course structure and the instructional strategy, as shown in Figure 4.13.

FIGURE 4.13. OVERALL SCHEME OF LEARNING ACTIVITIES FOR A COURSE.

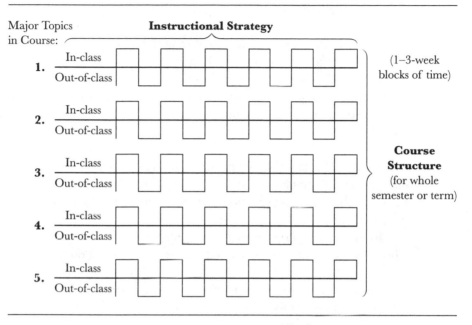

This diagram indicates that one needs to identify the main topics in the course, select an effective sequence of learning activities that stretch out over one to three weeks of class time (that is, an instructional strategy), and then repeat the strategy for each of the main topics. The overall scheme of learning activities naturally needs to be adjusted to fit the time structure and circumstances for any given teaching situation. But all courses need some kind of overall scheme that takes the chosen strategy and applies it to each of the main topics that make up the structure of the course.

Need for Differentiation and Integration. The diagram in Figure 4.13 also reveals another important principle of good course design: the need for differentiation and integration among the learning activities.

The need for *differentiation* shows up in two ways:

- First, the course needs *variety* in the types of learning activities from day to day, within each topical block of time. Courses where all the class sessions do more or less the same thing have a low level of differentiation.
- Second, the course needs a pattern of *development* in the complexity and challenge of the learning, from Unit 1 through Unit 5. As students move through

the sequence of topics, they need to work on problems and learning tasks that become increasingly more complex and reflect the interaction among the topics encountered.

Similarly, the course needs *integration*, both within each topical block of time and in the progression through each of the topical units. That is, the individual activities need to be connected as they work toward the conclusion of each topical unit, and the topic of each new unit needs to be connected and integrated with the preceding topics as the sequence works toward the conclusion of the whole course.

Creating a Schedule of Activities. Once you have developed this general scheme of learning activities for the whole course, you can lay out a more detailed week-by-week schedule of activities for the whole term. To do this, the form in Exhibit 4.5 can be helpful.

In my own experience and in working with others, it seems to be helpful, when filling out this form, to ask and answer the following questions in this order:

1. What activities need to come first, that is, *how should the course begin?* This will allow you to identify the learning activities for the first week or two.
2. What activities do you want to conclude with, that is, *how should the course end?* These activities should be planned for the last week or two.
3. What activities should constitute the *middle* of the course? Now you can lay out the activities for the instructional strategy you have chosen around the sequence of topics that form the course structure.

There are two remaining suggestions for creating this form of course activities. First, it obviously needs to be adjusted to the time structure of a given course. If the course meets twice a week for fifteen weeks or four weekends in a row, the form needs to be adjusted to reflect this structure and filled out accordingly.

Second, leave some blank spaces or unscheduled time in the course. This will make it much easier to adjust when some activities or topics take longer than expected, when a particular class session gets cancelled for some reason, or when you simply come up with a creative idea during the course for something that would be exciting to add.

What you have now is a good basic plan or design for the course. You have built strong primary components for the course (the initial phase), and then you have organized these components into a meaningful sequence of learning activities (the intermediate phase). In the next phase of the design process you will address some important additional tasks, but the basic design for the course is in place.

EXHIBIT 4.5. SEQUENCING THE LEARNING ACTIVITIES IN A COURSE.

	Sessions per Week					
Week	Class Session	Between Classes	Class Session	Between Classes	Class Session	Between Classes
1						
2						
3						
4						
5						
6						
7						
8						
9						
10						
11						
12						
13						
14						
15						
Finals						

Final Phase: Four Tasks to Finish the Design

Now that the intermediate phase of the design process has been finished, you need to take care of four remaining tasks to complete and refine the design for the course.

Step #9: Put Together the Grading System

Although I earlier urged the development of a feedback and assessment system that goes beyond just grading and contributes to the learning process, teachers in nearly all institutions still need to turn in grades. They therefore need to put together a grading system that is both fair and educationally valid. Following a few simple rules should help with this.

First, the list of graded items should be diverse. Students learn in different ways and differ in how they best show what they know. Course grading systems that rely solely on one or two exams, be they multiple-choice or essay, penalize students who are better able to show their abilities in other ways.

Second, the list of graded items should reflect as much as possible the full range of learning goals and learning activities. If you want students to learn how to apply the content and how to integrate it with other realms of knowledge, they should receive course grade credit for showing they have learned how to do that. Not all learning activities needed to be graded, but if you really want students to engage in a particular learning activity, say, writing weekly journals, that needs to be reflected somehow in the course grade.

> *Steps in Integrated Course Design*
>
> Initial Phase: Building Components Parts
> 1. Situational Factors
> 2. Learning Goals
> 3. Feedback & Assessment
> 4. Teaching & Learning Activities
> 5. Integrate the Component Parts
>
> Intermediate Phase: Coherent Whole
> 6. Course Structure
> 7. Teaching Strategy
> 8. Overall Set of Learning Activities
>
> **Final Phase: Four Remaining Tasks**
> **9. Grading System**
> **10. Possible Problems**
> **11. Write Syllabus**
> **12. Evaluation of Course and Teaching**

Finally, the relative weight of each item on the course grade should reflect the relative importance of that activity. Presumably all graded items are important, but some are more important than others. For example, a culminating project that involves all the major realms of learning in the course is more important than a weekly quiz. If so, this should be reflected in the relative weights of the items in the course grading system.

To show what a grading system might look like that incorporates these recommendations, Exhibit 4.6 shows the grading system that I used in my world geography course. This has several different kinds of graded activities, including

EXHIBIT 4.6. GRADING SYSTEM FOR A GEOGRAPHY COURSE.

	Points:
1. Basic Individual Activities	
• Test: Major places in the world	10
• Test: Using an atlas	10
• Keeping a course journal	10
• Reading exercises (2)	5
2. Major Individual Activities	
• Tests on readings (individual, given every two weeks)	20
• Individual essays ($N = 5$, 1–2 pp. each)	20
• Final Exam	10
3. Group Activities	
• Tests on readings (group, given every two weeks)	35
• Regional briefings (2)	10
• Culminating research and presentation project	20
TOTAL:	150

Grading Scale (points):

A = 139–150
B = 128–138
C = 116–127
D = 105–115
F = 104 or less

some that relate to each major learning goal, and the weight of the individual items reflects the relative importance of each activity.

Step #10: Identify What Might Go Wrong

It is always good, before implementing any course design, to give it one final check and review. Are there any operational problems that you can identify and correct ahead of time?

It is not always easy to detect operational problems in advance, but when you can, it avoids trouble later on. Some of the ones I have experienced or observed in others' courses are such things as setting up a good assignment but not allowing students enough time to complete it. Or having too few copies of the reading material in the library reserve so that when all the students try to access it at the same time, they can't. Trying to anticipate and solve problems like these ahead of time will help the course run a lot smoother.

Step #11: Write the Syllabus

Once you have the course designed and ready to go, you need to communicate information about the course to the students. This means writing a course syllabus that contains the information students need in order to understand what the course is all about, where you are trying to go with the course, and how it is going to operate.

Different people have different ideas about what should and should not be in a syllabus. My view is that it needs to contain enough information so students can do what you want them to do, along with the policies that set the ground rules for course operation. Using these guidelines, I recommend that syllabi include the following:

- General management information—the teacher's name, office hours, phone, e-mail address, and so on
- Goals for the course
- Structure and sequence of class activities, including due dates for major assignments, tests, and projects
- Text and other required reading material
- Grading procedures
- Course policies: attendance, work turned in late, make-up exams, penalties for academic misconduct, and the like

Your institution may require some additional statements. My university, for example, asks all professors to include a statement on their syllabi for students with physical or learning disabilities.

Step #12: Plan an Evaluation of the Course and Your Teaching

Every time you teach, you have an opportunity to learn about teaching and about yourself as a teacher. To take advantage of this opportunity to learn and grow, you need to plan a thorough evaluation of the course itself and of your own teaching. And this means going well beyond simply looking at the means from student ratings at the end of the course. I have written more extensively elsewhere about evaluating one's own teaching (Fink, 1995) and evaluating teaching in general (Fink, 2001), but some of the key ideas on evaluation are useful to summarize here.

Midterm Assessment. For starters, you should think about collecting information from the students in the middle of the course as well as at the end. This kind of formative assessment will allow you to address any major concerns students might have while there is still time for them to benefit from any changes that need to be made. You can formulate a simple set of open-ended questions or use some of the published questionnaires that have been created specifically for midterm use (TABS; Weimer, Parrott, and Keens, 1988).

Multiple Sources of Information. When you are trying to assess the quality of your teaching, it is important to consider multiple sources of information. The easiest and most common resource is to collect questionnaires from students. But it is also possible for someone, either the teacher or someone else, to interview the whole class or a representative sample of students. The SGID (Small Group Instructional Diagnosis) is designed specifically for this purpose (Diamond, 2002).

Besides collecting information from students, it's interesting to audiotape or videotape a class session to find out what *really* happens there—what you do and how you talk while leading a class. In addition, a careful analysis of patterns of correct and incorrect responses on tests can sometimes identify particular areas of learning (or nonlearning) that are critical for student success. And, finally, having a colleague or an instructional consultant observe your teaching and give you feedback can also contribute special insights. These are people who do not have to worry about doing the work of teacher or of the students; hence they can bring their extensive knowledge of the subject and of teaching in general to bear on the task of identifying what is going well and what you might do to improve.

Finally, as you formulate questions, either for students or for outside observers, it can be helpful to focus their attention of four important aspects of your activities as a teacher:

- To what degree are your goals for the course being achieved?
- How effective are particular learning activities and your overall instructional strategy?
- Are the feedback and assessment procedures helpful and fair?
- How effectively do you interact with students?

With that, you have finished all three phases of the course design process. If all has gone well, you should have a plan of teaching and learning activities that is both feasible and powerful. It will be one that is possible for both you and the students to implement and will achieve significant kinds of student learning.

Two General Tips

As teachers undertake the challenge of designing more significant learning experiences, I have observed two practices that significantly facilitate the whole process: involving students and devising a simple graphic for the central theme of the course.

Involve Students

The whole premise of this book, that teachers should design courses to maximize significant learning, creates a new requirement for teaching a course. It is imperative to involve the students in the shaping and implementation of the course. If the only goal is foundational knowledge or maybe even application learning, it may be possible to continue treating students as objects that the teacher is going to do something to. But when you raise your goals to include such things as the human dimension, caring, and self-directed learning, it is necessary to treat students as *subjects* who are essential partners in the process.

At minimum this means sharing the goals and your teaching strategy with the students in the class. But to make the course really run well, students will need to add their own goals to your list of important course goals, help select the type and form of feedback and assessment that would be useful for them, and participate in analyzing and rethinking the teaching and learning strategies that would be most effective for them.

An analogy that may be useful here is the relationship between a coach and a sports team. In any sport, any and all points scored will be scored by the players, not by the coach. The coach is responsible for having a game plan. However, the game plan, to be implemented, must first of all be understood by the whole team. But even a good game plan may need to be modified from time to time, based on the ongoing dialogue between the coach and the team.

The basic point for the teacher is to keep the dialogue open with the class about all aspects of the course design. Make sure they understand what your game plan is and the reasons you have designed the course the way you have. But then make sure that you interact with students throughout the course, about the course. From time to time, they will come up with good ideas for changing the way the course operates. And they will appreciate you for listening to them and being open to their suggestions. Doing this will make the course a shared, collaborative experience.

Use Common Themes or Graphics to Clarify the Focus of the Course

Once the general structure has been created, the teacher still needs to find a way to help students clearly see and understand the central focus of the whole course. The simplest way to do this is to find a theme, question, or graphic that reflects the main focus of the whole course. A few examples will illustrate what this means.

Using an Integrating Question. Two engineering professors co-taught a seminar on leadership for the graduate students in their research group (Sabatini and Knox, 1999). At the start of the course they posed a key question: "What is leadership?" They had students write their own personal ideas on this question (reflective dialogue with self) and then held a whole-class discussion (reflective dialogue with others) in which the students tried to merge their individual responses into a generally agreed-upon list of the characteristics of effective leaders. The second activity consisted of reading a biography of Abraham Lincoln (getting new information and ideas). The group then revisited their list of the important characteristics of leaders to see if they felt a need to add, delete, or modify their original statements, and they did make changes. Throughout the seminar the class went back and forth between reading new material and revisiting their ideas on leadership. In this case, a question ("What is leadership?") served as the mechanism for integrating the goals, learning activities, and assessment.

Using a Graphic. In my course on world regional geography, I developed a diagram that reflected my understanding of what a "region" is (see Figure 4.14). This

FIGURE 4.14. GRAPHIC OF A CENTRAL COURSE CONCEPT: "A REGION."

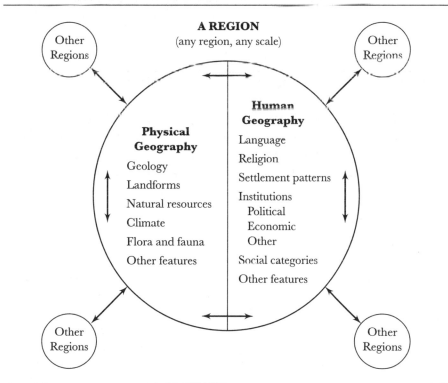

model says, in essence, that any region consists of physical factors, human factors, and interaction with other regions. The model is dynamic in that the individual components of *physical* geography affect each other (the internal vertical arrows), as do the components of *human* geography. There is also a strong interaction between the human and physical factors (the horizontal arrow). Finally the region itself interacts with other regions (the diagonal arrows, outside the main region).

As this class studied different regions, discussed newspaper stories in relation to different regions, and did research projects on specific regions, this model guided the effort to identify the information and questions needed to understand a given region. In this example, a graphic served as a unifying mechanism.

Mary Beaudry (2000) has written about the value of a good graphic image for communicating the organization and structure of the subject of a course. She argues that teachers should shift their attention from the question of "How much content is enough?" to "How should my course content be organized?" She argues that a good course graphic is potentially very valuable as a way of communicating the organization of the content.

Finding or developing some mechanism, whether it be a question, a theme, or a graphic, will allow you to greatly assist students in making the necessary connections between the goals, teaching and learning activities, and feedback and assessment.

Benefits of This Model of Course Design

Now that you have seen the whole integrated course design process, I can step back from the model and discuss some of its specific benefits. It allows teachers to diagnose their courses and identify the sources of teaching problems, and it has a number of other features that make it generally attractive.

Understanding the Sources of Teaching Problems

When I work with teachers, either in workshops or in one-on-one consulting, we often encounter an "Aha" moment after laying out this model of course design. We look at what they have done previously and can often identify the reasons why their students are not responding better. In many cases, they have been aiming their course at low-level learning goals (just "learn the content"), using audit-ive assessment procedures, or offering students nothing more than passive forms of learning. As a result, the course was perceived as boring and not very important. In turn the students were not motivated and had no energy in the class.

Having this model allows teachers to see that poor student motivation is a symptom of a problem but not the root problem. The root problem is poor course design. Learning how to design courses properly will eliminate or at least diminish many common teaching problems.

Additional Benefits

This model has a number of other benefits as well. Whether you are a faculty member working on your own teaching or an instructional consultant trying to advise other faculty members, it is advantageous to have a model of the course design process that is

- *Simple:* The basic model of integrated course design is relatively simple and easy to remember. It consists of four basic components and they are connected in a straightforward manner.
- *Holistic:* Even though the basic model is simple, it unpacks in a way that allows it to incorporate and address much of the complexity of high-quality teaching.
- *Integrative:* It shows the relationships among the main elements of the course and reveals how they affect and interact with each other.
- *Practical:* It shows teachers what they need to do to create significant learning experiences for students, both in the design phase and eventually when they actually teach the course.
- *Normative:* It provides specific criteria for determining whether a specific design is a good design.

Integrated Course Design: A Summary

That completes my discussion of the model of integrated course design. Since this has been a lengthy discussion, it may be helpful to review the whole process briefly and make some general comments about it.

The Overall Course Design Process

Perhaps a useful way of both reviewing the course design process and helping readers remember the structure is by a series of questions. As shown in Exhibit 4.7, the design process can be thought of as twelve questions, sorted into the three phases.

As presented here, the task of designing an effective and powerful course involves going through three phases. In the initial phase, the teacher needs to build strong primary components. This involves doing a thorough analysis of the situational factors, creating a set of powerful learning goals, creating effective teaching

EXHIBIT 4.7. KEY QUESTIONS TO ASK WHEN DESIGNING A COURSE.

Initial Phase: Building Strong Primary Components

1. *Where are you?* Size up the situational factors.
2. *Where do you want to go?* What are the learning goals for the course? Ideally, what would you like students to get out of this course?
3. *How would you know if you got there?* That is, how would you and the students know if they are achieving these goals? This is the feedback and assessment question.
4. *How are you going to get there?* Select or develop the learning activities that you will need to achieve these goals.
5. *Who and what can help?* Find resources.

Intermediate Phase: Assembling the Components into a Dynamic, Coherent Whole

6. *What are the major topics in this course?* Create a thematic course structure for the course. Identify the four to seven major topics, ideas, or themes for the course.
7. *What will the students need to do?* Assemble the specific learning activities into an effective instructional strategy.
8. *What is the overall scheme of learning activities?* Dynamically integrate the course structure and the instructional strategy for the whole course.

Final Phase: Taking Care of Important Details

9. *How are you going to grade?* Develop your grading system.
10. *What could go wrong?* Anticipate possible problems in the design.
11. *How will students know what you're planning to do?* Now write the syllabus.
12. *How will you know how the course is going? How it went?* Plan an evaluation of the course itself and of your own teaching performance.

and learning activities, and formulating effective feedback and assessment procedures. The final part of this phase is to make sure the four components reflect and support each other.

In the intermediate phase, the activities in the component parts are assembled into a dynamic and coherent whole. To do that, it's necessary to create a meaningful course structure, select or create a powerful instructional strategy, and then put these to together into an overall scheme of learning for the course. When this has been done, the teacher is in a position to lay out the full sequence of learning activities for the course.

The final phase calls for the completion of four important tasks. The teacher needs to put together a grading system, debug possible problems, write the syllabus, and plan an evaluation of the course.

If each of these three phases can be completed in an effective fashion, the result should be a course that leads to student learning experiences that are truly significant!

What Changes Are Being Recommended?

I am quite aware that designing and teaching a course in the way described here represents a major change from the way most teachers traditionally operate. Although more will be said in the next chapter about how to make such changes, what are the key changes being recommended? I would summarize these in terms of seven important changes:

- *Set more ambitious learning goals.* Use the taxonomy of significant learning to imagine and set goals that include but go well beyond simply wanting students to master the content of the course.
- *Enlarge the kinds of learning activities you use.* Use the activities shown in Exhibit 4.1, strive to go beyond the box of providing indirect sources of information and ideas, and include activities that provide students with experiences and opportunities for reflection.
- *Create rich learning experiences.* Be creative and search for powerful Doing and Observing experiences that allow students to acquire multiple kinds of significant learning, all at the same time.
- *Provide multiple opportunities for in-depth reflection on the learning process.* Give serious consideration to the use of one-minute papers, periodic journal writing, and learning portfolios. Students need to repeatedly reflect by themselves and with others about what they have learned, how they learn best now and might learn more effectively in the future, and what the meaning of the whole learning experience is.
- *Find alternative ways to introduce students to the content of the course.* Students will always need to acquire new information and ideas, the content of the course. But look for ways to do this that can be done out of class, thereby freeing up valuable class time for experiential and reflective kinds of learning activities.
- *Create a coherent and meaningful course structure.* Identify the four to seven most important concepts, issues, or topics in the course. This provides the overall course structure within which the instructional strategy and learning activities work. When possible, formulate a question or graphic that can provide unity and coherence in the course.
- *Select or create a dynamic instructional strategy.* Look for or create a strategy that puts specific learning activities into a particular sequence that can build increasing energy at each step of the course.

The basic principles being espoused here are to incorporate as much *significant learning, active learning,* and *educative assessment* as possible, and then put all of this into an effective and powerful *instructional strategy* that operates within a meaningful and coherent *course structure.*

Good Course Design and "Flow" Experiences

During the last decade or so, Mihaly Csikszentmihalyi (1990, 1996, 1997) has attracted considerable attention in intellectual circles with his concept of "flow." This concept is a useful way to indicate how a well-designed learning experience can be connected to learners' efforts to improve their quality of life. This is true whether the learning experience is self-generated or teacher-generated.

Csikszentmihalyi starts with the view that the quality of our lives depends both on what we do and how we experience what we do. Sometimes people do their usual life activities (working, taking care of themselves, playing games or otherwise taking advantage of leisure) but experience those activities in a very special way. These special moments happen when there is a harmony in what we feel (our emotions), what we wish (our goals or intentions), and what we think (our cognitive mental operations). These exceptional moments, when all factors are aligned, are called "flow experiences" (1997, chapters 1 and 2). When people have a flow experience, they are totally absorbed in what they are doing; all their psychic energy is flowing in one right direction; and they lose all self-consciousness and sense of time. This can happen to people in very different walks of life and in different kinds of situations. But when it happens, their descriptions of it are very similar.

However, flow experiences are not created at will. They are experiences that happen to a person. But some activities make it more likely for flow to occur, and these are called "flow activities." What are the characteristics of flow activities?

First, flow activities are activities that allow a person to focus on goals that are clear and compatible. Second, they provide immediate feedback that makes it clear how well you are doing. Third, flow tends to occur when the balance between high challenges and high skills is just right. (see Figure 4.15).

When these three conditions are met, a person's attention becomes very focused, ordered, and invested in the task at hand. Self-consciousness and time disappear. The person experiences "flow" and the "serenity that comes when heart, will and mind are on the same page" (Csikszentmihalyi, 1997, p. 28).

Now, how is all this connected to issues of good instructional design? Interestingly, Csikszentmihalyi felt compelled to comment on the relationship between flow and learning even though he was writing about psychology, not education.

FIGURE 4.15. "FLOW" EXPERIENCES IN RELATION TO CHALLENGES AND SKILLS.

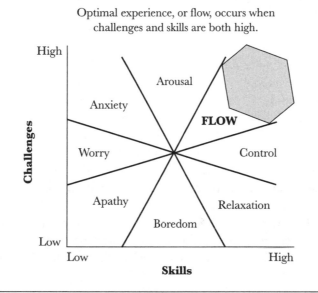

Optimal experience, or flow, occurs when challenges and skills are both high.

Source: Csikszentmihalyi, 1997, p. 31. Copyright © 1997 Mihaly Csikszentmihalyi. Reprinted by permission of Basic Books, a member of Perseus Books, LLC.

He believes that flow naturally leads to personal growth and acts as a magnet for learning (Csikszentmihalyi, 1997, pp. 32–33). Why is this? It goes to the issue of the balance between challenges and skills.

When facing a high challenge (which is necessary to achieve flow), a person has to learn new and better skills. Once greater skills have developed, the person is ready for new challenges, which call for the learning of additional or better skills. And the cycle continues on and on.

Once we see the connection between flow and learning, we can then identify the role of good course design. If teachers can design instruction that increases the likelihood of students' experiencing flow in their learning, exciting things can happen. How might a teacher do this? If we look at the characteristics that Csikszentmihalyi identified as important for flow activities, we can see how the ideas on course design presented earlier in this chapter at least offer some suggestions.

First, it is necessary to obtain accurate information about students and other *situational factors* to find the right level of challenge and the right kind of support needed. Knowing accurately what students can and cannot do at the start of the instructional sequence is critical, so the teacher can set the challenge at a level where students have to stretch a bit but not too far. Similarly, the teacher needs to find out how a particular set of students learn so the right kinds of learning activities can be provided for developing the skills needed.

Second, we need to provide the right kind of *goals*. The taxonomy of significant learning offers one potentially valuable way of identifying such goals. Teachers who can learn how to incorporate goals for such things as learning how to learn, developing new values and interests, enhancing human interaction capabilities, and the rest are in a good position to offer "clear, compatible" goals that can stretch learners in meaningful ways.

Third, the right kind of *feedback and assessment* offers learners immediate and meaningful information on how well they are doing. Having clear criteria and standards—and involving students in both the development and application of these criteria to their own work—gives them the third important ingredient for flow activities.

Fourth, the right kind of *teaching and learning activities* will offer learners the right level of challenge along with proper support for developing the skills to meet these challenges. Teachers need to create learning activities that challenge students but then complement these with other activities that help students develop the skills necessary to meet these challenges.

What this means is that if teachers design their instruction properly, they can create the conditions in which flow activities are likely to occur. If students can begin to experience flow in their learning, this experience will lead to the realization of a need for more challenges and more learning. And that will set in motion the sort of synergistic, positive cycle of events that teachers barely allow themselves to dream about now.

An exciting prospect to imagine and consider!

CHAPTER FIVE

CHANGING THE WAY WE TEACH

In the first chapter of this book I issued an invitation to readers to consider changing the way they think about teaching. In the next three chapters I laid out some ideas on significant learning and integrated course design to provide content and direction for this new way of thinking. However, teachers who are ready to respond to this invitation will still face a number of important questions associated with the process of making substantial changes in the way they teach:

Question #1: Is it really possible to change my teaching in a way that will both achieve the kinds of learning described in the taxonomy of significant learning and build the kinds of courses that exemplify the principles of good course design? It feels like it might be just pie-in-the-sky dreaming.

Preliminary answer: Yes, this kind of student learning can be achieved. You can be sure it's possible because bits and pieces of significant learning are already being achieved by innovative and caring teachers. This chapter provides a specific description of what these teachers are doing with course design that allows them to achieve multiple kinds of significant learning.

Question #2: But can *I* do it? The challenge of changing the way I have been teaching for several years—changing *myself*—sounds quite difficult.

Preliminary answer: Yes, it is difficult to change ingrained patterns of behavior that have been created and developed over many years. But it's useful to remember, first of all, that it's not a matter of changing everything, only some things. Second, although it is difficult, everyone undergoes various kinds of change in a lifetime, and some of that change is intentional. This shows that change is possible—including change in the manner of teaching, if it seems desirable enough. To help with the task of intentionally changing teaching, it's necessary to first examine some of the barriers to self-change that people often encounter. This chapter provides a description of two specific challenges to self-change and offers suggestions for dealing with them.

Question #3: What does it look like when people change how they teach? Can you give me a model?

Preliminary answer: Yes. This chapter contains a detailed description of one professor who deliberately and intentionally undertook to change the way he had been teaching for many years. This description includes some of the key conversations he and I had, the insights we developed, the dead ends we ran into, the changes he made, and the impact of those changes on his students. The comments also include a summary of the lessons we learned about how to make this process of change easier and more effective.

Question #4: If I do make the changes suggested here, will it really make a significant difference in what happens in a course? Or will it just end up being "much ado about nothing" after all the smoke clears away?

Preliminary answer: You will eventually have to answer this question in your own heart. But I am convinced that it *will* make a difference, a significant difference. In the final section of this chapter, I present evidence that convinces me that it will make a substantial difference.

Is It Really Possible?

The first question I want to address is whether it really is possible to achieve the exciting kinds of learning described in Chapter Two. To most readers, having such learning occur on a regular basis sounds like a dream, one that is perhaps too good to be true. To answer this question, I have drawn material from published descriptions of twenty-two courses in which teachers are already accomplishing significant kinds of learning and share my analysis of what these teachers are doing that is responsible for their success. A brief description of these courses is provided in Exhibit 5.1. (Note: A fuller description of each course—including an analysis of the kinds of learning promoted, the components of active learning used, and the citation for the published description—has been put online at http://www.significantlearning.org so readers who are interested can pursue this material in more depth.)

The primary criteria for including courses in this selection were that the teacher seemed to succeed in promoting learning that went beyond foundational

EXHIBIT 5.1. SELECTED COURSES
THAT PROMOTE SIGNIFICANT LEARNING.

1. NATURAL SCIENCES

- *Biology for Science Literacy:* Students work in small groups on term-long investigations including analyses of socially important scientific issues, using scientific concepts, reasoning, and their own values.

- *Multidisciplinary Geology:* In this team-taught course, students gather materials and data on field trips and then learn how to construct knowledge in geology, physics, and chemistry.

- *Chemistry Senior Seminar:* Over three terms, students do increasingly independent research and formal presentations based on primary literature in the field.

- *Honors Course on Technological Innovations:* Students engage in a simulation of being stranded on an island. They have to figure out how to survive, organize their society, and build an airplane to fly off the island.

- *Nursing—Cultural Issues in Childbearing:* Students use films and books to explore the ethical and cultural issues of childbearing for women and their families as well as for the nurses themselves.

- *Medicine—Problem-Based Learning Curriculum:* Students work in small groups on realistic patient problems and learn how to solve new medical problems.

- *Geology—Applied Hydrology:* Students use fieldwork and other data to investigate a real drainage basin and eventually present a paper at a statewide hydrology conference.

2. SOCIAL SCIENCES

- *Different Perspectives on the Environment:* Students keep journals on their personal experiences with nature while reading varied and often conflicting views on the relationship between people and their environments.

- *Business—Integrated Business Core:* In a practicum course (one of four courses in the core), beginning business majors start up and run a real business with real dollars during one semester.

- *Business—Its Culture Revealed by the Humanities:* Students use film, literature, history, and psychology to develop new perspectives on the human meaning of common business issues.

- *Education—Introduction to Teaching:* Prospective teachers engage in multiple activities to explore three fundamental questions: What does it mean to teach? What are schools for? What do teachers need to know?

- *Building Character and Spirituality through Aerobics:* Students work on physical and spiritual fitness by developing goals for themselves and assisting others.

- *Tax Law:* Students study the Internal Revenue Code and regulations by translating them into their own words, applying them to specific situations, and creating a flow chart of how they work.

- *Law School and Women's Issues:* Upper-level students analyze their own previous curricular experience and ask what would have happened if the feminist perspective were taken seriously.

EXHIBIT 5.1. SELECTED COURSES
THAT PROMOTE SIGNIFICANT LEARNING, Cont'd.

3. HUMANITIES

- *English—Seeking the Meaning of Shakespeare:* Students use psychodrama and the ideas of multiple intelligences to pursue an emotional as well as a cognitive understanding of Shakespeare's plays.

- *English—Linking World Problems and Literature:* Students learn about a foreign region (Yugoslavia) and then raise funds for relief work in that region by compiling and marketing an anthology of contemporary authors.

- *English—Fiction and an Imaginary Town:* Students write about an imaginary town, drawing from their experiences in their own community.

- *English—Intolerance and Service Learning:* Students study the sources of prejudice, engage in community service, and put together a "Tolerance Fair" that is presented in the public schools of the community.

- *Cultural Diversity and Philosophy:* Students study primary sources from diverse cultures concerning views of the self, human beings in relation to each other, and human beings in relation to the nonhuman world.

- *German Culture and Song:* Students examine authentic cultural issues in contemporary Germany by exploring popular culture via newspapers, magazine articles, and popular music.

- *Spanish—Role-Playing Literary Figures:* At a key point in this course, students engage in a role-play—in Spanish, portraying characters in a simulated trial of the central figure, an abusive *Comendador.*

- *Art History—Myth, Religion, and Art:* Students work on weekly problems that explore the relationships between spiritual beliefs and artistic works, drawing on material from different world cultures and historical periods.

knowledge and included important aspects of active learning. Unfortunately, very few of the published descriptions included in-depth comments about the feedback and assessment aspects of the courses, so I have not attempted to analyze the courses for these factors.

It is important to note that the teachers in this sample were obviously not aware of the prescriptions for significant learning or integrated course design presented in this book. Presumably they were following their own instincts or some other model of teaching and learning to help them create significant learning goals and effective learning activities. Nonetheless, as will be seen in the comments that follow, their goals, activities, and results are very consistent with the language of significant learning and the model of integrated course design presented in this book.

For this reason, their examples provide valuable lessons for teachers who want to create more significant learning experiences for their students. To identify these lessons, I take each kind of significant learning and examine what the teachers are doing in these courses that promote that kind of learning.

Learning How to Learn

As noted in Chapter Two, the phrase "learning how to learn" has three distinct meanings: how to be a better student, how to conduct inquiry and construct knowledge in certain disciplines or fields, and how to be a self-directing learner. A number of teachers in this set of twenty-one courses created ways to promote each of these versions.

Becoming a Better Student. Several of the teachers in the sample took a deliberate approach to helping people become better students. They provided explicit attention to the learning process in the initial course in a curriculum. As a result, their students did better in subsequent courses in the curriculum. An excellent example of this phenomenon occurs in the Integrated Business Core (IBC) for beginning business majors. Although the teachers in this team-taught program do not spend a significant amount of class time explicitly addressing the question of "how to be a *good* student," they do put students in the position of having to learn a lot of material on their own, and the students excel. As a result, professors in later courses note that IBC students are able to get organized for effective learning much more quickly than students who have not been in IBC.

Similarly, the law school students who review their previous courses from a feminist perspective spend time asking: *What* am I learning? What else *could* I learn? And what *should* I be learning? Although the teacher does not indicate in the published article whether students do in fact learn how to be better students, having students search for answers to such questions in middle of their program and reflect on the implications of the answers seems likely to enhance their subsequent learning experiences.

Learning How to Inquire and Construct Knowledge. A second meaning of "learning how to learn" is for students to learn how to engage in inquiry and the construction of knowledge in a certain domain of human endeavor. Several courses deliberately supported this kind of learning. For example, students in the biology, geology, and chemistry courses are all asked to formulate questions and then to work on answering them. The latter part of this task requires students to learn how to search for and identify relevant information and then to analyze that information in order to answer a question or solve a problem. And students in the art history course are given multiple problems to research concerning the relationship between religion, art, and architecture.

In all of these examples, the teachers give students practice in conducting inquiry (a form of "doing" experience in the model of active learning) and then give them constructive feedback on how well they are engaging in the process of inquiry.

In a few of these courses, special attention is given to how knowledge is constructed in particular disciplines. For example, the multidisciplinary geology course has students collect sample material from field trips and then, with different teachers, analyze those materials in terms of what they can learn about geology, physics, and chemistry. In each case, students are learning forms of analysis peculiar to each discipline. At the end of each unit, students discuss what was learned and how it was learned.

Becoming Self-Directing Learners. Although none of the courses in the sample focus explicitly on helping students become self-directing learners, several do pay direct attention to the learning process. For example, the subject of the education course is obviously "teaching and learning," but this course also asks students to reflect on their own learning as well and prompts them to explore the impact of their own learning processes on how they should teach in the future.

A number of other courses, for example, the honors course on technology, the law curriculum and feminism course, and the multidisciplinary geology course, all have students keep learning logs where they reflect on what they are learning, what they could or should be learning, and how they are learning. This procedure can definitely increase students' self-awareness as learners.

The next step in helping students become self-directing learners is to have them think toward the future and identify what else they need or want to learn, that is, develop a *learning agenda*. The students must also identify specific actions for learning those items on their agenda (that is, develop a plan of action). For example, the specific action could be reading a book on the topic, finding information on the Internet, talking to an expert or experienced person, observing something, or trying to do something oneself.

One example of helping students along the road to becoming self-directing learners comes from a strategy I used a few years ago. I was teaching a course on college teaching attended by a dozen or so graduate students from across campus, all of whom wanted to become college teachers. During the course, I had them browse through several books on college teaching, just to note the range of topics one could study in relation to this subject. Then I asked them to select the three topics that seemed most important and write a brief essay on why these three topics were important for them to learn. Later each student created a teaching portfolio as a concluding project for the course. In the final section of the portfolio, they were to write about what they were going to do in the future to become better as a college teacher. To do this, they had to identify what they wanted or needed to learn (that is, their learning agenda) and what they could do to learn that (that is, a learning strategy or plan of action).

Nearly all of the students later commented that creating this portfolio as a whole and especially doing that final section was one of the most valuable assignments in the whole course. It moved them well along the road toward becoming self-directing learners. And many of them later told me that they implemented their learning agendas within a year or two after the conclusion of the course.

Caring

The teachers in the sample frequently taught in a way that made students excited. That is, the teachers found ways to increase the degree to which students cared about what they were learning. How did they do this?

Although there were clear differences in the specific techniques used, there is also a general pattern that follows a two-step sequence. In each case where the learning experience has a strong motivating impact, the teacher first does something to connect students with their own feelings about the topic at hand and then has the students take an action that was informed or influenced by the first step.

In terms of the model of active learning, the first step is usually accomplished by letting students indirectly observe some phenomena by bringing stories to the students, often in the form of films, novels, or role-playing. In one case ("English and Service Learning"), students engage in direct, rather than indirect, observations of interactions between different social groups in a community while performing community service. The second step of this general sequence constitutes a "doing" experience, in which the students create something, propose an action, or reshape some ideas on the subject of the course.

Following is a list of examples that show, in more concrete terms, how this general pattern works to help students care about what they are learning in different kinds of courses:

• In the English class "Linking World Problems and Literature," students hear stories about the turmoil and tragedies in Yugoslavia from a visitor who recently returned from there. (Hearing these stories connects students with their feelings about the topic.) The class then engages in a variety of projects to raise awareness in the United States and also to assist the visitor. They compile an anthology, sell the anthology to various outlets, and contribute the profits to a relief organization working in Yugoslavia.

• In the Honors class studying technology, students have to imagine what it would be like to be stranded on a deserted island and need a way to get out. (Like other simulations, this one is designed in part to connect students with their feelings.) They are then challenged to figure out how to survive, how to organize their society, and how to design an airplane that will get them off the island, by using only the limited materials available to them (a "doing" experience). (Note: The simulation relaxes the time constraints in this project—students only need to learn what all would have to be done for such things as manufacturing the fuel and the metal for building the engine, if they had enough time. The final exam doesn't involve leaving the ground.)

• In the nursing class that focuses on childbearing in different cultures, students view films about and read stories written by women in different cultures. The students then have to identify the multiple meanings of childbirth for women and decide how these meanings would affect their future professional work as nurses.

• In the senior capstone course in English titled "Intolerance in America," students engage in a variety of community service activities, allowing them to see the effect of intolerance on people. Then as a culminating project, students create a "Tolerance Fair" that consists of different ways of displaying information on the topic. The fair is taken to public schools in the area.

Human Dimension

When teachers want students to enhance their human interaction capabilities, they have to find ways to help them become more self-aware and other-aware in relation to the subject being studied. Sometimes the activities used are especially effective in helping students learn about themselves *or* about others. But more often students find that learning about either one helps them learn about both.

To heighten self-awareness, teachers put students in imaginary situations or in simulated roles (an indirect "doing" or "observing" experience) and then have them reflect, often through the use of learning logs, on how these situations or roles make them feel. That is, the students engage in "dialogue with self." Generally these new situations or roles create new perspectives, so students are prompted to compare these new perspectives to their own previous thoughts, feelings, or beliefs.

Similarly, to heighten students' other-awareness, teachers find ways to bring in the stories of others via an indirect "observing" experience, for example, film or literature, and then have students talk with their classmates ("dialogue with others") in an effort to find the meaning that certain events have for others. When activities that are aimed at learning about self and about others are combined, the impact is especially strong.

Some examples will show how these ideas work in practice.

• In the environmental studies course, students read literature that advocates different and sometimes conflicting views about nature and what policies society should have toward the environment. The students also engage in a structured debate designed to help them identify with views that differ from their own (identifying with others, that is, increasing other-awareness). At the same time the students are prompted to reflect on their own experience with nature and keep a learning log in which they reflect on the meaning of their experiences. By comparing their own ideas with the new ideas being encountered in class and exploring their reaction to all the varied viewpoints, they are reflecting with themselves about themselves.

• In a course on philosophy and cultural diversity, students read some of the traditional European philosophers (for example, Descartes, Locke, Camus) but also read philosophical statements by representatives of other cultural viewpoints: Black Elk (Native American), Malcolm X (African American), Anzaldua (Latin American), Majaj (Arab American). One interesting twist is that these readings are deliberately selected to include statements concerning our relation to non-human Others as well as to human Others. In this case, the reading materials introduce new perspectives on personal identity, relating to other humans, and one's relationship with nonhuman Others. Both learning logs and class discussions are used to help students more fully understand the perspective of others in order to heighten their own sense of self-awareness and to reflect on how they want their Self to grow, change, and become.

• The teacher in the aerobics class makes learning about oneself and learning about others a direct part of the course. She has students set some short- and long-term goals related to their physical selves but also related to other aspects of their lives, for example, their spiritual selves. By so doing, she in essence prompts students to attend to what they want their Self to become. During the course, students meet with the teacher to discuss their progress on their goals (Dialogue with Others). In a second assignment, each student has to team up with another student and create a new aerobic routine for the whole class to use. Working with another to create something new (doing) that would help the rest of the class requires students to attend to the question of learning how to interact with others in a positive, constructive way.

• In an intermediate-level German course, the teacher embeds the usual attention to linguistic competence in a larger context of learning about popular culture, especially through music. Each unit has a humanistic theme or topic (for example, German perceptions of foreigners), and each unit goes through three stages. In the first, students look inward (that is, explore Self) to identify their own experience and their knowledge of the theme. The last two stages use a feature song, linked with German newspaper and magazine articles, to explore German expressions on the theme. By combining activities that heighten self-awareness with activities that heighten other-awareness, the students develop a much greater knowledge and understanding of human interactions in German culture, as well as enhanced listening, reading, writing, and speaking skills.

• In a fiction-writing course, the teacher wants students to acquire new perspectives on the meaning of community and citizenship while creating fiction. So he has students write stories in which they create an imaginary town. As students populate their towns and homes with characters, they find they need to look closely at their own families and communities for inspiration, rather than to established authors. The students also rely on classmates to give feedback on the cohesiveness and realness of the many events in their stories. Hence students have to interact with themselves (in their inner reflections on their own lives) and with others (in the community as well as with classmates) in order to create an image, a story of what community is like, and what roles individuals can and do play in it.

Integration

Several of the courses described in the case studies generate integration kinds of learning, although they differ in terms of *what* they are connecting. Generally integration is accomplished in a two-part sequence. First, students have to learn about each of the subjects being connected. Second, students have to give focused attention to making the connections. In some cases, this means just comparing two or more subjects, that is, identifying similarities and differences. In others, attention is focused on the interaction among two or more subjects.

When learning about different subjects, in the first part of this sequence, students engage in the usual activities of reading or listening to lectures (receiving information and ideas) and sometimes in a special form of "doing" experience: field-based activities, lab work, complex projects, and the like. In the second part, students have to engage in thinking, writing, reflecting (Dialogue with Self), and in small group or whole class discussions (Dialogue with Others). Sometimes special "doing" projects are also used. It is in this second step that students integrate the material from the first step.

Here are some examples of integration learning from the case studies:

• In the multidisciplinary geology course, non-major students study—in sequence—geology, physics, and chemistry. The focus of the course is on local geology, but the team of three teachers uses a sequence of fieldwork, classroom explanations, lab work, and class discussions to present each discipline. As the class works through the different disciplines, much of the discussion is focused on a comparison of how each of the three disciplines construct or create knowledge. Hence, in this case, integration is primarily a comparison of three different ways of knowing.

• In the course titled "Biology for Science Literacy," students work through a series of concept activities, investigative activities, and issue-oriented activities. Throughout these activities, the teacher helps students learn how to make informal and thoughtful decisions on issues relating to science that are consistent with their own values. In this case, students are exploring the connections or interactions between scientific knowledge, policy issues, and the students' own personal values.

• In an art history course titled "Myth, Religion, and Art," students examine the many ways in which religious beliefs affect the creation of works of art. In addition to attending a traditional lecture and slide presentation, students work through a weekly series of problems aimed at exploring different questions about the relationship between art and religious belief. In this case, students are integrating a broadened understanding of different religious beliefs and various forms of art, religion and art in different cultures around the world, and the past with the present.

Application

Many of the courses described in the published literature on college teaching were selected in part because they devised special means for promoting some kind of application. Of the courses selected, 80 percent involved work on application learning, which is defined here as learning how to engage in one or more kinds of thinking (creative, critical, and practical), developing an important skill, or managing a complex project.

The patterns by which this was accomplished were quite consistent and clear. Students engage in some kind of "doing" activity that allows them to have repeated practice with whatever kind of application learning is the goal; then the students receive feedback, preferably feedback that is prompt and criteria-based.

Thinking Abilities. Several of the courses in the sample create activities intended to help students develop one of the three kinds of thinking abilities described in Chapter Two:

• *Critical thinking:* Students in the chemistry senior seminar are given repeated opportunities to critically assess published articles on a variety of topics.

• *Creative thinking:* Business students in the course linking business and the humanities have to create fictional but realistic businesses after examining business operations from multiple perspectives. Students in a course on writing fiction have a major project in which they individually write a story around an imaginary town.

• *Practical thinking:* Students in a medical school with a Problem-Based Learning curriculum are given carefully designed patient problems. They must examine the information they are given, decide what additional information might be helpful, consult medical textbooks, and propose a diagnosis and therapy—all aimed at solving the patient's problem.

Skills. Other courses offer students opportunities to develop a number of skills, often related to communication:

• *Data gathering:* Students in the multidisciplinary geology course have a number of field trips and lab exercises. These activities give students practice in developing their ability for making and recording field observations, reading topographic maps, and operating lab equipment.

• *Foreign language:* In the course on German culture, students work extensively on building the full set of communication competencies: reading, writing, listening, and speaking.

Managing Complex Projects. Several courses present students with the challenge of learning how to manage large, open-ended complex projects:

• In the course on creative writing in relation to Yugoslavia, the class decided to compile and market an anthology of contemporary American authors. This required students to solicit manuscripts, prepare the design and layout of the anthology, develop promotion strategies, and choose a charity to receive the proceeds.

• Beginning business majors in the Integrated Business Core have a semester-long project in which they form a real company to market a real product or service. As described in Chapter Four, the students in each company must decide what to sell, organize the company, obtain real operating funds from a local bank, produce and market the product or service, and close out the business—all within sixteen weeks. (They also select a charity and do volunteer work for that charity, which adds to the complexity of the project.)

• Students in the honors course on technology engage in a major simulation. The simulation indicates that the students are members of a government project who have crash-landed on a deserted island. They have figure out how to survive, organize their society, and build an airplane from available resources in order to get off the island. By the end of the semester, each group has to submit a final portfolio that includes completed plans for the airplane, the research that they completed during the semester, a model of the airplane, and a learning log.

Foundational Knowledge

My assumption is that all courses, good or bad, make some provision for covering their stated subject matter. Nonetheless, there is still an important question about learning foundational knowledge.

Given the fact that some courses spend all their time and energy on supporting only one kind of learning (foundational knowledge), we need to know how the courses described here manage to free up time for other kinds of significant learning without abandoning the goal of also furthering foundational knowledge? Presumably they have to create some alternative way for students to move on to more significant kinds of learning without spending all their time acquiring foundational knowledge. Therefore, I reviewed the cases with this question in mind and found some interesting lessons.

Make Better Use of Out-of-Class Time. In the preceding chapter I discussed Walvoord's analysis of a common problem in higher education: that teachers never seem to have much time to spend on teaching students how to use the content because all their class time is devoted to communicating that content.

To help solve this problem, many of the teachers in the case studies move the initial exposure to the content to outside-of-class time. And they are quite successful in convincing students to comply. For example, "Workshop Biology" has no lectures to provide students with exposure to the content. Instead, students have outside assigned readings; class time is then devoted to working on a series of exercises that provide a variety of questions and problems.

In "Tax Law," students study the laws beforehand and then spend the majority of class time applying them to case problems and integrating the several procedures into a flow chart. Students in the Shakespeare course read his plays before class and then engage in multilayered dramatizations of selected portions of the text in class.

The key to getting students to do the necessary work and reading before class seems to lie in devising the right kind of in-class activities. Students need to know that the reading done beforehand will be absolutely necessary to do the in-class work *and* that the in-class work is an important and valuable kind of work. If the teacher can devise this kind of activity, the majority of the students will do the required work out of class, either as preparatory work before class or as follow-up work after class.

The Content Can Be Provided in Different Forms. Many of the teachers in the sample used the traditional means of providing content, that is, readings and lectures, as a means of helping students gain contact with important information and ideas about the phenomenon or subject being studied. But several were creative in finding other ways.

The German course, for instance, uses current magazines, journals, and newspapers to give students examples of authentic, contemporary writing in German on issues of importance in popular German culture. Several courses use film, either documentary-type films or dramatic films. Films can provide information directly about phenomena, for example, documenting interviews with childbearing women about their experiences, or they can provide it indirectly through fictitious but realistic portrayals of relevant phenomena. For example, "Business as Revealed in the Humanities" used the film *The Great Gatsby* to provide insights on the complex interactions that affect the economic behavior of individuals and organizations. Other courses use the familiar activities of field experiences and lab work to put students in a "doing" situation where they gather their own data and information about the subject.

Link the Content to Other Learning Activities. In the vast majority of these courses, the activity through which students gain foundational knowledge is also linked in a structured and sequenced way with activities aimed at promoting other kinds of significant learning. This linking adds the educational energy necessary for engaging in multiple kinds of learning.

• Students in the Integrated Business Core learn important basic concepts in the three core courses on management, marketing, and legal studies. And these basic concepts are used immediately in the practicum course, where students start and operate a real business. Also, within the three core courses, teachers use team-based learning, where students' early reading assignments are quickly followed by several application exercises. In this approach there are essentially no lectures, only an occasional ten- to fifteen-minute explanation of concepts that students have had difficulty understanding on their own.

• In the course on Spanish literature, students first read a given play in Spanish. This is followed by other key activities: watching a film version of the play, reading critical essays on the play, writing an essay that interprets events in the play from the perspective of one character, and then engaging in a ninety-minute role-play. In this exercise, one of the main characters is put on trial, pro and con arguments are heard from various characters and perspectives, and a discussion is followed by a judgment of guilt or innocence—all in Spanish.

• In the introductory teacher education course for prospective teachers, the role of content and field experiences is dramatically changed in order to promote a more critically reflective attitude toward students' professional activities and professional development. The course begins by having students look carefully at their own beliefs and assumptions about teaching and learning by using personal reflection, class discussion, case studies, and videotapes of classroom instruction. It is only after students have created individual and group lists of key questions and topics that the teachers introduce material from the education literature and assign students to be participant observers in classrooms. The effort to gain foundational knowledge is delayed in this case until students have developed a strong internal sense of what they need to know and why they need to know that.

• Students in the art history course meet once a week for three hours at a time. This large block of time follows a particular sequence each week. In the first hour, small groups of students discuss their response to the preceding week's problem. New foundational knowledge is introduced in the second hour; the teacher presents information on a new topic, usually accompanied by slides. Then, in the third and final hour, the groups start working on a new problem related to the new topic in which they explore the relationships between religious ideas and religious architecture. In this case, new foundational knowledge is introduced by the teacher and followed immediately by students' learning how to use that knowledge in an application-type problem, using a small group format.

• Students in the chemistry senior seminar course meet one hour per week throughout three ten-week quarters. They follow a sequence that begins with each individual student selecting a discussion topic from a long list on the general subject. The teacher provides one key article on the topic and the student eventually leads a discussion on that article and topic. Following the class discussion, the student turns in a short research paper (four to six pages) on the same topic. This sequence is repeated for each of the three quarters, with students taking more and more responsibility for selecting their own topics. In this course, students gain their foundational knowledge through their own research and by participating in class discussions led by other students. Their individual research is also linked to the activity of leading a class discussion and writing a summary paper.

To provide a quick overview of what these teachers have done to promote specific kinds of significant learning, the lessons are summarized in Exhibit 5.2. This analysis should give all teachers both the hope that such ambitious goals are feasible and some clear ideas on how to achieve such goals in their own courses. These teachers used their own intuition and ideas on good course design (especially the experience and reflective dialogue components of active learning) in ways that were creative, appropriate for their subject matter, and effective in terms of promoting significant learning. If others can do it, then it is at least possible that you can do it too—and you have the advantage of having access to the ideas in this book.

EXHIBIT 5.2. PROCEDURES FOR
PROMOTING SPECIFIC KINDS OF SIGNIFICANT LEARNING.

1. Learning How to Learn
   a. Becoming a better student. These particular courses did not frequently promote this in a direct way. A few did indirectly by creating a course at the beginning of a curriculum sequence that specifically addressed learning issues. This presumably was helpful to students as they took courses later in the curriculum.
   b. Inquiring and constructing knowledge in a specific subject matter. Have students practice engaging in inquiry, with feedback, and also analyze how knowledge is created or constructed in this subject matter.
   c. Becoming a self-directing learner. Again, these particular courses did not frequently make a specific effort to promote this kind of learning. Those that came close offered students opportunities to reflect on their own learning processes—that is, become more self-aware as learners—and practice building a learning agenda and strategy, with feedback on the process.

2. Caring
   a. Connect students to their own feelings about a topic.
   b. Have students take some kind of action that is informed by the first step.

3. The Human Dimension
   a. Allow students to build a new connection with themselves or with others by putting them in an imagined or simulated situation or by giving them the chance to hear the stories of others (that is, through indirect doing or observing).
   b. Have students reflect on these situations or stories: How do these situations or stories impact the students themselves? Do they generate new thoughts, feelings, actions, or beliefs?

4. Integration
   a. Learn about the various subjects being connected.
   b. Reflect and think about the connection: What are the similarities and differences? What interactions are occurring?

5. Application
   a. Give students repeated practice.
   b. Provide feedback on student practice.

6. Foundational Knowledge
   a. Make better use of out-of-class time.
   b. Provide the content in various forms.
   c. Link the content to other course activities.

The preceding discussion identified ways of teaching significant learning, which leads to the question of how to assess this kind of learning. The published descriptions of the courses in this sample did not contain detailed information about this question. Therefore I solicited ideas from a group of twenty-five faculty developers on a focused version of this question: What could teachers do to determine whether a specific kind of significant learning was occurring or not? The results of this initial effort to develop feedback and assessment procedures for new kinds of learning are shown in Exhibit 5.3.

Our discussion brought forth two important points. The first is that, as one moves beyond foundational knowledge and application learning, there are assessment procedures available that are valid but not as consistently reliable as we would like. For example, multiple-choice tests can be reliable indicators of foundational knowledge, whereas journal writing can be a valid but not always reliable indicator of whether students have come to care about the subject more. The second point is that some but not all of these procedures are appropriate in the grading system for the course. In most cases, wanting students to become more excited about the subject (caring) and to discover the personal and social implications of the subject (human dimension) are highly desirable learning goals; nonetheless, you may not want to use them as a basis for assigning the course grade.

How Can I Overcome the Challenges of Change?

For many people, this new way of teaching may represent a major departure from their current practice, and that means making big changes. I see two key challenges here: accepting the risk of doing something new, and maintaining a positive self-image throughout the change process. It's useful to do some careful thinking about both in advance.

Handling the Risk Factor

Following the suggestions presented in this book can generate a great deal of anxiety and uncertainty. Do I really know how to do this? Will it work if I do try it? What if it fails miserably? Such uncertainty can be quite unsettling. All innovation inherently carries risk, and taking risks is scary. On the other hand, avoiding any innovation condemns one to stagnation, which leads to an inability to improve and grow professionally as a teacher. To improve requires trying new ways of teaching, that is, being innovative. And being innovative inevitably entails some level of risk, a potentially unsettling process.

The solution to this dilemma lies in being deliberate about the type of innovation and about the level of risk to accept. Size up your political situation (Are

EXHIBIT 5.3. ASSESSMENT PROCEDURES FOR SIGNIFICANT LEARNING.

Learning How to Learn:
- Personal reflections. Usually gathered after a learning activity or whole course, these can be generated in writing, class discussions, online exchanges, learning portfolios, or even in SGIDs (Small Group Instructional Diagnoses).
- Learning portfolios.
- Performance in problem-based learning.
- Case problems about learning: Learn something new; document the procedures used and the results.

Caring:
- Personal reflections.
- Standardized questionnaires, for example, about interests, attitudes, or values.
- Learning portfolios.

Human Dimension:
- This has two aspects: the personal dimension (Self) and social dimension (Others).
- Information about changes in the *personal dimension* can be elicited in two basic ways:
  Personal reflections.
  Standardized questionnaires on factors such as self-confidence can be completed before and after an activity to measure any change.
- Information about a student's learning in the *social dimension* can be collected from students themselves or from others, for example, from other members on a team project.
- Learning portfolios can address both aspects of human dimension learning.

Integration:
- Have students identify the interactions or relationships between "X" and "Y." Then assess the clarity and extent of what they have integrated. This can be done via such activities as:
  Reflective writing
  Incomplete but progressive cases
  Concept maps
  Some portions of Problem-Based Learning apply here
  Interdisciplinary cases (Using authentic problems if possible)
  Capstone projects
  Work on real-life examples

Application:
- Have students *do* whatever you want them to learn to do.
- Then assess what they do with clear criteria and standards. This can be done via such things as:
  Simulations
  Demonstrations
  Team projects
  Case studies
  Explication activities (for example, in literature)
  Writing
  Some Classroom Assessment Techniques (CATs)

Foundational Knowledge:
- Traditional kinds of paper-and-pencil tests
- Drill and oral questions
- Some Classroom Assessment Techniques (CATs)

you tenured or not?) and your own psychological capabilities (How much risk can you comfortably handle?), and from this, first decide how much risk you can afford to take. Then, based on that information, decide what amount and what kinds of innovation offer the prospect of significant improvement in the quantity and quality of your students' learning without exceeding your acceptable level of risk.

Figure 5.1 outlines what is involved here. At any given moment, everyone is always at the far left-hand side of this diagram. But we are also always faced with the question of how much change and how much risk we are willing to accept in order to grow and improve.

Bonwell and Eison, writing about active learning in 1991, identified "risk" as perhaps the greatest of all the barriers confronting teachers who want to use more active learning (pp. 62–64). They noted that there were two types of risk involved—how the students will react to new ways of learning and how the faculty member will feel about the new ways of teaching. The risk with the students is that they may not participate willingly, may not learn as much (that is, not cover as much content), or may not learn as well. In addition, the teacher risks feeling not in control, not having the necessary skills, or being viewed by others as not fulfilling the proper role of a teacher.

These are all risks that can be successfully met and overcome. Bonwell, in a later publication (1992–93), offered three strategies for lowering the risk when trying new ways of teaching:

• Choose a lower-risk learning activity. For example, taking a periodic pause during a lecture to have students do something in pairs is less risky than having students do a role-play.
• Choose an activity that involves less in-class time. Shorter activities are less risky than longer activities.

FIGURE 5.1. RISK AND INNOVATION.

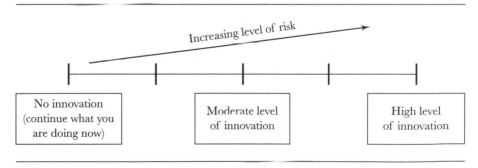

- Structure the activity carefully. If you can think ahead and anticipate possible directions the activity might go, and then put parameters or boundaries around it so that it will probably go where you want it to, there will be less risk.

Accepting the Need for Continuous Change

A second requirement for those trying to improve their teaching is the recognition that what they really need is not to make *a* change but to *continually change.* Doing this involves a major restructuring in how you think about teaching and about yourself as a teacher.

Robert Kegan (1994) has some stimulating ideas about multiple orders of consciousness that have relevance here. He postulates five orders of consciousness, three of which are reached by adults in varying proportions. In the third order, people interpret and create life experiences based on inferences about what they should do, with the "should" coming from various sources of authority: parents, the law, social identity, and so on. People who reach the fourth level of consciousness (not the majority of adults, according to Kegan) engage in "self-authorship," creating meaning in life according to their own sense of Self. But there exists yet another, fifth level of consciousness in which people find multiplicity in their own (and in others') sense of Self. These people author, or create, not just their Self but *changes* in it. That is, they consciously and deliberately engage in continuous self-transformation.

It's interesting to apply these ideas to the challenge of deciding how to teach. For instance, my own research (Fink, 1984), confirmed by others (Boice, 1992, p. 76), indicates that most new college teachers begin their teaching careers by following the lead of teachers they had as students. They emulate the teachers they admired and do the opposite of teachers they disliked. I interpret this behavior as exemplifying third-order consciousness. These teachers make meaning in their teaching by following the authority of their former teachers, that is, new teachers often teach the way their teachers taught.

These teachers usually find their own style of teaching after a few years, based on their own experience and a clearer sense of what kind of teacher they themselves want to be. This seems closer to Kegan's fourth order of consciousness, authoring one's own teaching style and one's own sense of Self as a teacher.

But people who are ready for the fifth order of consciousness recognize that they need to continually learn *new* ways of teaching, which means continually making small changes and periodically making major changes. Is this feasible? Do teachers really do this?

The answer is that really good teachers do. Some dramatic examples of this come from a new book on team-based learning (Michaelsen, Knight, and Fink,

2002). In a couple of the chapters in that book, teachers described why they had changed the way they taught, even though they previously had personal styles of teaching that were both excellent and mature. These were people who had won teaching awards, generally based on their excellence as lecturers. This was a way of teaching with which they were comfortable and which students obviously admired because they gave the professors high ratings. But eventually these teachers became uneasy about their perceptions of low-quality student learning. Even though their *teaching* was called good, student *learning* was not so good. As a result, they began looking for ideas on what they might do differently.

When these particular teachers encountered what they took to be a powerful new idea about teaching (in this case, the strategy of team-based learning), they decided to try it. They were well aware of the high risk involved in giving up a familiar way of teaching that in one sense was still working quite well. At the outset, they were not sure how the students would react to the new strategy, nor were they sure how they themselves would find it. Even so they had the courage to take that risk in hope of achieving a greater good: higher-quality student learning. In these particular cases the innovation worked and quickly became their new, preferred way of teaching. The new teaching strategy then continued as their preferred way of teaching because it reinforced what was now their criterion for good teaching: not their own comfort level but the quality of student learning.

What this all means for teachers who strive to be excellent is that they need to accept the fact that they will never "get there." Teaching well, to use an old adage, is not a destination but a journey. Even though there will likely be very good experiences along the way, one has to always look at oneself and in essence say: "This was good but not as good as it could be. I need to keep on working at it, to find some way of taking it to the next level of excellence."

How Do I Change? A Case Study

To shed some light on the question of how to proceed once your mind is made up to try for new ways of teaching, I will share a close look at one professor who undertook such a change. This review examines the process by which he attempted to change, the nature of the specific changes he made in his course, and the effects of those changes on student learning.

This teacher, physics professor John Furneaux, contacted me during the spring before he was to teach a two-semester course. He knew I was writing a book on course design and offered his course as an opportunity to test my ideas. Therefore, we engaged in a joint effort that began in the spring and continued until the end of his course.

Preliminary Discussions

We began by focusing on each of the primary components of course design and how they fit together. John brought to these discussions some ideas about areas of his teaching he definitely wanted to change. But he was also open to additional suggestions.

Situational Factors. The course he wanted to redesign was "Electronics Lab," a sophomore-level, two-semester course for physics majors that typically enrolled twenty to thirty students at a time. In terms of the general curriculum, this course played a key role for majors. It was here that students were supposed to learn how to understand and then actually make some of the electronic measuring devices that they would use in the research aspects of their upper-division courses in physics.

Since John had taught the course before, he had a reasonably detailed knowledge of the students, what knowledge they brought into the course, and where they would have occasion to use that knowledge later.

Learning Goals. John had heard about and was particularly stimulated by the idea of "context rich problem solving" proposed by physics educators at the University of Minnesota. (See http://groups.physics.umn.edu/physed/index.html.) He knew that he wanted his students to learn how to solve authentic, meaningful kinds of problems rather than typical end-of-chapter kinds of problems. He was also intrigued by and attracted to the taxonomy of significant learning when I introduced this concept.

John knew that one of his key goals had to do with application learning. He wanted students to learn how to do things. He wanted them to know how to use the computer to build electronic equipment for use in real, meaningful physics projects. Somewhat to my surprise, he found even the human dimension learning goals applicable in a hard-core science course like physics. John wanted students to understand that science is a human enterprise and therefore has a human face to it. In other words, scientists have both noble and petty personalities. He wanted his students to develop a self-image of themselves as people who can do serious science. He also believed they needed to learn how to interact with others on intellectual projects because that is the way much of today's major scientific research takes place.

Third, as we explored the goal of having students learn how to learn, this translated for John into having students learn how to use electronic equipment to create knowledge. Before we could proceed, however, we found that we had to spend time asking ourselves, "What do physicists mean by *knowledge?*" This was a critically important issue since helping students learn how to generate knowledge was the second of John's two fundamental goals for this course.

Teaching and Learning Activities. John brought two ideas to our initial discussion about the kinds of teaching and learning activities he wanted to use. Clearly he was dissatisfied with the cookbook exercises that had been used before and wanted to replace them with more challenging, authentic, and meaningful projects.

Second, computer programs are now available to design electronic equipment. John wanted students to learn how to use these programs to collect and manipulate data for the purpose of designing measuring devices. And he wanted to do this in the context of focused, real projects. This is the kind of activity physicists do in their labs, and this is what students will do later in the undergraduate curriculum. Hence he wanted this course to emulate, as closely as possible, what students would be doing in their subsequent physics labs.

He was also somewhat familiar with the use of small groups in teaching. But he wanted to expand and refine his understanding of this form of learning so as to use it more effectively in this class.

Feedback and Assessment Procedures. John did not bring many strong ideas about what he wanted to do in regard to feedback and assessment. But he was quite attracted to several of the ideas embodied in the concept of educative assessment: giving students opportunities for self-assessment, having clear criteria and standards, frequent and immediate feedback, and so forth.

Creating a Rough Draft of the Course Design. At our second meeting, a month later, we worked to create an expanded set of significant learning goals and used my four-column worksheet (see Exhibit A.1 in Appendix A) to identify the goals, relevant feedback and assessment activities for each goal, and appropriate teaching and learning activities. The resulting outline (see Exhibit 5.4) created a perspective on the course that he found exciting. It was certainly more ambitious in terms of student learning than what had been done before. But it was also internally cohesive; that is, the second and third columns identified the specific activities or tools needed to pull this adventure off, and the activities all seemed to be doable.

Developing a Course Structure and an Instructional Strategy. Having taught the course before, John knew the full list of important topics on the subject. But, with prompting from the ideas on course structure, he also identified what he considered to be the major topics that incorporated subtopics and laid out a thematic structure for the whole two semesters.

EXHIBIT 5.4. INITIAL COURSE
DESIGN FOR "ELECTRONICS LAB" COURSE.

Goals	Feedback and Assessment	Teaching and Learning Activities
1. Develop familiarity with electronic techniques. A. Know the terminology. B. Operate the technology. C. Know and describe how the technology works.	A. Paper-and-pencil tests. B. Lab: Do it. C. Paper and pencil: describe.	A. Readings, lectures. B. Lab exercises. C. Explain technology to others, orally or in writing.
2. Use the technology to generate knowledge. A. Use technology to answer questions. B. Design technology for real projects. C. Assess validity of data techniques and information and answers. D. Identify and assess own assumptions.	A. Teacher gives a question; students *use* technology to answer question. B. Teacher gives a question; students *design* technology. C. Teacher gives example of a procedures or results; students assess the data, information, techniques, and answers. D. Same; students identify and assess their assumptions.	For all of these: • Practice doing, with feedback. • Observe others. • Assess own and others' "doing" performance. • Assess data, information, techniques, answers, and assumptions.
3. Understand what *knowledge* is. A. Students create a model of knowledge. B. Test complex questions.	In discussion, teacher finds out if students can: A. Create a model of knowledge. B. Use their model to answer questions about knowledge.	For all of these: • Reflect. • Create a model of knowledge. • Use their models to answer questions.
4. Personal and social nature of science. A. Understand the individual nature of science. B. Understand how social dynamics work in scientific work.	A. Write an essay titled "Human Dimensions of the Work of Science." B. Have informal discussion, in small groups, outside of class.	For all of these: • Journal writing. • Reflect on the individual and social nature of their own small groups. • Read accounts of the work of scientists. • In small groups, discuss own activities, reading material.

EXHIBIT 5.4. INITIAL COURSE
DESIGN FOR "ELECTRONICS LAB" COURSE, Cont'd.

Goals	Feedback and Assessment	Teaching and Learning Activities
5. Learning how to learn. A. What would you *like* to learn? B. In particular situations: • *What* would you learn? • *How* would you learn that?	A. Journals, essays B. Teacher gives a hypothetical situation; students address: • What does one need to learn in that situation? • How would one learn that?	For all of these: • Use context-rich problems. • Use scientific method procedures.

Note: Technology in this course refers both to computer technology and to electronic measuring technology.

Then, keeping in mind the several kinds of learning he wanted to promote, he created a sequence of activities that he repeated, with some modifications, for each of the major themes or topics. His strategy had four phases. The general aspects of this strategy can be described as follows, using the topic of *resistance* to unify the examples.

1. Look at the concept and the specific electronic device involved.
   • Example: Examine resistors and diodes.
2. Measure the properties of that device.
3. Use the device to measure a physical property.
   • Example: Use resistors as transducers, to measure temperature.
4. Use the measure of one physical property to create knowledge about another physical property.
   • Example: Use your ability to measure temperature to calculate the heat capacity of a selected material.
   • Use the information about heat capacity to identify the kind of metal the material consists of.

In essence, John was getting students to work through the multiple layers of inquiry involved in creating knowledge in physics. Students had to learn first about basic measuring devices because that was the explicit subject of the course. Then they learned how to use this knowledge to make measurements and collect data about the properties of physical phenomena. They also used that data to make larger inferences about the principles and patterns of physical processes.

With this work accomplished, John had a basic design for his course. He was then ready to begin implementing it.

First Semester

Once he got into the semester, John found himself continuing to think of additional learning activities he wanted to introduce and of novel ways of bundling several activities. He also uncovered some of the problems in his original design. For example, when he began to introduce the idea of using computers to design electronic apparatus, which was one of his major course goals, he discovered just how far he had overestimated the level of incoming knowledge. "When students first began this course," he told me, "I asked them to show me what they would do to 'use electronic equipment and the computer to measure the temperature of the air in this room.' Their response, at that stage, was to run over to the thermostat on the wall, read the temperature, and then type it into the computer and send it to me in an e-mail."

I asked John what he had hoped the students would have done in response to such a question. The answer to this question, it seemed to me, would likely be a good description of what he wanted students to be able to do at the end of the course. He said he wanted students to go to the computer, use the program to design an electronic apparatus to measure temperature, use that design to build an actual piece of equipment, use the equipment to measure air temperature, and then assess how well the instrument did what they intended. Clarifying this ultimate learning goal was extremely helpful in refining the course later on.

On the other hand, several of his ideas did work well. In line with the idea of active learning and creating rich learning experiences, John had each of the student groups design and build a series of measuring devices. This assignment was both challenging and open-ended in terms of what students were supposed to do, quite unlike the cookbook exercises that they had done before. But to add a touch of playfulness and reality at the same time, he created a simulated employer, the "Nielsen Brothers Holding Company," for the student groups to work for. ("Nielsen" is the name of the physics department building.) Periodically this company would send the students project requests for equipment that could conduct certain measuring tasks. The student groups were to figure out how to respond to these requests, that is, they had to design, construct, and assess an instrument that would measure certain properties.

Another of John's projects that went exceptionally well was the assignment for his students, who were sophomores, to design a learning unit for the "students just behind them," that is, for students in a freshman physics course. This assignment turned out to be a key project that had some powerful educational overtones. In this particular course John was trying to increase students' awareness of multiple levels of learning. However, he not only wanted them to learn about electronic measuring devices, he wanted them to learn about the relationship between these devices and the process of generating knowledge in physics. In addition, he wanted them to go up another level to being aware of the relationship between their ability to generate knowledge (that is, their ability to learn) and the structure of the learning experiences in a course.

To accomplish this goal, John had students design a teaching and learning unit for new physics students. In the process of creating this learning unit, these sophomore-level students were forced to think through the issues of *what* freshman-level students should learn (goals), *how* they could learn (teaching and learning activities), and what kind of *feedback* they should receive (feedback and assessment). As a result of thinking through these issues for other learners, the "Electronics Lab" students simultaneously became more thoughtful and conscious about these same issues and processes in their own learning.

John shared the ideas he received from me about good course design with his sophomores to help them complete this activity. With this guidance, they worked in small groups and came up with some very creative units. The project prompted the students to review and deepen their knowledge of the physics concepts presented in the introductory course. At the same time, it helped them solidify their own knowledge of electronics and increase their understanding of the process of learning while they created something truly helpful to other students.

Reflective Dialogue. Another significant change from earlier incarnations of the course was the frequent use of reflective dialogue. For example, the students were asked to periodically reflect on the course and its specific activities in short writing assignments. After doing the writing, they shared their individual reflections with other members of the class. A concluding assignment at the end of the course was to reflect on the course as a whole and write an extended essay in the form of a learning portfolio.

Feedback and Assessment Procedures. John made some extensive changes in the procedures he used to assess the students' progress and give them feedback. The most significant change was to incorporate procedures for educative assessment. He provided the students with a high level of feedback and gave them multiple opportunities to engage in self-assessment of their own work.

The first occasion for self-assessment occurred when the students created their first measuring instrument, an interface box. When they were finished, all the groups put the boxes they had created on a table in the center of the room. The class then held a whole-class discussion to generate a list of criteria and a set of procedures that would allow them to assess the boxes. Then all the groups, using the criteria and procedures developed by the class, assessed each box. Grades for the exercise were based on both the group assessments and the instructor's assessment of the instruments.

As the students worked to assess each box, they were starting the process of developing their own criteria for what constitutes quality in electronic devices, an important feature of the feedback and assessment process that would be further strengthened later on. Another important aspect of this whole project was that the boxes that the students had constructed were instruments that the students would use and have to rely on in all subsequent exercises in the course. Hence it was clear to the students that this task was important. Knowing that they had to have interface boxes that worked properly made both the construction and assessment aspects of the exercise quite relevant and valuable for the students.

Mid-Semester Assessment of the Course. As part of his effort to keep a high level of dialogue between himself and the students, John did a mid-semester evaluation of the course. He made a special point of asking the students to be very honest with their responses. The students cooperated by candidly telling him what they thought worked well and what did not.

The fact that John asked his students what they thought and felt about the course—and then actually listened and responded to them—made the students realize that they were an integral part of the experiment. As a result, they were very supportive of his efforts to solve the problems that existed.

Second Semester

John learned a lot from the experiences of the first semester and from the feedback he obtained from his students. With that, he and I continued to work at refining the course for the second semester.

In the process we revisited the issue of learning goals. As I listened to John talk about what he really wanted students to be able to *do*, it became clearer that his primary goal for the course was focused on application learning. Together we formulated the following primary learning goal:

> BY THE END OF THIS COURSE, STUDENTS SHOULD
> BE ABLE TO *DESIGN, CONSTRUCT,* AND *ASSESS* ELECTRONIC
> APPARATUS TO MEASURE PHYSICAL PROPERTIES.

The creation of this learning objective struck John as "really hitting the nail on the head." With this clearer formulation of the primary goal, we were able to start work on creating criteria and standards for the key parts of this goal: design, construct, and assess.

Refining Criteria and Standards. The clearer the statement of criteria and standards we could come up with for the application goal, the better the job of measuring student performance John could do. To construct the new standards and criteria, we followed Walvoord and Anderson's recommendations (1998, chapter 5). To get started, I asked John to describe how a typical student would behave who does *not* know how to do a good job of designing, constructing, and assessing—that is, a student at the beginning of the course, or one who had snoozed through it. Then describe what a student would do who *does* know how to do a good job at the tasks. His descriptive responses to these two questions gave us the material we needed to construct the criteria for assessing the students' application learning, that is, their ability to design, construct, and assess. Then for each of these, he worked up a set of standards. These were short statements on a scale of 0 to 3, describing different levels of quality performance on each criterion. Here are the basic *criteria* for each of the three general application goals:

I. Design
  A. Conceptualize problem.
  B. Use a computer program to design a solution.
    1. Effectively
    2. Efficiently
  C. Identify the accuracy and precision that are needed for the measurement and available from the experiment.
II. Construct: The equipment constructed by students should be
  A. Effective
    1. Measure properly and accurately.
    2. Measure only the intended property.
  B. Efficient
    1. Use few wires.
    2. Take a small amount of time.
  C. Robust (durable)
  D. Reliable
  E. Useful in the future
III. Analyze and Assess
  A. Determine how well the apparatus works.
  B. Determine how it can be improved.

Then for each of the criteria, John developed specific *standards*. These described different levels of quality performance for each of the criteria. Here are the high (++) and low (−−) ends of the standards for three of the criteria:

- I.A. Conceptualize a design problem.
    ++ Considers errors, accuracy, and precision first. Still focused on the immediate but considers improvements as an afterthought.
    −− Cannot start or continue even with a few hints. Needs everything laid out.
- II.C. Construct a robust (durable) instrument.
    ++ Reliability and durability questions are considered as part of planning process and are incorporated at each step.
    −− Reliability and durability are completely beyond thinking and understanding.
- III.A. Determine how well the apparatus works.
    ++ Thinks of what is necessary for a given measurement and makes sure that data are obtained to definitely answer the question at hand if possible.
    −− Does not understand or give consideration to this question.

The development of the reformulated application goal as well as the creation of associated criteria and standards had a powerful impact for John. It gave him the clarity and tools he needed for a variety of assessment tasks. With these tools, the students could engage in self-assessment with more focus and clarity. As the teacher of the course, John was able to assess student performance with more confidence and more focus. Going a step further, John assembled a group of colleagues from other departments on campus who were interested in pedagogical research. The task he had for his colleagues was to assist with generating a fuller and deeper assessment of the course. The outcome of that assessment is described in the following section.

Impact of the Changes Made

At the end of the second semester John conducted a thorough assessment of the course and the changes he made. With assistance from colleagues with expertise in educational assessment and data analysis, he gathered data on student performance, student perceptions of their own performance, and student assessment of the course. Three general points came through very strongly: the course did succeed in generating significant learning, the students were clearly aware that the course was different from other courses, and—good as these results were for a first-time effort—the course was capable of becoming even better in the future because of the quality of the feedback from the assessment effort.

Significant Learning Achieved. John also made his own assessment of how well the students achieved various kinds of significant learning. Based on the products of their work and his general observations in class, he was satisfied that the students had achieved the kinds of goals he had set for the course, especially in terms of learning how to design, build, and assess electronic measuring devices.

He also gave the students a questionnaire, asking whether they thought they had achieved different kinds of significant learning. On a scale of 1–6 (6 = high), the majority of the students gave the course a high rating, a 4 or 5, on each of nine kinds of significant learning (see Figure 5.2).

The comments indicate why the students rated each kind of learning as high as they did. A few of their comments are shown here, grouped according to the kind of significant learning they were addressing:

Foundational Knowledge

> "I am no longer entirely bewildered by everyday electronic items . . . and can distinguish the basic function of the internal workings of remote controls, toasters, and the antiquated wiring of my old Buick."

Application

> "Coming into the course I knew little about electronics. Now I am able to design and construct working circuits using operational amplifiers, LEDs, and photodiodes that are clean and simple."

Integration

> "I now have taken the knowledge from this course and started applying it to areas of personal interest at home, for example, building radios."

> "The relationships between theory and reality finally clicked this semester. The ability to analyze real-world systems forces an understanding of how electricity really works."

Caring

> "I was never one for electrical science, and I have come to appreciate it more."

> "Updating the labs has me excited about electronics."

Human Dimension (Self)

> "I have a greater grasp of my own computer programming skills. I also learned that I enjoy teaching others."

FIGURE 5.2. STUDENT RATINGS OF SIGNIFICANT LEARNING.

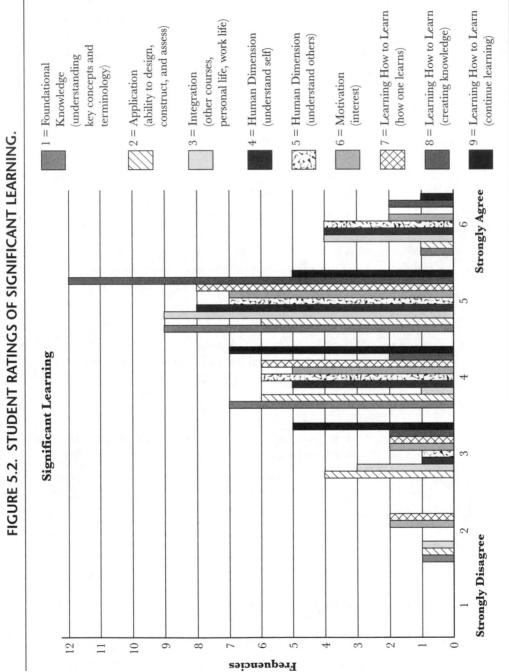

"I learned how I react within a group and what I can and cannot (or will and will not) do under pressure."

Human Dimension (Others)

"I had to figure out how to motivate other group members, and we had to work harder to pick up slack."

"I learned that it can . . . be beneficial to consult with other minds when I am lacking in knowledge."

Learning How to Learn (How One Learns)

"I've learned that reading a book does not create the ability to create a circuit that does what you want it to do."

"My usual strategies of reading documentation, systematic elimination of variables, and educated guessing served me fairly well in this course."

Learning How to Learn (Creating Knowledge)

"Upgrading the freshman lab by interfacing a time mechanism with Labview made it easier to see how data from electronic devices is used to create knowledge."

"Using the transducers enlightened [me about] the methods physicists use to obtain data."

Learning How to Learn (Becoming a Self-Directed Learner)

"I tried to independently build a current amp. This showed me that to continue learning electronics, I need to use reference books and ask professors who are more experienced for advice."

"I suppose that I need to continue with digital stuff, but I think that I need to study much more analog."

My conclusion from the data shown in Figure 5.2 and the student comments is that the course did succeed in promoting significant learning to a major degree.

This Course Was Different. The students were quite clear in their end-of-semester learning portfolios that they perceived this course to be quite different from other courses they had had. One student expressed this view quite well: "Let students know [in the future] that this course will in no way resemble an ordinary course.

. . . All students will have certain expectations about the format of the course. I think the best way to handle these notions is to dispel them as soon as possible. Let them know that the structure of this course will in no way resemble their ideas about the learning process."

The course had different and more meaningful goals, extensive group work, a high level of hands-on projects, and frequent involvement of the students in generating and responding to ongoing assessment. All together, these changes made it clear to the students that this course was indeed different from traditional courses, even traditional lab courses.

The Present and the Future. John was able to generate an impressive number of important changes in this course during the first time around. But even though he did have the benefit of good ideas from his department's seminars on teaching and from access to a coach with a clear sense of what integrated course design means, he still had to translate this information into specific activities in a specific course.

For example, John was able to formulate significant learning goals, generate coherent and meaningful active learning projects, and find ways to engage the students in educative assessment. The result was close to our hopes: a high level of achievement of significant learning. The majority of the students rated the course as a 4 or 5 on a 6-point scale for each kind of significant learning.

In addition, John was also learning as he went along. Even before the end of the course, he was well aware of things he wanted to change in future versions: modify specific projects, regulate the group work somewhat differently, and so on. My expectation is that with these second-order improvements, the results should be even more impressive the next time he teaches it.

John now has a clear sense of where he wants to go, what tools he needs to get there, and how to get the information he needs to continue improving the course. In a word, he is on a strong, well-founded learning curve.

Lessons Learned on How to Change

Based on this case study (which is still under way and, like all good innovations, will never be totally finished), it is important to ask what it teaches about the process of making substantial changes in how one teaches. What lessons does it provide for others?

The Value of Dialogue. First, being able to talk with someone else when working on a major change project is very powerful. In this case, we had a content expert (John) and a course design specialist (me). The value of dialogue about such a project comes in part from the varied expertise that different people bring to the task and in part from the opportunity to engage in dialogue with someone who is not in the course, that is, who is not a student or coteacher. This outside person can ask, as I tried to do, probing questions about the meaning of terms (for example, What do you mean by "knowledge"?), ideas, plans for teaching and learning activities, possible problems, and so on. In our situation, it was helpful having someone with a few years of experience as a campus-based instructional consultant. On campuses without such a person, one might engage a fellow faculty member interested in creative and innovative approaches to teaching.

The Value of Focusing on the Primary Components of Course Design. It is good to start this change process by thinking carefully, at a level that is appropriate for the teacher involved, about the primary components of integrated course design: situational factors, learning goals, teaching and learning activities, and feedback and assessment. Teachers like John —who have a fair amount of teaching experience and have thought extensively about teaching—can start at a more advanced level in terms of the kinds of goals they want to achieve and kinds of innovations they want to experiment with. Teachers who do not yet have these advantages should strive to be more cognizant of what their goals really are, even if they are traditional goals. They should think carefully about the relationships among all the components: the teaching situation, their goals, the feedback needed to determine how their teaching procedures are working, and what modifications they might make in how they teach.

The Willingness to Start Without a Fully Refined Design. We had to accept an initial course design that was not totally worked out in detail. However, we did have the best ideas we could come up with on three components of course design: goals, feedback and assessment, and teaching and learning activities. We knew these were an early draft of the ideas but decided they were good enough to get started. But we (read: John) had to live with the uncertainty that comes with starting the course with ideas that were still in a somewhat nebulous form.

The Need for Sustained Effort and Searching. The teacher (again, John) had to continuously monitor the course. With this information, the two of us searched for ways to refine and enhance our understanding of the goals. We also searched for ways to create more powerful forms of active learning and educative assessment. The big breakthrough, in this case, came when we developed a clearer sense of the fundamental application purpose of the course and then developed clear, specific criteria and standards. Given the fact that the basic components of a good course design were already in place, a significant improvement in this one component allowed a synergistic improvement to take place in the other components.

◆ ◆ ◆

The primary point of describing John's experience is to help readers see that it is possible to make substantial changes in the way one teaches. It is also important to have a good understanding of how the change process works. In this case, using the ideas of significant learning and integrated course design succeeded in helping this teacher find new and different ways of teaching. The integration of course design and significant learning resulted in better student learning, a clear student perception that the course was different and better, and the creation of an environment in which the students were highly engaged.

Will It Make Any Difference?

Given the challenge of implementing all the changes necessary to promote significant learning, a reader may ask: "Will it really make any significant difference after all? Will my class really be substantially different and better? Or will the results look pretty much like what happens ordinarily, that is, will it still be business as usual?"

These are legitimate questions and ones that need to be addressed. My belief is that these procedures will definitely make a difference, that a teacher's dreams for something special can happen—if the teacher carefully and systematically works through each of the steps in the course design process. What is the basis for this belief and this hope?

The experience of the teachers in the case studies and the experience of the physics teacher just described all indicate that doing things in a different way really can make an important educational difference for students. But to shed further light on this question, let me share two additional examples of teaching that support this belief. One comes from the world of music and the other from sociology.

A Curriculum for Band and Orchestra Directors

At the University of Oklahoma the music education program has developed a two-year (four-semester) curriculum for students who intend to be band and orchestra directors in public schools. The students usually enroll in this curriculum during their sophomore and junior years. The first year is a pair of two-credit courses, and the second year consists of two three-credit courses.

Goals. The primary focus of the course is on application goals. Students need to develop "the necessary conducting skills, instrumental pedagogy, and organizational skills to be successful in the public school instrumental music classroom (band or orchestra)" (M. Raiber, personal communication). But to achieve these application goals, students clearly need all the other forms of significant learning. They need:

- *Foundational knowledge:* Knowledge about the various instruments, conducting techniques, and the like.
- *Integration:* Ability to integrate individual instruments and players into the whole band or orchestra and the music into the whole school curriculum.
- *The human dimension:* A clear understanding of themselves as player, teacher, and conductor, plus an ability to interact with others—students, parents, administrators, and so on.
- *Caring:* An interest and excitement about music and young people and a professional attitude toward their responsibilities.
- *Learning how to learn:* As novice teachers, they obviously need to know how to keep on learning how to improve the various abilities required for this profession.

Teaching and Learning Activities. The curriculum has a high level of "doing" experiences. The people who designed this version of the curriculum believed that students in this program needed much more conducting experience than was previously the case. Therefore students spend a lot of time working with other students one-on-one, in small groups, and in large groups. This practice time gradually increases in complexity, taking on more and more of the challenge of full responsibility for conducting as the program progresses.

Although this program does not rely heavily on textbook information for presenting information and ideas, students do get lots of information in class about how to perform on various instruments, conduct in various situations, and so on. They are expected to keep notes, type them up, and keep them in a notebook with multiple tabs for the many topics about which they are learning.

Students also engage in extensive reflective dialogue about what they are learning. They keep "reflective teaching journals" with entries expected after every class. Students are asked to "reflect on any thoughts about teaching at the beginning of each semester: hopes, fears, self-evaluations, interesting teaching techniques they have witnessed, interesting experiences with students or teachers, and their own accomplishments and triumphs. The journal continues to serve as a reflective tool throughout their undergraduate teaching career and serves as a record of professional development" (M. Raiber, personal communication).

Each student is later asked to put together a learning portfolio, using material from the journal as well as anything else appropriate.

Feedback and Assessment. This program is full of authentic assessment. Students frequently engage in various kinds of conducting situations with real students and real music. Periodically they conduct in full formal performances.

The students also receive extensive feedback. Their conducting performances are audiotaped or videotaped, and they receive frequent oral and written feedback from the teacher, as well as oral feedback from their peers. Students are regularly asked to engage in self-assessment. They analyze and assess their own performance in writing after listening to and watching the recordings of their performance. Clear and specific criteria and standards are developed or provided for these various forms of assessment.

Results? This well-developed sequence of learning activities produces several kinds of positive results. The first is that the students finish the program with a high level of self-confidence. They know they can conduct well because they have already done it, many times.

For this particular curriculum, research has been conducted on the longer-term impact of the program (S. Paul and others, 2001). Students from four nationally known music education programs participated in a study that related four special kinds of learning activities (two kinds of "doing" experiences and two kinds of reflective feedback) to the performance of the students during their first year after graduation as actual music teachers in the public schools. For data on their performance, the teachers were videotaped and then rated with the "Survey of Teaching Effectiveness," an instrument that had previously been developed and tested by members of the National Association for Music Education.

The data was analyzed at two levels. Each of the four learning activities individually had a positive relationship to high-quality performance during the first year. But the major impact of the program on student learning occurred only when the four learning factors were combined. All the participants were sorted into three groups (High, Medium, and Low) according to the number of times they had engaged in the four learning activities. On a scale ranging from 10 (low) to 50 (high), the mean for the "Low" and "Medium" groups ranged from 25 to 28. The mean for the "High" group was 40. Graduates from the program described in this section fell primarily into this latter group. Clearly the combined use of significant learning goals, active learning methods, and extensive educative feedback and assessment made a difference, a significant difference, in the readiness of these students to fulfill an important role in our public schools.

Service Learning in Sociology

One of the more visible practitioners of service learning is José Calderon, an associate professor of sociology and Chicano studies at Pitzer College in Claremont, California. He has had some experiences in his own life, working with Cesar Chavez and the United Farm Workers, that changed his life and changed what he wanted to do as a teacher (Calderon, 1999; also described in Enos, 1999).

Calderon has students who, although they come from a variety of social backgrounds, have not had much exposure to people different from themselves. One of his general goals is to broaden their social experience. He has done this, in part, by incorporating service learning into one of his major courses, "Rural and Urban Ethnic Movements."

Goals. In terms of significant learning goals, Calderon clearly puts a major emphasis on helping students learn about the human dimension of a multicultural, modern society. He wants students to better understand themselves and the values and limitations of their own experiences that have resulted from particular social processes and to develop a deeper understanding of people who live in social situations very different from their own. Again, though, he realizes that to accomplish this goal, he needs to support the other kinds of significant learning goals as well. Students need *foundational knowledge* about social difference and multiculturalism. They need to develop their abilities for critical and creative thinking and managing complex projects (*application*). Another very important goal is *integration*, with students learning how to integrate labor union activities, community development, and university resources. Students often become conscious of the need to change their value system (*caring*). And they *learn how to learn* by becoming more self-conscious of the role of new social experiences, critical analysis of their own ideas, and so on in their own knowledge and future education.

Teaching and Learning Activities. This course includes all the components of active learning. The service learning component allows students to gain rich, powerful forms of experience, both "doing" and "observing," by working and living with farm workers for several weeks. They do a lot of reading about social theory and about the sociology of farm workers that provides the students with new information and ideas. Finally, they engage in extensive reflective dialogue with themselves and with others. They keep journals, write several reflective essays, and hold frequent discussions that allow them to reflect on the subject and on their own learning processes. "Why is it that one group of people treats another group of people a certain way? Why is it that I have never learned about the outrageous treatment of farmworkers, even though I have attended a 'good' public school system?"

One other rich learning experience occurs when students, in return for the union's hospitality and shared knowledge, present a reflection of what they have learned, through the medium of theater. The students have to learn how to work together, how to think critically about what they have learned, and be creative in developing a dramatic form for communicating their feelings and ideas.

Feedback and Assessment. Students are working in an authentic situation that provides them with meaningful feedback on their performance in a natural, frequent way. They also get feedback from their peers and instructor on the quality of both their learning and their performance within the farmworkers' community. Based on this, they are able to engage in self-assessment using their reflective journals.

Results? Calderon has described a number of major changes in students that have resulted from their experiences in this course. First, as noted, some students (especially those from more affluent backgrounds) begin to ask serious questions about their prior schooling and the social processes that seem to put blinders on their own education. Other students, with backgrounds similar to the farmworkers', find that the university can help them find solutions to long-standing social problems. Second, students begin to realize their political potential. If they get organized, they truly can have a political impact in various communities. Finally, students frequently develop a new and powerful set of life values. To exemplify this, Calderon shared the story of one student who initially was very conservative and questioned even the legitimacy of unions. While enrolled in the course, he participated in the service-learning alternative spring break. Sometime later he wrote a letter to Calderon and described how this course and its associated experience had changed his entire life. He said that he had decided to change his career plans and go into social welfare kinds of work in order to empower people. Previously, his intent had been to work for corporate America and make lots of money (Calderon, 1999, p. 9).

Comments on These Two Case Studies

My hope is that these two case studies will convince readers that something special can happen when instruction is designed properly. In both these cases, the teachers used ambitious forms of significant learning goals, powerful forms of active learning, and meaningful forms of educative assessment. In particular, both used rich learning experiences and extensive opportunities for reflective dialogue, the two general strategies recommended in Chapter Four. As a result, in each case the students definitely had significant learning experiences that were clearly distinct and powerful.

Concluding Comments

I hope readers will derive three major lessons from the examples and analyses that have been presented in this chapter:

It truly is possible to design courses in ways that support significant learning. The teachers in the several case studies described here succeeded in generating multiple kinds of significant learning. If they can do it, in different kinds of teaching situations and with various kinds of subject matter, so can others.

It matters what teachers do to promote this more ambitious learning agenda. For starters, these teachers relied on active learning, especially on a greater and more creative use of rich learning experiences and reflective dialogue. In addition, I know that the teacher on my own campus used educative assessment, and I suspect that the teachers in the published reports did likewise. This suggests that the model of integrated course design is indeed effective in showing what one needs to do to promote better quality learning. It can provide a road map for improving one's courses.

It can and will make a difference if one does set significant learning goals and does use the components of active learning and educative assessment. It will make a big difference in the quality of your students' learning experiences. The students in these courses knew and understood that they had had a different kind of learning experience, and they saw the special value of what they had learned this way.

To conclude this chapter, I want to share something from my experience of working with teachers that is a major part of the reason I have written this book. I have seen teachers succeed in making substantial changes in the way they teach, and it is an awesome event to behold. I have seen the dedication it takes on their part and the need for the right kind of new ideas. But more important, I have seen the impact that making such change has on both teachers and students. Their students become more engaged in the course and learn more. The teachers rediscover the joy of teaching when they see the kind of learning that results. These results have been achieved both by teachers who had problems they wanted to solve and also by teachers who, although they were already good, were committed to becoming even better.

My hope is that the stories presented here will persuade readers to be courageous enough to accept the invitation to change the way they teach and that the ideas and examples will help them find ways to generate the kinds of learning they desire for their students.

CHAPTER SIX

BETTER ORGANIZATIONAL SUPPORT FOR FACULTY

The new ways of teaching described here make a real difference in both student learning and teacher satisfaction. However, to have any chance of making these changes into a widespread reality, faculty will need better support from the various organizations in higher education that shape the context within which they work.

In this chapter, I have two audiences in mind: faculty members who are ready to take on a leadership role and work for organizational change and the people who are already decision makers in various organizations in higher education. Colleges and universities are the key organizations that need to make changes because they provide the immediate context for faculty work. But a number of other organizations have major influence as well: accrediting organizations, funding agencies, disciplinary associations, and the numerous journals that publish material on college teaching. If faculty members can work with administrators in these various organizations, meaningful changes can be made that will greatly enhance the context for faculty teaching throughout higher education.

The reason these organizations need to give serious attention to their role in supporting faculty change is quite clear: faculty members are the ones in charge of the courses and curricula that constitute the core of our educational programs. *Until and unless the faculty changes, nothing significant has happened* in terms of improving the quality of educational programs in colleges and universities.

Hence faculty members themselves and organizational leaders need to gain a clearer picture of the problems faculty face in their current situation and what support faculty need. Such an analysis will then allow us to explore ways in which the key organizations can work together to provide that support.

Problems Faculty Face at the Present Time

Faculty members face a number of problems that everyone needs to understand and appreciate. The first is that faculty can be creatures of habit just as much as anyone else. Even as students sometimes go through the motions of taking a course without giving much thought to what they are doing, so too faculty members can go through the motions of teaching rather mindlessly. They can follow their own usual patterns without taking time (or being able to take the time) to closely examine the quality of what they are doing or to learn about ideas that would provide better alternatives.

Faculty who do rethink their assumptions about teaching often face a second barrier, that of receiving little or no encouragement from others. Their colleagues do not spend much time talking to each other about teaching, other than to complain about students. They do not compare notes on new ideas they are trying or celebrate one another's success in trying something new.

But faculty in departments that do care about good teaching frequently encounter another problem: finding enough *time* to spend on learning about and preparing for different ways of teaching. The prevailing view of faculty work in most institutions includes only teaching, research, and service. This view does not provide any "in-load" time for faculty to work on their own professional development in teaching or anything else.

And those highly motivated individuals who decide to make time anyway, even if it means doing so on an overload basis, can easily find themselves overwhelmed by the multitude of good books, articles, and ideas available on college teaching these days. Where should they start? Who is available to help them decide where to start? Where can they get a conceptual framework about the big picture of teaching that will allow them to determine which of the many ideas in the large and growing literature on college teaching are major ideas and which offer supporting details?

When faculty do find and try an innovative idea, they sometimes run into uncooperative students. When students have not thought about their own learning and what kind of teaching best supports good learning, they too can object when someone changes the game and creates a new situation with new rules and new expectations.

A final serious problem remains even for those faculty members who try a new way of teaching that succeeds. Sometimes they are faced with a faculty culture and colleagues who either do not care or are jealous, or who attribute their efforts and success to impure motives such as pandering to students or spending their time on teaching rather than on research.

Not all of these problems exist at all colleges and universities. But my visits to many different campuses have convinced me that faculty in every institution face some of these problems and sometimes all of them.

What Do Faculty Need?

If the present situation is going to be changed, six critical conditions need to be addressed. What is it that faculty need?

- *Awareness:* The first requirement is that faculty members become aware of their own need to learn and change and, later, of their need to support organizational changes that affect the context within which they operate.
- *Encouragement:* Faculty need to know that others value their professional development as teachers and their ability to teach effectively.
- *Time:* Faculty need help in finding the time necessary for learning about teaching and for revising their courses and institutional curricula.
- *Resources:* Faculty need access to consulting services, support groups, reading material, and workshops and conferences that give them the intellectual and emotional resources necessary for change.
- *Cooperative students:* Faculty need students who understand and are mindful about what constitutes good learning and good teaching.
- *Recognition and reward:* Faculty need to be formally recognized and rewarded both for making the effort to improve and for any success they achieve in becoming more effective teachers.

These six conditions are mutually reinforcing. This means that all six conditions need to be improved if we want to have a major impact on the ability of faculty to change. Achieving this will require coordinated efforts by all the major organizations involved in higher education.

What organizational changes are needed to better support faculty efforts to improve their teaching? The rest of this chapter will present some ideas in response to this question. Most attention will be given to changes needed in colleges and universities for two reasons: these institutions have an immediate and direct influence on college teachers, and faculty themselves have a reasonably good chance of making changes at this level if they work together. But other organizations also play a key role and can provide important kinds of support that colleges and universities cannot provide by themselves. Therefore I will share some ideas about what these organizations can do as well.

At the end of this chapter, I will show how the contributions of each of these organizations can come together to help faculty members gear up for the task of creating new and more powerful learning experiences for students.

Support from Colleges and Universities

The way in which colleges and universities are organized and operate is the single most significant factor affecting how well faculty members are able to change and improve the way they teach. These institutions constitute the immediate context within which faculty work. The implication of this is clear: for faculty to learn how to create and offer better courses and educational programs, these institutions must examine the ways they support—or create barriers to—faculty change and then modify current practices as appropriate. This view is simply recognition of the fact that *effective instructional development is linked to and depends on effective organizational development.*

The many decision makers and leaders within these institutions—administrators, faculty leaders, instructional consultants, student development personnel, and so on—have to continuously ask themselves, "What can we do, individually and collectively, to help the faculty and students create more significant learning experiences?"

As institutional leaders ponder this question, they need to consider holistic, multidimensional responses by the institution and a few specific actions with direct impact on the faculty's readiness and ability to create better educational programs.

A Multidimensional Institutional Response

Given current changes in higher education, it will be imperative in the years and decades ahead for the leaders in all institutions of higher education to continuously rethink how their institution operates. Business as usual will no longer suffice. The best response to the challenges that lie ahead will be for the leaders to learn how to make a multidimensional response by the institution. The value and importance of making a holistic institutional response cannot be overemphasized. If only one aspect of operations changes while other dimensions stay the same, the original change will not last and the institution will return to business as usual before long.

After reviewing a number of perspectives on organizational effectiveness (Kotter, 1996; Creech, 1994; Heifitz, 1994) and thinking about how to adapt these perspectives to institutions of higher education, I have developed the model of institutional effectiveness shown in Figure 6.1. This model provides a conceptual framework for identifying the key aspects of an institution's operation that need attention.

Basically this model suggests that if a college or university wants to be an effective provider of higher education, it must first have a clear and measurable vision of what constitutes good *educational goals* for it as a particular kind of institution. Then it needs to create the *educational programs* that will meet those educational goals and the *organizational structure* and the *policies and procedures* that will support those programs, and then engage in a serious *assessment* of the degree to which it is achieving its educational goals.

If faculty leaders and institutional administrators see the value of making a multidimensional response to the changing environment of higher education, what might such a response entail? Here are several ideas to consider when doing this, backed up by examples from three institutions that have made a multidimensional response to their educational goals and to the need for change—Alverno College in Wisconsin, Pitzer College in California, and Syracuse University in New York— along with some from my own institution.

FIGURE 6.1. A MULTIDIMENSIONAL MODEL OF INSTITUTIONAL EFFECTIVENESS.

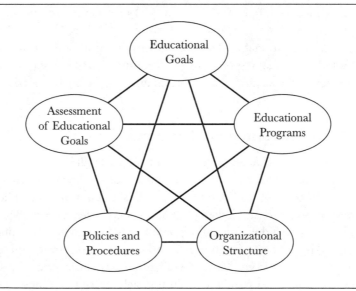

Create a Set of Educational Goals Focused on the Learning Needs of Individuals and Society. As institutions learn how to operate in a more competitive environment, they will need to start by thinking more about the educational needs of individuals and society and try to meet those needs, rather than starting with ideas that grow out of their existing structure and resources.

At the present time, few institutions have a clear set of educational goals. When you ask faculty or students what the educational goals of their institution are, most will say they have no idea. Some people at small colleges will say it is to "offer a good liberal education"; those at large universities may respond by saying the goals are to "provide a full range of high quality educational opportunities" (an actual quote from the Web site of a large institution). Sometimes individual departments or programs have clearly stated goals, but often the whole institution does not. This still leaves a problem for students, though, because they take courses from the whole institution and it is the whole institution that defines and creates their general education program. When there is no coherent sense of educational purpose at the institutional level, students frequently end up feeling that the pieces of their education have been very fragmented, isolated, and unrelated to each other. This was the primary criticism of American higher education offered by an AAC commission some years ago (AAC, 1985).

As institutions try to formulate a vision of what would constitute good educational goals in the face of diversity, change, and the periodic criticism that they are turning into professional "vocational" schools, it is important to keep in mind the three fundamental goals that students and society have always had for educational services:

- Enhance the quality of individual lives.
- Prepare people to contribute to the multiple communities of which they will be a part.
- Prepare people for the world of work.

One organization that has also attempted to offer guidance to institutions in terms of identifying worthwhile educational goals is the National Association of State Universities and Land-Grant Colleges. A statement in one of the association's commissioned studies (NASULGC, 1997) recognized the importance of these same three educational goals by describing what universities should do to offer an "education of value": "This university will provide graduates with an education that fits them with the skills, attitudes, and values required for success in life, citizenship, and work or further education" (p. viii). My language simply broadens these goals a bit. "Success in life" is equivalent to what I call "enhancing the quality of individual life"; "citizenship" is what I call "preparing people to contribute to multiple communities"; and success in "work" is the same as my "preparing people for the world of work."

My basic recommendation, like the AAC and NASULGC reports, is that colleges and universities need educational goals for the whole institution that meet three general criteria. These educational goals need to be learning-centered, inclusive of a broad range of educational needs, and yet specific enough to be measurable. It is impossible to design programs that generate a good education until the institution knows what it means by a "good education." What might such educational goals look like?

To answer this question, I will offer examples of goals from three institutions that illustrate what institution-wide goals might look like and will describe the institutional adjustments these institutions made to support those goals.

The first institution is Alverno College in Milwaukee, Wisconsin, one of the best-known examples of an institution that has recreated itself in a new, different, and effective form (Mentkowski, 1999). Institutional leaders started this process in the 1970s by formulating their educational goals around eight abilities that they wanted all their graduates to have. These eight abilities have been modified slightly over time, but they have had a high degree of stability. The current set lists communication, analysis, problem solving, valuing in decision making, social interaction, global perspective, effective citizenship, and aesthetic response. To graduate from Alverno, students must demonstrate at least a moderate level of proficiency in all eight of these abilities and a high proficiency in four of them.

A second example is Pitzer College in Claremont, California. Since its founding in 1963, the college has tried to create an undergraduate education program that offers and integrates three objectives: an interdisciplinary perspective, an intercultural perspective, and a concern with ethical implications and social consequences of the relationship between knowledge and action (Enos, 1999, p. 60).

The third example is Syracuse University (Wright, 2001). Although proud of its long history as a research university and member of the AAU, Syracuse was experiencing falling student enrollments and reduced revenues in the early 1990s. After some in-depth soul-searching by both faculty members and administrators, the university decided it had been funding research on the backs of undergraduates who were paying dearly to attend this high-tuition private university. They acknowledged that their students deserved a better education. Eventually both the faculty and administrators made the decision to pursue a more balanced set of goals, that is, to become a "student-centered research university." Although this new educational goal is less specific than the earlier examples, it nonetheless provided a sufficient basis for making substantial organizational changes.

If faculty and administrators in colleges and universities can formulate an institution-wide vision of educational goals that meet the criteria of being learning-centered, inclusive of important educational needs, and measurable, the institution's leaders will be in a good position to examine the other aspects of their operation and determine other changes that need to be made to make that vision a reality.

Create Educational Programs Capable of Implementing the Educational Goals. While writing this book, I happened to be working with my daughter to find a college for her to attend after finishing high school. She had a geographic preference (north central states) and a particular major in mind (interior design). We were also looking for a college that had a good general or liberal education program. When we looked at the catalogs and Web sites of many colleges, most had very attractive statements about what their general education program aimed to accomplish. But when we looked at the *programs* for delivering on those promises, the programs looked pretty much alike and not adequate to the stated goals. What most had was the usual curricular structure in which students are required to meet some distribution requirements and select a major.

What was not visible was any programmatic adjustment that would strongly promote students' capabilities in critical thinking, communication, writing, computer literacy, global perspectives, multicultural living, and so forth. We were looking for something more than taking a single course that in some way or another related to one of these goals. If there was going to be "writing across the curriculum" (or critical thinking, global perspectives, or anything else across the curriculum), where was the curricular structure that provided multiple opportunities to achieve the intended learning goals and that coordinated or connected these experiences? We also wanted an institution with a strong faculty development program, so the faculty would know how to implement the curriculum. (Note: The only institution that met all our criteria was the Western College Program at Miami University of Ohio. My daughter applied to that program, was accepted, and is attending classes there as I write.)

What the good colleges are doing and others need to do is to look carefully at the kind of learning they would like to see in their graduates and then ask themselves: What kinds of learning experiences would our students need to have to achieve these goals? Where in our curriculum are the desired skills, knowledge, and attitudes going to be acquired and developed? How can we coordinate curricular learning with special experiences provided through extracurricular and co-curricular activities, housing programs, and student organizations?

Some colleges have instituted freshman year and even senior year courses in which students are encouraged to become more self-aware as learners and reflect on what they are currently learning, what else they need to learn, and how they might best learn that. Perhaps we need a new kind of course that runs continuously throughout the undergraduate program that will enable students to reflect on and connect their various learning experiences across time.

To return to the three examples, the faculty at Alverno has worked hard for many years to incorporate opportunities for students to develop their eight abilities within all the courses in the college. The descriptions of courses in the college catalog indicate which abilities are incorporated into each course. Hence when students select their courses, they look at what opportunities a given course offers to further their eight abilities as well as at the subject matter of the course. Students also enroll in special courses throughout their undergraduate program where they think about what they are learning in their courses and put together learning portfolios that document their level of achievement for each of the eight abilities.

At Pitzer, the faculty participate in various development activities that enable them to create courses that are truly interdisciplinary, intercultural, and capable of helping students develop the concern for the ethical and social implications of particular kinds of knowledge that constitute the core educational goals of the college.

Administrators at Syracuse provided funds to help departments make the changes necessary to provide more student-centered educational programs. Departments responded in several ways. They revised their own mission statements; introductory courses were modified to emphasize computer skills and critical thinking skills; large courses added more recitation sections; freshman seminars were revised; and academic support was increased for all courses.

Create an Organizational Structure That Fully Supports the Programs Needed.
If institutions decide to create curricula and programs that address a more focused set of educational goals, they will need new and different organizational units to properly support those programs. Most colleges and universities rely on one and only one kind of unit to deliver educational programs: discipline-based departments. These units are extremely powerful. They are responsible for the recruitment and selection of new faculty, the ongoing support of faculty, periodic evaluation, and eventually the powerful decisions about faculty tenure and promotion. They control the educational offerings within the institution and farm their faculty out on a voluntary basis to serve on the campuswide committees that make decisions about campuswide educational offerings, such as the institution's general education committee. The result? Relatively strong departmental programs and weak coherence in programs that operate at the institution-wide level.

What changes might a college or university make in its organizational structure? Two kinds of changes need to be considered. The first relates to different ways of delivering instruction. The second relates to providing better support for the professional development of faculty; I will discuss it in the next section in the context of four specific recommendations for colleges and universities.

The founders of Pitzer College decided not to have traditional academic departments at all. Rather, given their educational goal of offering an interdisciplinary curriculum, they set up field groups. These are groups of faculty members with various disciplinary backgrounds who have common research and teaching interests. Their belief is that traditional academic departments would lead to academic entrenchment and that this is antithetical to the educational goals of their institution.

At Alverno College, the leaders decided not to eliminate traditional departments but to complement them with another kind of organizational unit. They continue to have traditional academic departments, but nearly all faculty members are also members of another department focused on one of the college's eight educational abilities. Hence their faculty are members of two departments. The latter units are inherently cross-disciplinary and therefore counter the academic entrenchment that might otherwise occur.

Syracuse University did not change its overall organizational structure, but it did expand its Center for the Support of Teaching and Learning to provide better support for faculty and students. With twenty staff members, this center is now one of the largest of its kind in the country.

These examples indicate some of the organizational experimentation that institutions are engaging in to find more effective organizational structures to support their particular educational goals. When this has been accomplished, institutions then need to examine the fourth component of a multidimensional response: institutional policies and procedures.

Create Policies and Procedures That Allow Faculty to Work Effectively. At the present time, most institutions have policies and procedures that—although not intended for that purpose—have the effect of creating major barriers to serious faculty work on changing educational programs. Policies and procedures in many areas need to be changed, but two areas have a particularly strong impact on the ability of the faculty to promote significant learning: policies related to faculty work and to the evaluation of teaching. These are so significant that I will present more extended comments about each of them later in this chapter.

Conduct Institutional Assessment Related to the Institution's Educational Goals. Currently very few institutions assess their graduates to determine whether these graduates have achieved the kind of learning intended by the institution. Instead, they rely on individual courses to ensure that quality learning is occurring, or in some cases, department-level assessment of graduating seniors is made in relation to departmental goals for majors. Is there a need for institution-wide assessment of graduates?

A report from the Education Commission of the States (ECS) on "Quality Assurance in Undergraduate Education" (1994) answers this question with an emphatic yes. This report comes from a conference on this topic cosponsored by the ECS with the Johnson Foundation, the National Governors' Association, and the National Conference of State Legislatures. Participants included state and federal policymakers and leaders from the corporate, philanthropic, higher education, and accreditation communities.

In the participants' view, undergraduate education is an extremely important part of higher education's overall set of responsibilities but one in which "perhaps the greatest improvements remain to be made" (p. 2). To make the improvements needed, colleges and universities need public support. But the public (meaning taxpayers, legislators, parents, and students), in exchange for that support, needs assurance that institutions are doing what they need to do to offer high-quality programs. This is the external reason for quality assurance. However, there are internal reasons and internal audiences that create a need for quality assurance as well. If the institution has established educational goals for undergraduates, then the institution itself needs to know whether these goals are being achieved or not. So, for both external and internal audiences, the institution needs to collect, interpret, and report appropriate kinds of evidence, indicating the degree to which its graduates are achieving the kinds of learning goals that indicate the institution has a quality program.

The ECS report made a number of recommendations for what institutions need to do to provide this kind of quality assurance (pp. 2–3). First, institutions need to formulate a set of educational goals for all graduates of the institution. The report offered suggestions for what these goals might be, stated in a language that would be meaningful to the public. They suggested that all college graduates need high-level communication, computational, and technological literacy; informational abilities that enable individuals to gain and apply new knowledge and skills as needed; the ability to arrive at informed judgments and to function in a global community; and the attitudes, dispositions, and readiness to address specific problems in complex, real-world settings. These goals, or whatever goals were formulated by an institution, would indicate what that institution means by a "quality" education. Second, the ECS report also suggested that the assessment of the institution's ability to achieve these goals should be an institution-wide responsibility, rather than being the responsibility of each individual department. Third, assessment procedures need to be developed that go beyond "current quality assurance practices."

Is it feasible for institutions to engage in this kind of assessment and quality assurance? The ECS report did not offer examples of this, but again, Alverno College is the best example of an institution doing this with which I happen to be familiar. Administrators and faculty leaders at Alverno created an Office of Research and Evaluation shortly after the college was reorganized in the 1970s. This office has several responsibilities, but primary among these is the task of regularly collecting information about the performance of graduates and then reporting those results in ways that help the rest of the college monitor and improve educational programs in the college. That office collects information about Alverno graduates on an ongoing basis, up to five years after graduation, in relation to the eight abilities that represent the educational goals of the college. This information goes well beyond most institutions' standard surveys of their graduates by asking specific questions about the eight abilities. They ask graduates to provide evidence of being action-oriented problem solvers and of being able to analyze situations from multiple perspectives. And they ask for evidence of being effective communicators and of having an aesthetic response. And so forth. They also ask the respondents to relate their capabilities to specific aspects of the educational curriculum at Alverno. "Which parts were effective in promoting specific abilities? Which need to be improved?"

This kind of assessment obviously goes beyond the casual approach to convincing others of institutional quality: quotes from outstanding faculty or former students, descriptions of the physical plant, photos of students engaged in learning, a list of high-profile trustees, citation in college guides, lists of growing financial resources, statistics about scores by entering students on standardized tests. It also goes beyond the next level of looking at general outcomes: retention rates, graduation rates, number and retention of minority students, accreditation, and so forth. The approach to assessment recommended by ECS moves the process to a third level where it in essence says: This institution is dedicated to promoting and achieving specific learning outcomes. How well do its graduates, as a group, reflect these outcomes, and do they happen as a result of its educational programs?

This kind of institutional assessment meets both internal needs and external needs, as mentioned by the ECS report. Program administrators get the kind of feedback they need to assess and improve specific programs. External constituencies such as funding agencies, community leaders, and prospective students and their parents get the information they need to assess the quality of student learning in this institution.

In terms of the actions needed to increase the educational effectiveness of an institution, this kind of assessment completes the link between the educational goals of the institution and its educational programs. In some cases, it will also shed light on the effectiveness of the institution's organizational structure and its policies and procedures. Hence this is a critical part of the whole effort of striving for organizational effectiveness.

Putting the Recommendations Together. To conclude this section, the five general recommendations made here constitute a multidimensional response that institutions can take to increase their effectiveness in promoting significant learning. The key to starting this whole series of changes is with the first component: developing a focused set of educational goals that is important, appropriate to the institution, and measurable.

Is it important for an institution to address each of these five dimensions of institutional effectiveness? Yes, all five aspects of organizational behavior must be in alignment for the institution to be really effective. Although many organizations have attempted organizational change, it is the ones that make a multidimensional response that are successful. Robert Diamond, the former vice chancellor at Syracuse, believes that that university was able to make the sweeping changes it did because of "the near perfect alignment of vision, mission, structures, rewards, dollars, and decisions" up and down the whole organizational structure (Wright, 2001, p. 41).

In some ways, organizations are like automobiles. The engine, the ignition system, the cooling system, the transmission, the electrical system, the brakes, and so on—all have to individually be in good working order *and* they all have to work together for the vehicle to work properly. The same is true of institutions of higher education. They must have all of these features:

- *Educational goals* that are significant and measurable
- *Educational programs* capable of implementing those goals
- *Organizational structure* that properly supports those programs
- *Policies and procedures* that support the effort of faculty and others to implement and support those programs
- *Institution-wide assessment* that gives internal and external audiences meaningful information about the quality of learning provided in that institution.

Omit any one of these and the ability of the institution to provide quality educational programs will be greatly diminished. And conversely, any institution that can put all five of these factors in alignment will have a truly extraordinary program, one that will draw a large amount of attention because of its ability to provide educational services of extraordinarily high quality.

Four Specific Recommendations

Within the broad outline of a multidimensional response, though, four courses of action deserve special attention because they have such a significant impact on the ability of the faculty to implement effective educational programs. These recommendations concern procedures related to faculty work in general, procedures for evaluating teaching, the establishment of institution-wide teaching and learning centers, and coordinating student development with instructional development.

Change Procedures Related to Faculty Work and Faculty Evaluation

The single most important action institutions can take to improve instruction, in my view, is to change several procedures that influence faculty work. The need for changes in this realm of institutional operation are apparent from faculty comments and feelings in different situations.

When I give workshops on teaching at campuses around the country, participants often respond with comments like the following: "These are obviously good ideas. But frankly my institution does not recognize nor reward me for *improving* my teaching. They only reward me for getting publications out and for teaching my courses, not improving them." In this situation, faculty members feel that institutional evaluation procedures discourage them from improving their teaching—an activity that most observers would deem as highly desirable.

The need for change can also be seen in the feelings that many faculty and administrators have at annual faculty evaluation time. On most campuses, this process consumes a significant amount of everyone's time, creates a lot of negative feelings in both the evaluated and the evaluators, but ends up not being used as the basis for anything except giving very modest pay raises.

Situations such as these suggest a number of problems related to both the way expectations are set up for faculty work and then how that work is evaluated. These problems compound each other and need to be unraveled if we want to find an effective solution. The problem begins with the fact that most institutions have more work for their faculty to do than they have faculty to do it. The institution then asks faculty to do everything that needs to be done, working under the obviously false but very attractive assumption that faculty time is infinitely elastic. Then, when it comes time to evaluate faculty work, the evaluators in essence say: "Thank you for doing all that, but for now, just show me how many publications you had this year and what your student evaluation scores are." (This is generally a request for the average scores from one or two global questions.) This creates understandable resentment among the faculty and reluctance to spend time on anything other than a very narrow range of activities in the future.

What can institutions do to change this situation? It would seem that administrators and faculty leaders need to rethink two fundamental questions related to faculty work:

- What does the institution really need its faculty to be doing?
- How can we encourage faculty to do that, in a way that meets the institution's needs and faculty needs at the same time?

Here are some ideas that can help in answering these questions and rethinking institutional procedures related to faculty work.

• *What does the institution need faculty to be doing?* At present, three overriding principles operate throughout much of higher education and direct our expectations of faculty work: teaching, research, and service. The problem is that this trio, while good in many ways, does not include any provision for faculty to learn how to do their work better. It basically ignores the idea that Stephen Covey has presented so powerfully in *The Seven Habits of Highly Effective People* (1990), which is that everyone needs to periodically take time out from doing their basic work to "sharpen the saw." Faculty too need to take time out from the basic work of teaching, research, and service to sharpen their saws, that is, to acquire new ideas and develop new skills that will enhance their ability to perform more effectively.

It may help to see the significance of this idea by using a long-term perspective when we think about faculty work. My assumption is that all faculty members have the potential to get better over time at what they do, as shown by the dashed line in Figure 6.2.

The fact is, though, that some faculty realize that potential and get better over time (the A group) but others do not (the B group). The latter improve somewhat during the initial years of their career but then plateau and, in time, decline in the quality of their work. As one person said: "There is no such thing as 'stasis' in faculty work; you are either getting better or getting worse." And in my experience, the people who get better do so because they work at it. They continually monitor the quality of their work, look for new ideas (in their teaching, their research, and their various organizational roles), incorporate these ideas, and—after five years,

FIGURE 6.2. QUALITY OF FACULTY WORK OVER TIME.

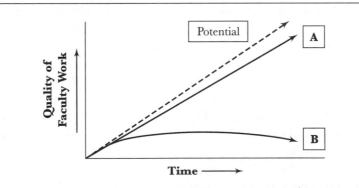

ten years, and so forth—continually become more effective and proficient in what they do. What can institutions do to encourage more of their faculty to be on a "growth curve" in all aspects of their professional work?

My recommendation is to add "professional development" as a major area in which faculty members are expected to spend some of their time each year. In essence, I am proposing to expand the basic trio of faculty work (teaching, research, and service) into a "governing quadrilateral" (teaching, research, service, and professional development). Since faculty competence is the foundation on which all of higher education rests, it is critically important for faculty members to continually expand and enhance that competence in the several realms of faculty work. How can institutions encourage professional development on a regular and continuous basis?

One procedure that would help immensely is to create a worksheet that identifies the major areas of faculty work and then to be sure that this worksheet includes professional development. An example of such a worksheet is shown in Exhibit 6.1. Such a form (or some variant of it) could be used both in the discussions of what faculty want and are expected to do and then, at the end of the year, in discussions of how their work went.

If such a procedure were used on a regular basis, faculty and administrators would be prompted to ask: What are some important areas of learning and professional development that might significantly enhance the quality of faculty work? Asking that question on a continual basis will greatly enhance the likelihood that faculty will do the work necessary to place and keep themselves on a growth curve professionally.

What are some of the areas in which faculty might improve their professional capabilities? Administrators and faculty leaders at each institution will want to generate their own list of such topics. But a group of department leaders on my campus addressed that question and came up with the following items:

It would enhance our institution's effectiveness if faculty could improve their capabilities in relation to the following four general areas of faculty work:

1. Teaching

- Basic skills (lecturing, leading discussions, making tests)
- Designing courses
- Designing curricula
- Interacting with students
- Responding to changes in this institution and in higher education generally

EXHIBIT 6.1. IMPORTANT AREAS OF FACULTY ACTIVITY.

Proportion
of Time:

1. **Teaching**   _____

   Includes the following kinds of activities:

   - Departmental teaching
   - University-wide teaching (outside the department)
   - Curriculum development
   - Supervising teaching assistants and interns
   - Advising undergraduate students
   - Advising graduate students

2. **Research and Creative Activity**   _____

   Includes the following kinds of activities:

   - Seeking financial support
   - Conducting research
   - Writing, presenting, and publishing
   - Creating and preparing artistic work
   - Exhibiting, presenting, and performing their work

3. **Service**   _____

   Includes the following kinds of activities:

   - Institutional service
   - Service in professional associations
   - Community service
   - University-community relations

4. **Professional Development**   _____

   Includes the following general areas of professional competence:

   - Teaching
   - Research
   - Service
   - Professional self-management

                                                       TOTAL: 100%

2. Research

- Seeking grants
- Writing skills (for grants and publications)
- Developing a publication strategy
- Mentoring
- Retraining for new kinds of research

3. Service

- Leadership
- How to help organizations change
- Presentation skills
- Conducting meetings

4. Professional Self-Management

- Time and stress management
- Seeking balance in work and personal life
- Developing negotiating skills and conflict resolution skills
- Putting first things first

If faculty regularly spent time learning about topics such as these as part of an ongoing professional development effort, they would put themselves on a growth curve professionally and our institutions would benefit enormously. This is important for professionals in all organizations, but it is critical in institutions where learning is the central focus of the whole institution.

   • *How can institutions meet faculty needs as well as institutional needs when setting expectations for and evaluating faculty work?* If leaders accept the idea of adding professional development to the list of expected faculty activities, the initial impact will be to exacerbate the problem: faculty will now have more to do rather than less! What can be done to resolve this situation? One essential action is to develop procedures and policies that make realistic estimates of the time required for various kinds of faculty work, and another is to make the setting of expectations and the evaluation of faculty work a joint endeavor between individual faculty members and the department (or other relevant academic unit).

Make Realistic Time Estimates. When faculty members have a long list of activities they want to do and the institution has a long list of activities it needs faculty to do, this can easily create a situation in which the lists are longer than the time available. This challenges us to make a realistic assessment of how much time is needed for specific kinds of activities and then to set priorities on which activities are most important.

If an institution decides to use a form like the one shown previously in Exhibit 6.1, listing different kinds of desired faculty activity, it needs to figure out how to make approximate but realistic estimates of the time required for different activities. I suggest starting with the two areas of teaching and professional development. Teaching has a certain fixed character to it when it comes to time, and we want to be sure a certain minimum amount of time is allotted for professional development. How, then, does one calculate the time required for teaching?

The 20 Percent Rule for Classroom Teaching. When you teach a certain number of courses, this encumbers a certain amount of time. How much time? I suggest using the "20 Percent Rule" for calculating the amount of time needed to teach a course. I have studied other teachers and my own work for many years, calculating how much time is needed to teach a course. This has led me to conclude that any teacher who teaches an ordinary, run-of-the-mill three-credit course and tries to do a good job will need to give it 20 percent of their time that term. This figure is based on the fact that such a course meets three hours a week, and most good teachers will spend another six hours per week in preparation and grading, on average, throughout the term. The resulting total of nine hours per week is 20 percent of a forty-five-hour work week, which is my approximation of the appropriate length of a work week for a professional academic. If the course has special features that increase the workload (high enrollment, frequent writing assignments, or the like), then the 20 percent should be increased. If it has features that decrease the workload (say there's a graduate assistant, or it is only a two-credit course), then the figure should be decreased. After the time for assigned courses has been calculated, similar allowance should be made for other teaching activities: supervising teaching assistants, advising graduate and undergraduate students, and the like.

One major factor that is almost always overlooked in this process is the impact of having a course that is a new preparation. When a faculty member teaches a course for the first time, it is a "new preparation" for that teacher. In such a case, the workload should be doubled! This is especially significant for new faculty members. Many of their courses are new preparations for them. If they have two such courses in one semester, each course has a workload equivalent of 40 percent, which means these two courses will require 80 percent of their work time that term. And this only includes the workload for their assigned courses; they still have advising, service, research. This is the major reason so many new faculty members are so seriously overloaded and are undergoing so much stress. This situation stifles any effort at creative teaching and promotes a teaching style exemplified by passive learning, easy grading, and lower-level learning. (For data from a nationwide study that shows the impact of new preparations on new faculty performance, see Fink, 1984, chapter 3.)

After the time needed for teaching activities has been calculated, the next step is to set aside time for professional development. In my view, this should never be less than 10 percent. At certain times in a career, when the faculty member is making a major career change, this might increase to 15, 20, or even 25 percent.

After the time needed for these two areas has been determined, the faculty member can see how much of their time is left and decide how to divide it between research and service. Both of these areas generally fall into the category of "do as much as you can." The advantage of having a worksheet like that shown in Exhibit 6.1 is that it allows the faculty member a much more realistic sense of how much time is really left for these other activities, and it allows the department to be more realistic in knowing how much research and service to expect from a given faculty member. It also provides a good basis for making appropriate adjustments when unexpected opportunities come along, for example, being elected to an office in a professional association. If one accepts such an opportunity, approximately how much time will it take? What changes need to be made in the rest of one's professional expectations? Having a worksheet like this gives the faculty member and department representatives a basis for making appropriate and realistic adjustments to such opportunities.

Make Expectations and Evaluation a Joint Effort. The second general response to the question of how to meet the needs of both faculty members and the institution is for them to work on this task together, making the setting of expectations and the evaluation of faculty work a joint effort by the individual faculty member and the department. Braskamp and Ory (1994), writing on the topic of faculty work, note that the root word of *assess* means to "sit down together." Consequently they too emphasize the value of making the process of setting expectations for and then assessing faculty work an explicit and collaborative endeavor.

In general, departments and institutions assume that faculty members all know what they are supposed to be doing and therefore do not spend much time working with individual faculty members on this issue. The problem with this benign neglect is that most faculty have more than they can do in a reasonable amount of time. Therefore they end up having to decide—by themselves—what the trade-offs should be. A better procedure would be for the faculty member and the department to decide, jointly and at the front end of the work year, what would be in the best interests of everyone for the faculty member to be doing. Then, when it comes time to do annual evaluations, these expectations have already been jointly decided and can serve as the basis for the evaluation. For this to happen, there needs to be regular dialogue between these two parties about specific expectations for faculty work and how that work is going to be evaluated.

My recommendation is for each faculty member to have regular, periodic discussions with the department chair or executive committee to identify the major areas where that faculty member's time should be spent. This process should start at the beginning of the performance or evaluation year with each faculty member generating a list of all the major activities he or she would like to undertake that year: teaching, advising, research, committees, whatever. Then, in a meeting with the chair or executive committee, the faculty member's list will be examined in terms of how well it contributes to departmental needs. If adjustments need to be made, these adjustments are negotiated then and there, at the beginning of the year with all affected parties present in the discussion. The resulting agreement, while subject to change during the year if special opportunities arise, then becomes the basis for an assessment of faculty work at the end of the year.

This procedure has several benefits. It gives individual faculty members a clearer sense of how they should spend their time during the year. It gives the department an effective mechanism for assuring that departmental priorities are being addressed and knowing who is responsible for any special projects. It also puts significant pressure on both the faculty and the department to become very clear as to what their real priorities are. One final benefit is that simply having this kind of discussion on a regular basis allows the department and the faculty to address all three of the other recommendations for evaluating faculty work: reconceptualizing the role of faculty evaluation in faculty work, making professional development a significant component of faculty work, and making sure everyone is using a realistic estimate of the time required for different areas of faculty work.

The Impact of Having New Procedures Related to Faculty Work. How well do these suggestions work for changing faculty attitudes and decisions regarding their work? One department on my campus participated in a pilot project with these suggestions and, after using them for two years, found them to be very valuable. The leaders in that department, Health and Sport Sciences, say that the major benefit is in the character of the discussions at faculty evaluation time. Instead of arguing and bickering over a rating that "should have been 3.6 instead of 3.5," the discussions are now focused on questions such as what activities would be most valuable for this faculty member to engage in next year and what resources can be found to promote success in those activities. A major side benefit has been that the process also encouraged the department to get serious about identifying its own priorities. And finally, it allowed individual faculty members to give thought to the question of what they could and should learn that would help them professionally and then engage in that activity—in-load—rather than as overload or on the run.

If similar policies and procedures for faculty evaluation were implemented throughout higher education, it would greatly increase the amount of time that faculty members would be able to devote to their own professional development. It would also build in time for them to use their new ideas and skills for the purpose of improving the courses and curricula on their campuses. The benefit to students would be enormous: better courses, better curricula, and more energized teachers.

Improve Procedures for Evaluating Teaching

The second major recommendation for institutional action concerns another area of policies and procedures, those used for evaluating teaching.

During the last few decades of the twentieth century, most colleges and universities in the United States adopted the practice of systematically obtaining student reactions to their courses and teachers. These quickly became the primary basis for evaluating the teaching of the faculty. However, as time has gone on, many faculty and administrators have become uneasy about student evaluations, even though they see it as an improvement on previous practice. Behind this heavy reliance of having students evaluate teaching lies a fundamental problem: institutions do not know what other criteria to use to evaluate teaching.

The basic problem is that academic departments and teachers face the task of having to evaluate teaching without the benefit of a shared vision and language for describing what constitutes "good teaching" and "good learning." As a result, they have let the default criterion become: How well do students like the teacher or the course, relative to other teachers and other courses? When this happens, departments take the mean scores from one or two global questions on the student questionnaire (such as "Overall, how good was this course [or teacher] compared to other courses [or teachers] you have had?"), and that becomes the whole basis for that year's evaluation of someone's teaching. This is an extremely narrow basis on which to judge an event as complex and multifaceted as college teaching! Perhaps more important, when faculty are evaluated this way, their attention is diverted away from student learning and focused inappropriately on *student approval*. How might this be changed?

A Learning-Centered Approach to Evaluating Teaching. The first step toward creating better procedures in this realm of institutional operation is to take a learning-centered approach. This would mean that the primary criterion for evaluating teaching should become the question: "Did a major proportion of the students have a significant learning experience?" This puts the primary spotlight where it ought to be, on the quality of student learning, not on the teacher's expertise, lecturing ability, or even ability to develop rapport with the students. These are all important, but they are secondary issues, not the primary issue.

To take a learning-centered approach to evaluating teaching, institutions will have to search for ways of collecting information about student learning and then assessing it. This will take some experimentation to find effective and efficient procedures. But I would offer two suggestions for facilitating this search. The first is that both the teacher and the students will need to provide the information needed. The teacher can collect and share samples of student work that indicate the types and range of student learning. Students can indicate on end-of-semester questionnaires how well they thought they had achieved various kinds of significant learning. But they can also contribute by assembling learning portfolios, if asked to do so by the teacher. Portfolios offer evidence about the kinds of student learning that occurred.

The second suggestion is that the taxonomy of significant learning can provide the language for interpreting and assessing multiple kinds of significant student learning. To what degree was the teacher able to guide students beyond the learning of foundational knowledge? Does student work show evidence of learning about application, integration, the human dimension, caring, and learning how to learn? If so, significant learning was occurring.

One of the most significant benefits of a learning-centered approach is that it uses the influence of the institution's evaluation procedures to direct faculty attention to where it should be: on thinking about ways they can increase the quantity and quality of student learning in their courses. Then, to the degree that the evaluation of faculty members' teaching indicates that certain aspects of their teaching need improvement, they will have a basis for selecting professional development activities that have a high likelihood of improving the quality of their teaching in a way that improves student learning.

Include Process and Context Issues. Although student learning should be the primary criterion in the evaluation of teaching, good evaluation procedures also require information about process and context issues. Since we are evaluating *teaching*, we need to know what the relationship is between the quality of student learning on one hand, and the teacher's activities and the context of the teaching, on the other.

Evaluating the *process* of teaching, that is, the teacher's activities, requires information about two key questions:

- Was the course well designed?
- Did the teacher interact well with students?

To answer the first question, evaluators will need to collect and examine course materials supplied by the teacher: the syllabus, sample class activities, exams, and so on. Criteria from the model of integrated course design can be used to assess the quality of these materials:

- Did the teacher do an in-depth analysis of the teaching situation?
- Were the learning goals focused on significant learning?
- Did the teacher use educative assessment activities when providing feedback and assessment to students?
- Did the teacher use teaching and learning activities that reflect the principles of active learning?
- Did the teacher use an effective teaching strategy? (And so forth.)

To answer the question about the nature of teacher-student interaction, evaluators may want to engage in classroom observations, but they can also collect information from the students, perhaps in the familiar form of student questionnaires. But the questions can now focus on questions arising from a solid conceptual framework of good teaching and good learning, for example, Did the teacher provide stimulating questions and ideas? Seem to care whether you learned or not? Make you feel included and comfortable in the class?

Finally, evaluators need to collect information about the *context* within which the faculty member's teaching took place. The context can have a major impact on the effectiveness of anyone's teaching. Factors such as the size of the class, the physical character of the classroom, the time and day of the class, and so on can make it harder or easier to accomplish one's purpose. Probably the simplest way to gauge the influence of these factors is simply to ask the teacher and the students whether they thought any specific contextual factors helped or hindered the course in particular ways.

Using a learning-centered approach to evaluating teaching and examining process and context issues would definitely improve the quality of the teaching evaluation procedures on most campuses. One major benefit of making this change is that it allows the institution's whole educational effort to become a more learning-centered process.

If the student questionnaires have questions about important kinds of learning on them, and the teaching evaluation process is driven by the central question of whether this teaching is promoting significant learning, then faculty and students will gradually begin to think about what they are doing individually and collectively in relation to the general goal of promoting more significant learning. When designing courses, faculty will be encouraged to ask themselves: Is this design going to promote the kind of significant learning that these students need and that this institution values? During the course, students and the teacher will be inclined to reflect: Are these activities the right kind of activities to promote significant learning? When the teacher makes a personal assessment of the course at the end of the term, the primary question will be: How well did this course succeed in promoting significant learning? Why or why not? When the evaluators look at the information provided by the teacher, their question becomes: Did this teacher and this course succeed in promoting significant learning?

An educational system where everyone is asking and searching for better answers to these questions would be an exciting place in which to teach and learn.

Establish Teaching and Learning Centers

The third specific recommendation for institutional action is to establish a campuswide program that can help faculty acquire new and better ideas about teaching and educational programs.

This recommendation directly supports the professional development of the faculty. If we want faculty to spend more time learning how to be more effective in their teaching and we want them to be able to spend that time efficiently and effectively, they need access to someone who can expedite that process. Having a campus office staffed by professionals who are familiar with the questions faculty have, are conversant with the literature on college teaching, and who know how to work with faculty individually and collectively can greatly increase the ability of faculty to learn what they need to learn quickly. Leaders in the professional organization that works most directly in this area, the Professional and Organizational Development (POD) Network in Higher Education, estimate that 30–40 percent of all institutions awarding undergraduate degrees have some kind of faculty development program at the present time. The additional good news is that this percentage seems to be steadily increasing.

Most institutions seem to be coming to the conclusion that it makes financial sense to invest in a faculty development program as a way of significantly increasing the capability of the single most costly and important resource in the institution—the faculty. The vast majority of new faculty members do not have any formal preparation for meeting their instructional responsibilities. Therefore a high level of in-service training is needed to create a faculty that is familiar with the theories, research, and practices of effective college teaching.

What are effective instructional development programs doing? Patricia Cross (2001) recently reviewed the proposals of 210 finalists for the prestigious Hesburgh Award, which is sponsored by TIAA/CREF to reward innovative and successful faculty development programs. Cross found that the activities of these effective programs could be categorized under three major headings:

Improving teaching by

- Applying knowledge about cognition and learning.
- Targeting particular groups of students.
- Targeting particular faculty.
- Developing a "personal vision" of teaching.

Redesigning courses to

- Adapt to new technologies.
- Developing new curricula or emphases.

Changing the learning environment of the institution by

- Creating "learning-centered" colleges.
- Developing a distinctive institutional mission focus.
- Focusing on student learning outcomes.
- Instituting incentives and rewards for teaching.

The three colleges discussed in this chapter have made extensive efforts to promote faculty development in institutionally relevant ways. Alverno has created a course schedule with a "class-free Friday." That leaves that day free for various faculty activities every week of the year. Much of that time is used for faculty development workshops, many of which are led by other faculty at Alverno. Pitzer offers intensive seminars to help faculty learn how to design their courses in ways that significantly incorporate multicultural learning into the student experience. They also have regular annual meetings and learning circles that allow faculty and students to learn more about how to make their service learning initiatives work as effectively as possible. And Syracuse University, as already mentioned, has created one of the largest teaching and learning centers in the United States.

Coordinate Student Development with Instructional Development

One final—and badly needed—change is focused on students rather than faculty. Faculty frequently report to me that students often become nervous and mildly anxious when they face a new and unfamiliar way of teaching. Students seem to get uneasy when someone appears to be changing the rules of the game. Many prefer a known challenge to an unknown challenge, even when the new way is intended to be more interesting and beneficial, and they can dig in their heels and resist efforts to get them to participate. When students react this way, it discourages faculty from trying new ways of teaching.

To have a situation in which both faculty and students are aware of and appreciate better ways of teaching and learning, the institution needs to find ways to educate students as well as faculty. Doing either one without the other only gets half of what we need. This is the reason institutions need to coordinate student development with faculty or instructional development.

How might this be done? At the present time, the responsibility for modifying student ideas and attitudes toward new and different ways of teaching lies solely with the teacher who wants to try something new. This practice is not effective because students are not likely to acquire positive attitudes about new ways of teaching if they only hear about such ideas from one of their many teachers. To make a widespread impact on student attitudes, institutions need to find or create mechanisms for educating a large proportion of their students on this topic.

This might be done through freshman year courses or ongoing courses focused on student learning throughout college. It could also be very helpful to enlist the support of the Office of Student Affairs that exists on most campuses. Such offices currently sponsor numerous activities aimed at student development, but these are not often coordinated with faculty development efforts.

It would be exciting if one or a combination of these programs could regularly and continually engage students in the question of how to be savvy agents of their own learning. In essence, students could be asked: "What can you do to help your teachers create significant learning experiences for you?" This would presumably lead to the question of what constitutes a "significant learning experience" in students' eyes and the related question of what kinds of teaching and learning activities are likely to foster such learning.

If students could develop more sophisticated ideas about significant kinds of learning and contemporary ideas on good teaching, it would be much easier for faculty to work with their classes to create powerful learning experiences. Also, at the end of the course, when students rate the teacher and the course, they would be able to appreciate and give high ratings to any teacher who made an effort to use such things as significant learning goals, active learning, and educative assessment (and presumably lower ratings to teachers who were not trying new and better ways of teaching).

◆ ◆ ◆

These four specific recommendations, especially when implemented in combination, will help faculty acquire a greater capability for creating more powerful courses and curricula in their institutions. A faculty evaluation system that incorporates professional development as a major area of expected faculty activity will give faculty the incentive and time to further their own learning about effective teaching and educational programs. Procedures for evaluating teaching that are learning-centered and include information about process and context will help focus the attention of everyone on the central question of how to promote more significant learning. Having a campuswide resource in the form of a faculty development or instructional development center will give faculty access to new and different ideas to use when they work on the task of creating better educational programs. And having students who know the value of good teaching and who are ready to cooperate with and give high ratings to teachers who make the effort to try and use better ideas on teaching would be extremely motivating to teachers.

Are These Actions Likely to Happen?

For colleges and universities to take the kinds of action I've described is a major undertaking. Making holistic, multidimensional changes in the way educational programs are created and supported, modifying traditional procedures related to faculty work and to the evaluation of teaching, establishing new centers for instructional development, and coordinating student development with faculty development will require time, energy, and commitment. Can we hope that such actions are at all likely to happen?

Historically colleges and universities have been conservative institutions; that is, they have been relatively slow to change the way they operate. However, a number of observers have noted that the whole context of higher education is changing, particularly in American higher education (Dolence and Norris, 1995; Duderstadt, 1999; Farrington, 1999). As noted in Chapter One of this book, Frank Newman has described four powerful sources of change currently operating on colleges and universities. If the observations and predications of Newman and others are accurate, institutions of higher education will face significant new pressures to become more open to change. And if this happens, faculty leaders and administrators will have an opportunity to initiate the kinds of organizational changes that can give faculty the support they need from their own institutions.

Helping Colleges and Universities Define Good Teaching

As campus leaders (meaning both administrators and faculty leaders) work to find ways to enhance teaching at their respective institutions, there is one specific arena in which certain national organizations could provide immense assistance.

As mentioned earlier, one primary problem that institutions face is the difficulty of formulating a definition of good teaching that will be acceptable across campus. If an institution tries to develop a common definition at the local level, the task will inevitably be given over to a committee. And, given the dominant tradition in American higher education of a content-centered perspective on teaching, the faculty on such committees would have great difficulty finding a definition that would apply across disciplines. Therefore a better approach is to develop a definition at the national level that can be picked up and used by individual institutions.

This is what has successfully happened in the last decade or so in public education. With the assistance of several national groups, the National Board for Professional Teaching Standards (NBPTS) developed a set of credible criteria for identifying teachers who are doing a truly excellent job in teaching, independent of level of teaching and subject matter. (For information on the history of this project, the standards themselves, and research on the impact of these standards, see the NBPTS Web site: http://www.nbpts.org.) Since these standards were published in 1989, local schools and even whole school districts have put money into programs that encourage as many teachers as possible to work to meet the new standards—and to be acknowledged and rewarded for doing so. And research indicates that the teaching done by NBPTS-certified teachers produces "deeper and more coherent student learning" than that done by teachers who applied for but were not awarded certification (AACTE, 2000).

National Prestige Based on Excellent Teaching

If a similar effort could be made in higher education, it would create the possibility of a powerful new measure for comparing institutions: the percentage of the faculty that has met national standards of excellence in teaching. How might this happen?

A number of the national organizations that interact with institutions of higher education are committed specifically to furthering excellence in educational programs. Prominent among these are the American Association of Higher Education (AAHE), the Association for the Study of Higher Education (ASHE), the Association of American Colleges and Universities (AAC&U), the American Council on Education (ACE), and the Professional and Organizational Development (POD) Network in Higher Education. These and similar organizations could collaborate in the development of a sophisticated but not overly complex definition of good teaching, with related criteria and procedures for identifying teachers who meet these criteria. With the credibility that such a product would have if backed by the prestige of several major organizations, leaders at individual institutions could adopt these as the basis for encouraging all faculty to work toward meeting such standards.

Some organization outside the institution, perhaps at the state or regional level, might need to evaluate the portfolios of faculty who apply to determine who has successfully met the standards. But if this can be done, then one measure of the quality of instruction at a given institution would be the percentage of its faculty to meet national standards for excellence in teaching.

Institutions and the public would be quick to recognize the significance of such a measure. This has already begun to happen as the result of another national project. The Pew Charitable Trust, with key personnel from AAHE, the National Center for Public Policy and Higher Education, and the Indiana University Center for Survey Research, collaborated to create the National Survey of Student Engagement (Kuh, 2001). The instrument has high credibility and is intended primarily for internal use by colleges and universities to improve the level of student engagement. But those institutions receiving high scores quickly recognized the value of publicizing those scores, and the public quickly recognized a good indicator of a high-quality institution when they saw it.

If a similar project could be mounted to measure the quality of teaching by college faculty, it would be a tremendous impetus to institutions of higher education to seriously support better teaching at those institutions.

Support from Other National Organizations

Several other national organizations could also play a significant role in the overall effort to promote better teaching. Four types of groups are especially well positioned to provide this support: accrediting agencies, funding agencies, disciplinary associations, and journals on college teaching. Some of them are already providing this sort of support, and the ideas in this book can further shape and improve the assistance they offer.

Accrediting Agencies

Accrediting agencies are potentially among the most powerful sources of change in higher education. Institutions must have accreditation, and society relies on accrediting agencies to ensure that accredited institutions are in fact providing quality educational programs. Hence these agencies face a very important but daunting task. How do you define *quality*—and how do you determine whether whole institutions and whole programs are providing it? Recent and current challenges faced by accrediting agencies indicate both the potential for influence and the complexity of using this influence to effect change.

One recent review of reform in higher education identified accrediting agents as the primary outside influence that encouraged colleges and universities to take the assessment movement seriously during the 1980s and 1990s (Lazerson, Wagener, and Shumanis, 2000). As a result of that influence, the vast majority of public and private institutions are now engaged in assessment activities. The downside is that these efforts have focused primarily on student progress through the system rather than on educational results. That is, data are usually collected on such things as the percentage of students progressing toward graduation, basic college readiness skills, and student satisfaction data, rather than on students' "higher order learning skills, affective development, or professional skills" (pp. 14–15).

The recent development of online learning and virtual universities is also going to exert strong pressure on accrediting agencies and higher education to resolve the quality issue. When students do not attend a physical campus and do not gain their education by accumulating a designated number of seat-time hours, what will accrediting agencies use as criteria to measure quality? This question came to a head when the North Central Accrediting Association awarded accreditation to Jones International University in 1999, the first accreditation ever for a "virtual university." ("'Virtual Institutions . . . ," 1999). This decision, the first of what will undoubtedly be a recurring challenge, has pushed both supporters and critics of virtual universities back to the basic question: What do students really need from a college education? How can you tell if they are getting that?

As accrediting agencies wrestle with this very fundamental issue of determining whether "quality" is present in a given institution, they would seem to have three options. First, they can focus primarily on input and process characteristics of the institution—number of Ph.D.'s on the faculty, books in the library, size of endowment, and so on. The problem with this option, of course, is that this kind of data completely ignores the question of whether these resources are being used effectively. The second option is to take the institution's own statement of educational goals at face value and simply determine whether the institution is meeting its own goals. This makes it easy for the accrediting agency but provides no assurance that the institution has selected significant learning goals. The third option is for the accrediting agency itself to set out some general principles about quality learning and ask whether students are achieving these and whether the institution has programs sufficient to support significant learning goals. This last option has some attractive features, but is it desirable? Is it a feasible option?

The Wingspread Conference mentioned in Chapter One, with representatives from the accreditation community, state and federal policymakers, and leaders from the corporate, philanthropic, and higher education communities, answered the desirability issue with a resounding yes (ECS, 1994). Noting that the public has strong need for a valid standard-setting process in higher education and that this process is in a "period of both crisis and real opportunity," the conference report stated, "For purposes of quality assurance, the paramount issue for every college or university is the performance of its graduates" (p. 3). The report goes on to list some examples of the kind of performance in question: technical competence in a given field, the ability to gain and apply new knowledge, attitudes of flexibility and adaptability, the ability to address specific problems in complex, real-world settings, and several others. In other words, this group concluded that accrediting agencies do need to set out a general statement of desirable kinds of learning and then use these as criteria for determining whether a given institution is providing a quality educational program.

The next question is whether such an agenda, even if desirable, is possible or feasible for an accrediting agency. As it turns out, a number of accrediting associations have already begun doing exactly this. ABET, the accrediting association for engineering programs, has issued a set of guidelines known as ABET 2000. These guidelines identify twelve specific kinds of learning that, in the organization's view, constitute high-quality learning and are applicable across the full range of engineering majors—electrical, civil, mechanical, and so on. From the year 2000 on, engineering programs being reviewed for accreditation must be able to show evidence that their students are achieving these kinds of learning and that the department or college has the kinds of courses and curricula to support these kinds of learning.

In December 2001, the Southern Association of Colleges and Schools adopted new Principles of Accreditation and reported them on its Web site (http://www.sacscoc.org/accrrevproj.asp, accessed in February 2002). These principles take some significant strides in the direction of calling for evidence of student learning and the professional development of faculty as teachers:

- The institution identifies expected outcomes for its educational programs and . . . assesses whether it achieves these outcomes [Outcome #16, on "Institutional Effectiveness"].
- Each educational program . . . establishes and evaluates program and learning outcomes [#1, under "Standards for All Educational Programs"].
- The institution identifies competencies within the general education core and provides evidence that graduates have attained those college-level competencies [#15, under "Standards Specific to Undergraduate Programs"].
- When determining acceptable qualifications of its faculty, an institution [considers] continuous documented excellence in teaching and other . . . competencies . . . that contribute to effective teaching and student learning outcomes [#20, under "Faculty"].
- The institution provides evidence of ongoing professional development of faculty as teachers, scholars, and practitioners [#22, under "Faculty"].

(Note: As this book was going to press, the North Central Association was publicly reviewing similar new criteria for the accreditation of colleges and universities in that region. See http://www.ncahigherlearningcommission.org/restructuring/.)

If and when other accrediting associations decide to take a learning-centered and improvement-oriented view of quality assurance, they will need a conceptual framework that is broad, flexible, and makes enough intuitive sense to be acceptable to a wide range of constituents. The taxonomy of significant learning has these characteristics. Had it been around at the time, the taxonomy could have been used to generate the ABET 2000 list of competencies. It is broad enough to include some competencies that were not included but could have been, and it is flexible enough to be translated into terms meaningful to engineers. And the general categories, such as acquiring foundational knowledge and learning how to learn, make sense to most people as constituting high-quality learning.

If accrediting agencies start requiring evidence of significant learning by students, this would generate a major influence for institutions to take a serious look at their educational goals, organizational structure, educational programs, and policies and procedures, and to start collecting information on what their students really were learning. That is, this requirement could prompt what I described earlier as a multidimensional response by institutions toward doing all the things necessary to provide a truly significant educational experience for their students.

Funding Agencies

Another powerful force for change is the collective influence of federal, corporate, and private funding agencies. These organizations provide funding for education-related projects, but they also stipulate the criteria for receiving those funds. If these agencies state in their criteria that all proposals need to show how the proposed activity would promote one or more kinds of significant learning, it would be a powerful stimulus for faculty to learn about different kinds of significant learning and think carefully about the learning outcomes of their projects.

One recent example of the influence of funding agencies was the requirement made a few years ago by the National Science Foundation (NSF) that all proposals for education-related projects include a strong plan for assessing the results. Later the NSF also set up a Web site with examples of good assessment plans to help educate faculty as to what constitutes good assessment. I have witnessed the effects of this requirement on the faculty on my own campus. Faculty members wanting to apply for NSF funding quickly began asking for help from my office, for example, about the meaning of *formative* and *summative* evaluation, and for support in setting up evaluation plans for their projects. Once they had learned about these concepts, they also began using them in their other educational work, whether it involved external funding or not.

If funding agencies decide to use their influence to promote better instructional design, they could construct their guidelines in a way that incorporated the key concepts involved in both integrated course design and significant learning. They could indicate that proposals need to indicate what kind of significant learning is going to be enhanced and share the taxonomy of significant learning as one framework for identifying different kinds of significant learning. They could state that the proposed activity needs to incorporate the principles of effective instructional design, that is, a thorough analysis of the instructional situation, clear and significant learning goals, active learning, and educative assessment.

Including such requirements would be a powerful stimulus for faculty to learn about the principles of good instructional design and to learn how to incorporate these into their funded—and unfunded—educational activities.

Disciplinary Associations

Disciplinary associations are a third type of organization that play a very important role in higher education. Faculty members work hard for recognition based on the social and professional norms of these organizations and avail themselves of the resources and services that they provide. As a result, these associations exert enormous influence on the attitudes and professional practice of faculty members everywhere.

Although most of these associations give some kind of attention to educational concerns, they vary enormously in the extent of that attention, in the kinds of services provided, and in the degree to which that attention is focused on teaching in higher education as opposed to public school teaching. Despite this variation, others have long recognized that these organizations have an important and widespread influence on faculty and have therefore tried to "influence that influence." During the 1990s two initiatives were launched with exactly that goal in mind.

In the United Kingdom, the Higher Education Funding Councils and the Department for Education and Employment have begun to fund special programs through the disciplines (Jenkins, 1996; Healey, 1998). One of the products of these initiatives has been the creation of "discipline networks" in several disciplines. These networks hold conferences, support the development of working papers, and publish in journals focused on the teaching of a particular discipline, for example, the *Journal of Geography in Higher Education.*

In the United States the Carnegie Foundation for the Advancement of Teaching is directing a similar but separate initiative. In 1998 the Carnegie Foundation established the CASTL Project (Carnegie Academy for the Scholarship of Teaching and Learning). One important component of this project is working collaboratively with the professional and scholarly societies to advance the scholarship of teaching within these organizations (Carnegie Web site: http://www.carnegiefoundation.org/CASTL/index.htm; accessed October 14, 2000).

What might these disciplinary associations do if they wanted to make a substantial and coordinated effort to enhance the quality of teaching and student learning within their respective disciplines and professions? Based on the different activities of these groups at the present time, a comprehensive effort would involve the following:

- Sponsor and organize research on effective teaching. (Example: the American Association of Physics Teachers.)
- Provide forums (conferences, journals, newsletters) for the public sharing and analysis of theoretical perspectives, research findings, and innovative practices. (Example: Most disciplinary associations do this now, although to different degrees.)
- Offer workshops for college teachers (local, regional, national, and international) to introduce new perspectives and develop important skills. (Example: American Society for Engineering Education.)
- Provide materials (books, papers, videos, CDs) that summarize and synthesize ideas on good practice. (Example: American Economics Association.)
- Address policy issues that exist and arise within local institutions that affect the work of teachers. (Example: How should one evaluate teaching? What should the role of teaching be in faculty evaluation? What role should professional development have in faculty work and evaluation?)

As disciplinary associations attempt such efforts, what ought the relationship be between their work and the substantial set of ideas and literature on college teaching in general that has emerged in the last few decades? My view is that the leaders within the disciplines ought to at least familiarize themselves with this literature and decide how it relates to teaching and learning within their own field. To ignore this body of ideas and literature is to risk limiting themselves to simply refining, restating, and reifying the traditional forms of teaching that exist and form a powerful voice within every discipline.

An example of the latter approach is the "AHA Statement on Excellent Classroom Teaching of History" issued in 1998 by the Teaching Division of the American Historical Association. While the four issues addressed in that statement are important (course content, historical thinking, classroom environment, and the evaluation of student performance), this statement on "Excellent Classroom Teaching" made no mention of the need for or value of such things as active learning, reflective writing, small group work, classroom assessment techniques, authentic assessment, learning portfolios, the need to evaluate one's own teaching, or any of the many other ideas that are now known to be important factors in high-quality student learning.

A better and more inclusive approach is exemplified by a leader within engineering education, Richard Felder. A retired but still active professor of chemical engineering at North Carolina State University, Felder has been doing workshops, alone and with others for over a decade, aimed at helping engineering faculty learn to be better teachers. His workshops have helped participants learn about small group work, active learning, authentic assessment, different student learning styles, and so on. He and his wife, a faculty development specialist, have been offering an average of over fifty workshops a year for the last several years, with a total attendance in excess of six hundred faculty a year. (Personal correspondence, October 2, 2000; for additional information see his Web site: http://www2.ncsu.edu/unity/lockers/users/f/felder/public/RMF.html; accessed September 2002.) This example illustrates how the right kind of leadership within a discipline can take ideas from the general field of college teaching and translate these ideas into terms and cases that are very meaningful for faculty within the context of a particular discipline.

How can the ideas in this book help in this effort? My hope is that the faculty members and others who provide the leadership for dealing with educational issues within specific disciplines will acquaint themselves with ideas about good teaching that exist outside their profession and not simply embalm themselves in the long-standing practices of the past. If they do make this effort to broaden their understanding, the ideas in this book can be very helpful. Teachers in all disciplines have to decide what they want their students to learn. The taxonomy of significant learning can provide teachers in all disciplines with a language for defining course goals that will enable these teachers to raise their sights on intended student learning. The model of integrated course design can provide a conceptual framework for undertaking this task in a powerful way, one that will allow them to take their courses to the next level of significance.

If the leaders like Rich Felder, who can be found within all the disciplines, can learn about these ideas and then translate and share with their fellow teachers whatever they find worthwhile, they can make a significant contribution to the overall effort of enhancing the quality of teaching and learning within higher education.

Journals on College Teaching

Another major resource for faculty on learning about teaching are the many journals on college teaching that have been established in the last century. Well over two hundred such journals exist in the United States alone, and other countries have similar journals as well. (For a list of these journals, see Cashin and Clegg, 1994; Deliberations Web site, maintained in England but including North American journals: http://www.lgu.ac.uk/deliberations/journals/index.html; access date October 14, 2002.) These journals are a primary outlet for the rapidly emerging interest in the "scholarship of teaching" as encouraged by the late Ernest Boyer (1990).

As noted in a perceptive analysis by Weimer (1993) of articles in several disciplinary journals on pedagogy, the vast majority of these essays are focused on *techniques*, that is, on ways of structuring a particular assignment or learning activity. Such essays are good in that they celebrate and honor the wisdom gained from reflective practice. However, Weimer thought the essays were also limited in several ways (pp. 45–46): the authors often did not reveal an awareness that these techniques had been written about elsewhere; they made no mention of the fact that the techniques could be used in other disciplines as well; and they provided little rationale or context for the particular technique, which limited the potential for transferability to other teachers. Similarly, when studying descriptions of courses for this book, I discovered that many essays were so focused on the particular teaching activity involved, what Weimer called "technique," that the essays often included only limited information about the teaching situation and only tangentially identified the specific learning goals for the course involved. In addition, they almost never included any significant information about the feedback and evaluation components of the course.

How might the articles in these journals be improved in a way that would make them more useful to other teachers? The basic recommendation is for the authors of such articles to look at their teaching more broadly and think about what they are doing as part of an instructional strategy and course design. As noted in Chapter Four, a teaching strategy is different from a teaching technique in that it is an interdependent sequence of learning activities that spans the entire course or learning program.

Thinking and writing about one's course design and teaching strategy would still allow authors to write about particular techniques. But it would place these techniques in a context that would allow readers to see the relationships between a given technique and the other components of the course as outlined in the model of integrated course design. Such an approach would also allow these scholars of teaching to address all the key components of a course: how to respond to teaching *situations* that are especially challenging; how to use or develop strategies that are successful in promoting important kinds of *learning goals;* how to identify the values and beliefs associated with a particular *instructional strategy;* and how to develop and use innovative ways of providing *feedback and assessment.* The particular ideas about significant learning, active learning, and educative assessment introduced in this book could be especially useful in these essays.

However, for potential authors to write essays that include this kind of context and rationale, the editors of these journals (who are often faculty members) will need to create new and broader guidelines for use by both writers and reviewers. These guidelines do not need to be complicated. They simply need to suggest that articles about specific courses should include information about important situational factors, the types of learning being promoted, the particular teaching and learning activities involved and how they were assembled into an effective strategy, and the feedback and assessment procedures used. It would also be especially helpful to know what *criteria* were used to evaluate the quality of student learning.

If editors, writers, and reviewers could work together in this way to raise the scope and level of discourse in journals on college teaching, readers would have a fuller understanding of the ideas and innovations being described and thereby be better equipped to actually use these ideas in their own teaching situations.

Bringing It All Together for Better Faculty Support

At the beginning of this chapter, I identified six faculty needs related to their ability to promote more significant learning: awareness, encouragement, time, intellectual and emotional support, cooperative students, and recognition and reward. Meeting all six of these needs will require the coordinated efforts of all the groups mentioned in this chapter and perhaps others; no one group is capable of changing all six conditions by itself. How do the actions suggested here for institutions of higher education and the other organizations involved in higher education all come together to meet these multiple needs?

Awareness

Creating awareness among faculty of the need to change is perhaps the most difficult, in part because it is the first step. Once faculty members are aware of the need to change, subsequent efforts to help them make needed changes become easier and more effective. But to start this process, faculty need to get the message—multiple times and from multiple sources—that it is important for them to be knowledgeable about teaching and learning and that they will be expected to be competent in putting together courses and curricula that meet high standards, perhaps higher than in years past.

First and foremost, this message needs to come from their home institution. Colleges and universities need to let their faculties know that the institution takes high-quality teaching and learning seriously. But this needs to be supported by more than public occasion rhetoric. The institution needs to examine (and change as necessary) its vision of its educational goals, educational programs, organizational structure, polices and procedures, and institutional assessment—all for the purpose of becoming more effective as an educational institution. Successful example? Alverno College.

Funding and accrediting agencies can also provide encouragement by informing applicants that the faculty in charge of educational programs and initiatives need to demonstrate a high level of competence in terms of current ideas on effective teaching and significant learning. Successful examples? The educational division of the National Science Foundation, the ABET 2000 criteria in engineering, and the recently approved Principles of Accreditation for the Southern Association of Colleges and Schools.

Disciplinary associations can support this effort by encouraging members to be both leaders of and consumers of conference sessions on teaching and learning within the discipline and to contribute articles and books to the scholarship of teaching within particular subject matter domains. Successful examples? The Carnegie Foundation's CASTL Project in the United States and the Learning and Teaching Support Network effort in Great Britain working with the disciplinary associations for this very purpose.

Encouragement

Faculty also need to believe that others value their efforts to learn about teaching and to become effective teachers. This means that the institution and individual academic units need to create a community and a culture among faculty that value good teaching and good learning. Such a culture would let individual faculty members know that it is acceptable and admirable to identify with the role of being an effective teacher and to be open and honest about the problems they are having, the ideas they are trying, and the help they need. The culture would include informal celebration of the successes that individuals have as teachers.

Institutions and individual academic units can encourage such a culture by organizing events that encourage faculty there to look at the question of what can be learned about being a better teacher and about offering better educational programs. Periodic departmental colloquia or collegewide conferences focused on teaching allow faculty to engage in dialogue about this aspect of their faculty role. Knowing that colleagues view high-quality teaching as a challenge worthy of sustained thought and action can be very motivating for everyone.

Time

The responsibility for helping faculty members find the time necessary both to learn about better teaching and to perform effectively lies primarily with the institution. The college or university as a whole and each individual academic unit need to find ways to add professional development to the traditional list of faculty expectations for doing teaching, research, and service. Then faculty members need to engage in a realistic discussion with their department chair or executive committee about how best to allocate their time among these four major areas of faculty responsibility. Successful examples? Departments on my own campus that have tried new procedures for integrating professional development with the evaluation of faculty work.

Support

Groups inside and outside institutions can provide the support that faculty will need when they are ready to learn more about teaching. A growing number of colleges and universities have teaching and learning centers or faculty development programs that offer individual consulting services, workshops, classroom observations, organized group discussions, reading material, and the like. These provide general ideas about better teaching as well as information about a particular faculty member's strengths and areas for possible improvement. Disciplinary associations can offer some of these same services with the advantage of being able to supply the language and examples needed to apply new ideas to the teaching of particular subjects. Journals on college teaching can provide a steady stream of new and emerging ideas about both general ideas and applications of these ideas in specific contexts.

Cooperative Students

The ultimate purpose of good teaching is to support good learning. But the learning itself is accomplished by students, not by teachers. Therefore effective teaching requires students who are knowledgeable about and capable of fulfilling their part of this whole effort. Many institutions, with support from national organizations and initiatives, have organized freshman year programs and even senior year programs for the purpose of developing students to the point where they can reflect on and take the action needed to support high-quality learning experiences. The general goal of having students who can work effectively with teachers and other students would be even further enhanced if institutions could increase the opportunities for students to learn about and reflect on what constitutes good teaching and learning. This suggests the desirability of having formal structures for students to engage in this kind of learning, not just at the beginning and end but throughout their college experience. Successful example? The learning portfolio requirement and associated support services for students at Alverno College.

Recognition and Reward

For faculty members to sustain an effort to improve teaching over time, they need to be recognized and rewarded for that effort. The primary responsibility for this task lies with colleges and universities, but disciplinary associations can add significant secondary support as well. However, for this effort to have a major impact, it needs to go beyond the presentation of a few teaching awards based on haphazard criteria like the ones that characterize many of these awards at the present time.

To improve the recognition and reward of teaching, institutions need to do two things. They need to clarify the criteria they use to define excellence in teaching, and they need to expand the opportunities for faculty members to achieve recognition and reward for excellent teaching.

Institutions need learning-centered criteria for identifying excellent teaching. This means that the ultimate question is: Has this teacher (or teaching) resulted in significant student learning? If so, the teaching is good; if not, it needs to be improved. To answer this question, the institution and the faculty will need to agree on what constitutes significant student learning. The taxonomy of significant learning is one appropriate way of answering this question. Faculty members then need to find ways to document the degree to which their students have achieved significant learning, whether that learning is defined in terms of this taxonomy or some other framework. In addition to this learning-centered criterion, the criteria should include two process factors: course design and teacher-student interaction. This would then call for faculty and members of the awards committee to understand what constitutes good course design and good teacher-student interaction and then know what kind of information would allow them to determine when each is present. Using these three criteria to define excellence in teaching would greatly clarify what the faculty needs to do to achieve recognition and what they had done when granted such recognition.

The second task, though, is to expand access to such recognition and reward. High-profile award ceremonies for good teaching can support the claim that the institution and at least some leaders within the institution value excellent teaching. The problem with this kind of recognition is that it is by definition limited to very few individuals. Institutions need to recognize and reward *all* faculty members who strive for and achieve excellence in teaching. This would require new procedures for identifying and rewarding everyone who achieves a high and well-defined level of excellence. To do this, institutions need to develop well-defined criteria and standards of good teaching that can be applied across disciplines and teaching situations. Administrators and faculty leaders can then encourage all faculty to work toward achieving these standards. And any faculty member who succeeds in meeting these standards should be recognized and rewarded promptly, with an appropriate title and, if possible, a financial award. This could lead to an attractive intrainstitutional dynamic in which departments engage in a friendly competition with each other for the highest percentage of faculty designated as effective teachers, just as many do now in terms of the amount of grant money they bring in or the number of faculty who have extensive publication records.

Some disciplinary associations also have teaching awards. They too could look at the possibility of making the criteria for these awards more learning-centered and look for evidence of good course design and teacher-student interactions. This could contribute to creating a disciplinary culture—a source of powerful influence on many faculty members—that truly understands what constitutes exemplary teaching and values it appropriately.

◆ ◆ ◆

Can all of this happen? In many ways, it seems like an impossible dream. But the good news is that almost all of the needed actions are already happening in various institutions and organizations. What is needed now is the leadership and vision to connect these separate events and make them part of a coordinated effort by many different groups to improve the quality of teaching and learning everywhere.

The first steps have already been taken. We can now see what the needs are and what the potential sources of support are. It is like working on a large jigsaw puzzle. We have a picture of our ultimate goal: we have all the pieces, face up and sorted by characteristics. What faculty and organizational leaders need to do now is spend the time and make the effort necessary to put them all together in the right way. The more actions that leaders in all the organizations involved in higher education can take to better support faculty, the more faculty will respond. In turn, faculty may even be ready to reciprocate by providing leadership within these various organizations to support the overall process.

An impossible dream? Maybe. But "impossible" dreams have come true before. . . .

CHAPTER SEVEN

THE HUMAN SIGNIFICANCE OF GOOD TEACHING AND LEARNING

Good teaching can be used to foster better learning. Those of us who work in higher education need to know why better teaching and learning are important because our answer will determine how we respond to the demands and calling of our profession. In my view, we need a perspective that relates teaching and learning to the quality of human life.

Parker Palmer, in *The Courage to Teach* (1998), uses a wonderful metaphor to describe what he tries to do in his teaching: "I [have] learned that my gift as a teacher is the ability to dance with my students, to co-create with them a context in which all of us teach and learn" (p. 72).

Teaching, Learning, and the Dance of Life

I would like to borrow this metaphor and extend it in a way that reveals the fundamental role that learning plays in life.

All human beings are in a dance called Life. We have all learned some of the steps involved in this dance, but there are always new and additional steps that need to be learned.

Some of the steps that have to be learned are the same for everyone and are cyclical in the sense that they are the same for each new generation. Members of each generation have to learn some of the same new things, new steps, as we grow and develop through the various stages of life. As youngsters we have to learn how to walk, how to talk, and how to respond to the different statements of our parents. As adolescents, we have to learn how to build relationships with people in our family and outside our family, how to accept responsibility, and how to set goals in life and work toward them. As young adults, we have to learn how to handle love relationships, make a living, and be a good spouse and perhaps a good parent. As mature adults, we have to learn more about what gives our life meaning, how to provide leadership in community groups of which we are a part, and how to let go of our children as they develop their own lives. As senior adults, we have to learn how to handle our growing physical limits, how to use increased leisure time in meaningful ways, and eventually how to handle the prospect of our own approaching mortality. The need to learn never stops. We have all faced or will face each of these learning challenges, as did our parents and grandparents and as will our children and grandchildren. How well people face and learn about these recurring life issues affects both the quality of their life and their interactions with others.

There are other steps in the Dance of Life, though, that are more linear in character and hence do change with time. As society and the world change, the members of each generation face situations that are new and different from those faced by preceding generations. People today, for example, face many learning needs that their parents and their grandparents did not face, at least not in terms of the specific content. Some examples will illustrate this point.

- *Technology:* People today have to learn how to use multiple kinds of technology in almost every aspect of their lives: automobiles, household appliances, TVs, VCRs, camcorders, computers, and so on and on.
- *Health care:* We have new opportunities and a need to learn about specific aspects of our physical condition (for example, calories, cholesterol, and cardiac arrest). But we also have to learn about and make choices among whole different approaches to medical treatment: traditional medicine, acupuncture, preventative health, physical therapy, chiropractors, and so on.
- *Adolescent life:* Parents, teachers, and children today face and have to learn about the enormous role and influence of drugs, violence, and sexuality in adolescent life that is completely different from what it was even a generation ago.
- *Quality of the environment:* Individuals and public bodies have to learn about the environmental impact of our activities and the impact of specific products we discard.
- *Organizational effectiveness:* As corporate, social, and political organizations have become larger and more complex, we have all found a need to learn more about organizational effectiveness and leadership than before.

- *Retirement:* People retiring are faced with more complex decisions about both investment strategies and public assistance programs for the elderly such as Medicaid and Medicare.

The learning challenges we face today as a result of such changes are quite different from the challenges faced by our ancestors and similarly will be quite different from those that will be faced by our children and grandchildren. This means that, for some kinds of learning, we cannot simply look at what our ancestors knew and learn that; we have to engage in completely new kinds of learning.

So everywhere one looks, people are either learning or needing to learn. In fact, one author has used *Learning as a Way of Being* as the title of a book on modern society (Vaill, 1996). What seems clear is that everyone, everywhere, needs to be learning all the time throughout their whole life—if they wish to live a full, meaningful, and effective life. When one stops learning, one stops living.

The Meaning and Significance of Good Learning

Given this universal and perpetual need to learn, how do people respond? They respond in a variety of ways, but in this variety we can see both similarities and differences. The similarity lies in the fact that almost everyone is learning all the time, both informally and formally. The difference lies in that some people learn what they need to learn while others don't. And an important aspect of successful learners seems to be that they develop a strong sense of themselves as learners.

How People Learn

What are the general ways in which we learn?

Individual, Informal Learning. Some of what we learn happens informally and even serendipitously, as we respond and react to everyday life experiences. Much of what we learn about ourselves and others results from our own interpretation, and sometimes misinterpretation, of specific events in life. Our sense of how people behave, who likes us and who does not, whether we see ourselves as smart and competent or dumb and inept—these are examples of the kinds of things we learn informally from our everyday experiences.

Individual, Intentional Learning. Another type of learning is more intentional but still individually controlled. Allen Tough (1979) has documented the widespread occurrence of what he called adult learning projects. He found that a large majority of adults routinely identify particular things they want to learn and then set about finding specific ways to learn about them.

An example of this kind of learning occurred to me some years ago when I was coaching my son's soccer teams. Like many parents of my generation, I was coaching a sport I had never played. Initially my skills at simply organizing practices and encouraging young kids were sufficient. But as the years went on, my son's teams (under my coaching) did not do as well as many other teams. Therefore I decided I needed to either get better or get out of coaching. So I looked around to see what learning resources were available. Eventually I found books, videotapes, and a community-based coaching clinic for coaches of youth soccer. I availed myself of these learning opportunities, and they made a big difference in my coaching ability. In Tough's terms, I had engaged in an adult learning project. I had formulated an individual learning goal and found resources to help me achieve that goal.

Formal Learning Programs. A third general form of learning occurs as the result of formal, structured learning opportunities organized by others. Individuals, groups within institutions, and whole institutions provide a variety of structured learning programs: courses, degree programs, workshops, seminars, training programs, and so on.

This latter, more formal kind of schooling experience plays an increasingly significant role in society and in individual lives. Almost every profession currently encourages continued learning by practitioners in the form of either mandated or voluntary professional development. Individuals choose to attend seminars and workshops that help them deal with specific issues in their personal lives: parenting, health care, psychological or family problems, money management, retirement, or whatever. Organizations are investing more and more resources in employee training programs, some directly and others only indirectly related to the job at hand, because they recognize the payoff of a better-educated workforce. To the degree that formal education programs are becoming increasingly important for the welfare of individual lives and society at large, it becomes critically important to learn how to make these programs as effective as possible.

One's Sense of Self as a Learner

While the three kinds of learning opportunities described in the preceding section are available to all of us, people respond to these opportunities in profoundly different ways. And one of the big differences lies in the strength of their sense of themselves as learners.

For some people, learning seems to happen to them. They have experiences and react to them. But overall they have a relatively weak and passive self-image when it comes to learning. They do not have a clear sense of what they need to learn or even of what they *want* to learn. They let others, in the form of parents, teachers, or friends, dictate what they learn and how they learn. Their learning is like sprinkling water here and there in the desert. Water goes into the ground, but nothing of significance comes of it. They are learning, but what they learn does not change, enhance, or transform their life in any significant way.

Other people have a more proactive sense of themselves as learners. As they go about their day-to-day living, they take responsibility for seeking out and learning what they need to learn. They have a sense of who they are and what they want to do in life. Based on this, they have a sense of *what* they need and want to learn, and they have—or know how to develop—appropriate strategies for learning. These people are called self-directed learners by some (Knowles, 1975) and intentional learners by others (Martinez, 1998).

Learning for this group of people is like watering a garden. They have decided what they want from their garden. They have prepared the soil, planted the seed, and then carefully watered the garden throughout the growing season. As the result of this kind of watering, they can, at the right time, harvest the plants and enjoy a tasty meal that nourishes both body and spirit.

Individuals can better respond to their inherent need to learn if they have a strong sense of themselves as learners. And society will be better off if people can develop a stronger sense of themselves as learners and thereby learn what they need to learn.

The Meaning and Significance of Good Teaching

Thus far I have been trying to make two closely related points. The first is that high-quality learning is absolutely essential for high-quality living; the second is that formal educational programs are becoming more and more important in society because people face a steadily increasing range of life issues that require new perspectives, knowledge, and skills. To the degree that this is true, it becomes imperative to find ways to make these educational programs as effective as possible. This is why state and local governments are working so hard to improve public schools and why there has been such a strong force behind the accountability movement in higher education. The public and civic leaders of society know that we need better learning, and that means we need better teaching.

It is clear, however, that "better teaching" has a dual meaning. On one hand, teachers need to be able to help people learn something that is truly significant, something I would call significant learning, in relation to the subject matter being studied. But in addition to that, teachers need to help students develop a strong and proactive sense of themselves as learners. The latter is absolutely necessary if we are to have any hope of creating learning organizations and, more broadly, a learning society. We need to have a critical mass of people who know the value of, and know how to self-consciously engage in, deliberate and intentional learning. Unless we learn how to promote this kind of learning, we will continue to have people who graduate from our schools knowing how to pass our courses but who continue on in life as second-rate learners.

A New Metaphor for Teaching

Metaphors are powerful ways of describing and making sense out of life, and over the years teachers have created a number of metaphors for what they do. Recently a popular metaphor has emerged to distinguish the new approaches to teaching from a more traditional approach: "Be a 'guide on the side' rather than a 'sage on the stage.'" This is a good metaphor in that it draws attention to the severe limits on significant learning when our teaching primarily focuses on lecturing. It also values the encouragement of students to become responsible for their own learning. However, the image of a "guide on the side" is also more passive than most good teachers seem to be. As a result, I have found myself looking for a new metaphor that captures this and other important characteristics as well. For example, teachers are often proactive and reactive at the same time. They are also in interdependent situations where each person involved is required to be competent in their individual role, yet the whole endeavor requires serious teamwork and coordinated effort.

Hence I would like to offer a new metaphor for teaching: the teacher as *helmsman* for the learning experience. (The concept comes from my experiences with whitewater rafting. I toyed with using *helmsperson* instead, in keeping with the gender sensitivity of our times, but that seemed more cumbersome and less effective than the original—and no one of either sex would use it afloat. Therefore I hope readers can accept this version as simply a generic and not a gender-specific term.) Negotiating white water, several people work together in a raft to maneuver it down a challenging river and stay away from rocks so they can reach a destination somewhere downstream. Most of the people work as "oarsmen" who paddle on one side of the raft or the other. Another person, usually the most experienced, serves as "helmsman." The job of the helmsman is to steer and to coordinate the efforts of the oarsmen.

The metaphor of the teacher-helmsman captures many of the important characteristics of the whole teaching situation as well as the interactions among the various actors. The whole group must see that they have an important and challenging job to do (significant learning); the helmsman (teacher) is a leader and plays an important role in coordinating the actions of everyone else. But the oarsmen (students) also have to understand both their individual role (to study and learn) and how to work together with others. That is, everyone has to support one another in the learning process. It is a coordinated team effort with the teacher playing an active leadership role.

Depending on the decision of the group and the leader, they can decide to take the raft on slow, level streams (easy learning), or they can take on rapid, steeper rivers (more challenging learning). The latter is more difficult but, when done successfully, is also more exciting and more rewarding.

To accomplish the latter kind of challenge successfully, everyone needs to discover one another's spirit in the process of learning and to discover the subject and what is to be learned about it. The helmsman in particular must discover what each individual is capable of and what the group is capable of collectively. The rowers (students) must discover what they themselves are capable of, what the others are capable of, what the leader is capable of—and how they can increase all those capabilities by working together as members of a spirit-discovering team with faith in one another.

The role of a metaphor is to symbolize important aspects of a task or situation. The metaphor of the teacher as helmsman offers a multifaceted vision of what teaching might be—when done at its best.

The Role of the Ideas in This Book

If we want learning that enhances one's ability to dance the Dance of Life and if we want learners who have a strong sense of themselves as learners, how can the ideas presented in this book be of help? I will comment on each of the three main topics: significant learning, integrated course design, and better organizational support.

Significant Learning

The taxonomy of significant learning offers a special language for describing what students might learn in our courses in a way that is capable of elevating our purposes in teaching. When teachers dream about what they *really* want their students to learn and when students reflect on what they learned from their really great teachers, both groups include understanding the subject but go beyond this and even beyond learning how to apply it. What is the range of different kinds of significant learning they refer to?

The taxonomy of significant learning identifies six kinds of significant learning that teachers can use to set more exciting educational goals for their instruction.

- *Foundational knowledge:* Understanding and remembering the key concepts, principles, relationships, and facts that constitute what is usually referred to as the content of the course.
- *Application:* Being able to engage in thinking about the subject, (for example, critical thinking, creative thinking, problem solving, and decision making), developing other key skills, and learning how to manage complex projects.
- *Integration:* Identifying the similarities and interactions between realms of knowledge, specific ideas, and people.
- *Human dimension:* Interacting with oneself and with others in new and better ways; discovering the personal and social implications of new knowledge.
- *Caring:* Changing one's interests, feelings, or values related to a subject.
- *Learning how to learn:* Acquiring better studenting skills, learning how to inquire and construct knowledge on a specific subject, and learning how to become a self-directing learner.

Being able to formulate learning goals such as these creates the possibility of students' having a significant learning experience. But having new, more ambitious goals will only lead to frustrated expectations unless we can link these goals to more powerful learning experiences in the course. And this is why teachers need to learn how to create more significant learning experiences.

Integrated Course Design

The model of integrated course design is a tool that enables teachers to support and promote significant learning. It has this capability because it incorporates and organizes several existing and potent ideas about teaching, for example, active learning and educative assessment, and then shows how to increase the impact of these (and other) ideas by connecting and integrating them.

In this model, the teacher creates the design for a course by carefully working through three phases of the design process:

Initial Phase: Build Strong Primary Components for the Course

1. Carefully analyze the situational factors.
2. Identify and set significant learning goals.
3. Create significant forms of feedback and assessment.
4. Create effective teaching and learning activities.
5. Integrate the four preceding components.

Intermediate Phase: Assemble These Components into an Overall Scheme of Learning Activities

6. Identify the thematic structure for the course.
7. Create or select a powerful instructional strategy.
8. Integrate the structure and the teaching strategy into an overall scheme of learning activities.

Final Phase: Finish Up the Remaining Tasks

9. Develop a fair grading system.
10. Debug possible problems.
11. Write the course syllabus.
12. Plan an evaluation of the course and of your teaching.

If teachers can learn how to design a course by carefully working through each of the steps involved in the three phases, they will have a very effective course design. The design will still need to be implemented, but the design will create the possibility of a truly significant learning experience for the students—and for the teacher as well.

Organizational Support

For faculty to spend the time and effort needed to learn new ways of teaching such as have been described here, they will need significantly more support from multiple organizations than they are receiving at the present time.

First, their own colleges and universities need to take certain steps to provide this support:

- Make sure the institution is organized and operates in a way that is internally in alignment.
- Support faculty efforts to learn about new ideas on teaching and learning by making professional development an integral part of faculty work and establishing centers that can help faculty learn new ideas about teaching and learning. (For a list of ideas that faculty can learn about, see Appendix B.)
- Have institutional leaders, especially department chairs, who can work with faculty in deciding how to make time available for professional development.
- Evaluate teaching in a way that will foster a faculty perspective on teaching that is focused on student learning and on what they need to do to further enhance the quality of their teaching.
- Develop mechanisms for educating students about what constitutes good teaching and learning, so they can cooperate with faculty who use new ideas.

The second source of faculty support needs to come from a variety of organizations involved in higher education.

National organizations with a focus on education could collaborate on a major national project to create a definition of good teaching that could be used by colleges and universities as they work to promote good teaching. This would need to be shaped in a way that is meaningful across a broad spectrum of disciplines and teaching situations and is still specific enough to distinguish good teaching from mediocre teaching. If such a definition were available, colleges and universities would at long last have a valid basis for recognizing and rewarding truly excellent teachers and for assessing the quality of instruction in those institutions.

Accrediting agencies need to continue a trend that is already in place. This is the policy of encouraging individual colleges and universities to provide evidence that students are achieving significant kinds of learning and that faculty are regularly engaging in professional development activities to learn how to teach as effectively as possible.

Funding agencies in government, corporate, and private organizations fund education-related projects. When these agencies describe the kinds of projects they are willing to fund, it would be helpful if they were to tell applicants to identify the kinds of significant learning that are going to be promoted in the project and indicate how the proposed activities reflect the principles of effective instructional design, such as active learning and educative assessment.

Disciplinary associations currently support efforts to improve teaching within their discipline in one way or another, but these associations could have an even bigger impact on the practice of teaching within their disciplines if their activities reflected the full range of possibilities: offering workshops that relate major ideas on college teaching to discipline-specific situations; sponsoring and organizing research on effective teaching; providing forums (conferences, journals, Web sites) in which practitioners can share their teaching concerns, experiments, research, and successes; providing materials (books, papers, videos, CDs) that summarize and synthesize ideas on good practice; and working collaboratively with local institutions and other national organizations to address policy issues that affect teaching.

The growing number of *journals on college teaching* could have an even bigger impact on the teaching of their readers if the editors, authors, and reviewers kept a few recommendations in mind: relate the article to some of the major ideas in the general literature on college teaching, broaden the focus from specific techniques to broader teaching strategies, and provide information on all the key components of instructional design (situational factors, learning goals, feedback and assessment, teaching and learning activities, and the relationships among these components).

If colleges and universities and the other organizations involved in higher education can provide this kind of support for faculty, I am convinced the faculty will respond by providing radically different and superior kinds of learning experiences for students.

Making the Most of Teacher-Student Interactions

As powerful as the ideas and recommendations on course design discussed thus far are, they are not enough by themselves to activate the full human significance of good teaching and learning. Good teaching and learning also require good interaction between teachers and students. At the present time, I see three concepts that seem capable of enhancing the way we interact with students as we implement the design of our instruction: teacher credibility, leadership, and the spiritual dimension of teaching.

Teacher Credibility

This is a concept adapted from communication research on speaker credibility or "source credibility" (Cooper and Simonds, 1998; Berlo, Lemert, and Mertz, 1969). The basic proposition is that whenever a speaker (or a teacher) is communicating with an audience, the audience is making decisions as to whether they find the speaker credible or believable. If they do, they attend to the speaker's comments and ideas; if not, they dismiss the speaker and spend their mental energy elsewhere. (Arletta Knight, who has a doctorate in instructional communication, has worked hard to bring the concept of teacher credibility from that discipline into the professional literature on college teaching. For a fuller statement on this concept, see her comments at http://www.ou.edu/tips/ideas/credibility.html; access date October 14, 2002.)

Communication researchers have gathered data on what makes particular speakers credible or not credible and performed a factor analysis on the data. Depending on the preferences of the researcher, they have come up with models that have three, four, or five primary factors. I like the three-factor version, which is similar to the one discussed by Kouzes and Posner in their book on leader credibility (1993). This version concludes that the primary factors affecting speaker credibility are competence, trustworthiness, and dynamism. When applied to teaching and learning situations, this concept suggests that students evaluate teachers and decide whether to buy into their teaching and courses depending on whether they perceive each teacher to be competent, trustworthy, and dynamic.

These three factors exist on two levels—and both levels matter. The teacher may in reality be (or not be) competent, trustworthy, or dynamic, and that is important. But it is also independently important whether the students *perceive* the teacher to be competent, trustworthy, and dynamic. Sometimes, for example, teachers who are in fact quite competent do something that makes the students perceive them as not being competent. If so, teacher credibility declines despite the teacher's actual competence.

The concept of teacher credibility leads us to ask the question: What kinds of teacher behavior affect student perceptions of competence, trustworthiness, and dynamism? Various audiences have discussed this question and generated the list of behaviors associated with each factor shown in Exhibit 7.1.

Many teachers have found that this concept and list of associated behaviors have enabled them to improve their relationship with their students. They can see things they are doing or not doing that may be causing problems, and these are often relatively easy to change. And the teachers who make these changes find that their relationship with students improves significantly thereafter. So this is a concept that has major value for enhancing teacher-student interactions.

EXHIBIT 7.1. CHARACTERISTICS THAT DESCRIBE TEACHER CREDIBILITY.

Competence	Trustworthiness	Dynamism
Knowledge of the subject	Have best interest of students at heart	Excited about subject

"Teachers are perceived as [competent/trustworthy/dynamic] if they . . . "

Competence	Trustworthiness	Dynamism
• Can explain complex material well	• Follow through on promises	• Have high energy
• Have good classroom management skills	• Give immediate feedback	• Are interesting
• Have the ability to answer student questions	• Offer a rational explanation for grading	• Are flexible, that is, can deviate to increase student interest
• Can reference significant works of others	• Show no biases, that is, teach from multiple perspectives	• Have good presentation skills
• Communicate well	• Treat all students the same	• Use a variety of teaching techniques
• Can "do" what they are teaching	• Never embarrass students	• Are sometimes unpredictable
• Have broad base of information	• Are flexible	• Relate positively to students
		• Add their own personality to the class

Leadership

A second general idea pertinent to the topic of teacher-student relationships is the concept of leadership. A teacher is generally seen by the university and by students as being the person in charge of a given course. This means it is possible for the teacher to think about the course as an opportunity to be a leader and to exert leadership skills.

For teachers who might want to use ideas from the literature on leadership to improve and guide their interactions with students, there are numerous theories and models available. Although I have not studied all the different leadership models, several of the ones I have studied offer ideas that are meaningful when applied to an educational setting.

One that I find particularly worthwhile for this purpose is the model of transformational leadership developed by Bernard Bass (1984, 1994, 1998). In his model, Bass describes four components of transformational leadership: idealized influence, inspirational motivation, intellectual stimulation, and individualized consideration (see Exhibit 7.2). When one looks at this list, it seems fairly easy to imagine that a teacher who is having problems in relationships with students could use these concepts to identify ways to relate to the students differently.

Other people may find other models of leadership that are more meaningful to them, and that is fine. My only point for the moment is that various concepts of leadership exist and have the potential for giving teachers a way to analyze and enhance their interactions with students.

The Spiritual Dimension of Teaching

In the past two decades Parker Palmer has been exploring and writing about education in a new and different way. Two of his books in particular have laid out the basic ideas in this particular perspective: *To Know as We Are Known* (1983) and the widely read *The Courage to Teach* (1998). In a general sense, Palmer says he is trying to enlarge our understanding of teaching by integrating three important dimensions: intellectual, emotional, and spiritual (1998, p. 4). When he writes about the spiritual dimension of life, he is referring to "the diverse ways we answer the heart's longing to be connected with the largeness of life—a longing that animates love and work, especially the work called teaching." (p. 5)

When one looks at teaching from this perspective, one sees the importance of new and different factors: love, prayerful education, wholeness, connectedness, an organic relationship between the knower and the known, and so forth. At the core of this novel language is a view that sees education as resulting from the interaction of three primary influences: the teacher, the student, and the subject. All of

EXHIBIT 7.2. TRANSFORMATIONAL LEADERSHIP: FOUR COMPONENTS AND ASSOCIATED BEHAVIORS.

1. Idealized Influence
   - Model your values when fulfilling the responsibilities of your role.
   - Act in a way that warrants admiration, respect, and trust.
   - Remember that others identify with and want to emulate the leader.

2. Inspirational Motivation
   - Motivate and inspire others by providing meaning and challenge to their work.
   - Arouse team spirit.
   - Display enthusiasm and optimism.
   - Get others involved in envisioning attractive future states.

3. Intellectual Stimulation
   - Stimulate others to be innovative and creative by questioning assumptions, reframing problems, and approaching old situations in new ways.
   - Never offer public criticism of individual mistakes.
   - Solicit new ideas from others.

4. Individualized Consideration
   - Pay special attention to each person's needs for achievement and growth.
   - Create new learning opportunities along with a supportive climate.
   - Recognize individual differences (in terms of needs and desires).
   - Encourage two-way exchanges in communication.
   - Listen effectively.

Source: Adapted from Bass, 1998.

these are interdependent—each connected and deeply affected by changes in the other two. But Palmer puts the subject at the center of this hub of relationships; he sees the teacher and the students as fellow learners trying to learn some truths about the subject.

To pursue the spiritual dimension of teaching, Palmer argues there are a number of actions that teachers can and need to take. They have to develop a strong personal identity and integrity. Then they have to learn how to create a community and learn how to engage in "knowing in community," "teaching in community," and "learning in community." All of this involves a highly developed ability to *listen* deeply, through contemplation and prayer, to the students and to the subject. The purpose of all this is to help the students develop an emotional, intellectual, and spiritual relationship with the subject, with the teacher, and with themselves individually and collectively.

Although Palmer is clearly the most visible and extensive writer on this topic, others have explored the question of how spirit and love might become part of the relationships and interactions that teachers have with their students. Vaill, in *Spirited Leading and Learning* (1998), has shared some ideas on the central importance of spirituality and learning for leaders in any organizational situation. Mary Rose O'Reilley has written two books that address this theme quite directly. In the first, *The Peaceable Classroom* (1993), she describes her efforts to create a nonviolent classroom that would allow students freedom to nourish an inner life. In her more recent book, *Radical Presence* (1998), she presents a vision of teaching as contemplative practice and a prophetic vocation.

◆ ◆ ◆

These three avenues—teacher credibility, leadership, and the spirituality of teaching—offer teachers multiple possibilities for thinking about and attempting to strengthen and improve their interactions with and relationships with their students. These, in combination with new ideas on designing learning experiences, can give teachers a powerful pair of competencies with which to approach the act of teaching. If teachers can develop and enhance both these aspects of their teaching, the result should be more powerful and exciting learning experiences not only for the students for the teacher as well.

Should We Abandon Traditional Ways of Teaching?

One important qualification needs to be added at this point. I have been emphasizing the need for teachers to learn new ideas about teaching, and in much of this book I have drawn a contrast between traditional practices in teaching and what can be accomplished with the addition of new ideas that have emerged from the scholarship of teaching in the last several years. And I believe that to be true.

But at the same time I also recognize and believe that, while they can be improved upon, these traditions also have good aspects in them that should by all means be retained. The humanities have a long tradition of looking closely at the text being studied and using discussion and essay writing to prompt in-depth self-reflection by students. A valuable part of the tradition in science is the use of empirical experiences, some of which occur in laboratory settings and others in various kinds of field experience. The social sciences have found great value in the use of case studies and other ways of bringing social reality into the classroom.

Used by themselves, these traditions have value but are limited in their impact. This impact can be greatly increased if they can be combined with and incorporated into a more powerful course design and implemented with more powerful forms of teacher-student interactions. Hence the real task for teachers is to learn about the new ideas, identify what is good in the traditions of their own particular discipline or realm of teaching, and then create a new form of teaching that combines the best of both.

The Principles and Spirit of Good Teaching

As we strive to build on but go beyond traditional ways of teaching, we will be forced to make choices. As we do this, we will need to identify the right principles and spirit of good teaching.

I recently heard a minister at a local church make some important distinctions that are relevant here, while talking about what he hoped members had received from their instruction for confirmation and baptism. He hoped they had learned some of the rules for good and righteous living. But beyond that, he also hoped they had learned some of the *principles* of good living, because rules cannot cover all the situations we find ourselves in. But even beyond that, he hoped people had found the right spirit for living a good and righteous life. For unless we want to live deeply and fully and spiritually, knowing all the rules and all the principles will have little value for us.

It seems to me that this same pattern can be applied to the act of teaching. I am not sure there is anything that qualifies as a rule of good teaching anymore. But there do seem to be a number of principles. In the area of course design, for example, I see a number of key principles. The basic components of a course design should incorporate active learning and educative assessment as a way of achieving significant learning goals. The structure of a course and the instructional strategy should be characterized by both differentiation and integration. And so on.

If these constitute some of the key principles of teaching, what might be said about the proper spirit of teaching? As I have sought the answer to this question, I have looked at what I thought was the right spirit in other realms of human activity. In every case, the key was having a spirit of love or passion for what one was doing. This might involve a love of music or painting (for an artist), a love of providing customers with high-quality products or service (for people in business), or a love of seeing people healthy (for doctors).

For teachers, having the right spirit also involves love. My good friend and colleague, Tom Boyd, a highly celebrated teacher, has written that good teachers have to love their subject, love their students, and love the teaching and learning process (1997). All three kinds of love are necessary; omit any one of them and the act of teaching can become tyrannical, directionless, or inept.

I might only add that one also needs to love and respect oneself. This gives one confidence to be a leader of others. The right kind of self-regard also induces an important dimension of humility, allowing us to recognize that, at any given time, we don't know everything there is to know about this subject, about the students, or about how to teach them about this subject. Finally, this kind of love enables us to accept our own limits and recognize that some of the learning needed will have to come from inside the students and from interactions among students, not just from their interactions with the teacher—and to trust that process.

A Dream of What Might Be, If . . .

Most people have read or seen video clips of Martin Luther King's famous "I Have a Dream" speech. It was an inspiring speech, not because it was his dream but because it gave all of us a clear and powerful image of a society that we could all value and work for, in this case, the image of an integrated, multicultural society where all people could truly experience freedom.

I too have a dream. But this dream is about teaching, learning, and higher education, and about the role that learning can play in the life of individuals and society. This is what I see in this dream:

I see people, all people, living their lives full of learning. At every step and stage of their lives, they recognize the need to learn; they see clearly how learning can enrich and empower their lives.

In addition to seeing the powerful link between high-quality living and high-quality learning, they also know *how* to learn what they need to learn. They are well aware of the different learning strategies available to them, and they know how to use these strategies: gaining new experiences, reflecting on the meaning of new and old experiences, acquiring new information and ideas, networking with other people, observing others who have special lessons to offer, and participating in formal educational programs.

People everywhere are able to operate this way because they have learned about the importance of life-related learning in both their formal and informal learning experiences. Their parents, friends, community associates, and formal teachers have all made it clear why continual learning is important and have clarified the different ways one can learn.

Although everyone plays an important role in this process, people in the role of formal teachers fulfill an especially critical role. They have responsibility for situations that are designed to be learning experiences. As they fill these roles, they support learning on multiple levels. The teachers help people learn, not only about the subject and topic at hand but also about the importance of learning and about special ways of continuing to learn. Consequently the students of these teachers become more aware of themselves as learners and develop into self-directing learners.

In this dream, teachers are able to generate such multidimensional learning experiences because they have sufficient preparation for fulfilling this role. They also have the internal and external incentives necessary to support their commitment to being and becoming effective teachers.

Teachers have the necessary preparation, support, and recognition because the organizations in which they work—schools, colleges, universities, churches, businesses, community organizations—recognize the importance of competent teaching and create the programs and make the organizational changes necessary to support the teachers.

And each individual organization is able to provide this support because all the organizations involved in education help each other work toward this common, shared goal. This coordination of effort happens because the leaders in society, education in general, and higher education in particular recognize the absolute importance of high-quality learning in society. For this reason, the leaders have learned to make the organizational changes that are needed.

This is a big dream. Right now, it is only a dream. But all major change starts with someone imagining a new and different way of doing things. If enough people see the same dream and decide the dream is worthwhile, things start to happen and changes begin to be made. If you can imagine it, you can do it.

My hope is that this book can stimulate your imagination and play a role in helping you find a new dream or several dreams that, for you, are worth pursuing. You may imagine a new way of being a teacher, a learner, or a leader in an educational organization. If you are a teacher and work seriously on the ideas and changes outlined in this book, my belief and expectation is that you will gradually become more and more competent as a course designer. And when you do that, you will increase your power and effectiveness as someone in charge of other people's learning experiences!

I also hope that you will examine the ideas in this book closely, not to determine whether they are true or false but to determine whether they are *useful*. These ideas should not be viewed as a doctrine that is right or wrong but rather as a raft that is capable of taking you to exciting places. If the ideas presented here do in fact turn out to be useful, they will enable teachers, learners, and organizational leaders to create learning experiences and educational programs that are truly capable of enriching and empowering people's lives.

This is my hope and my dream.

PLANNING YOUR COURSE: A DECISION GUIDE

Whenever teachers plan or design their courses, they are in essence making a series of decisions aimed at creating a design, which in this case consists of a plan of activities for what the teacher and students will do in a course. This guide identifies the several decisions involved in designing a course, places these decisions in an appropriate sequence, and suggests ways to make good decisions. I have grouped these decisions into three phases of the design process:

Initial Phase:	Building Strong Primary Components of the Course
Intermediate Phase:	Assembling the Components into a Dynamic, Coherent Whole
Final Phase:	Taking Care of Important Details

Initial Phase: Building Strong Primary Components

1. WHERE ARE YOU?

Size up the situational factors.

- *Specific context:* Number of students, kind of classroom, and so on.
- *General context:* Place in the curriculum, professional preparation, and so on.

- *Nature of the subject:* convergent or divergent, stable or rapidly changing?
- *Student characteristics:* Prior knowledge, attitudes, maturity, and so on.
- *Teacher characteristics:* Knowledge of and feelings toward subject and students; teaching philosophy, experience, and so on.
- *Special pedagogical challenge:* What is the special challenge to teaching this subject well?

2. WHERE DO YOU WANT TO GO?

What are your learning goals for the course? Ideally, what would you like students to get out of this course? Some possibilities:

- *Foundational knowledge:* Understanding of key content: facts, principles, concepts, and so on.
- *Application:* Thinking skills, other physical and intellectual skills, managing complex projects.
- *Integration:* Connecting ideas, information, realms of life, and so on.
- *Human dimension:* Knowing how to interact with oneself and with others.
- *Caring:* Making changes in one's feelings, interests, and values.
- *Learning how to learn:* Learning how to keep on learning after the course is over.

3. HOW WILL THE STUDENTS AND YOU KNOW IF THEY GET THERE?

How will you know if the students have achieved these goals? What kinds of feedback and assessment would be appropriate?

See Exhibit A.1 at the end of this appendix for one way of developing appropriate kinds of feedback and assessment for different kinds of goals.

- For each general goal specified here, what information can you gather that will tell you and each student about individual progress toward that goal? About how well the whole class is learning?
- For which goals are paper-and-pencil evaluations sufficient? Which need reflective writing? Performance assessment?
- What kind of feedback and assessment can you provide that will go beyond just providing a basis for the grade and will actually enhance the learning process?

4. HOW ARE YOU GOING TO GET THERE?

Select or develop learning activities that reflect the principles of active learning.

- How will students acquire the content, that is, the necessary information and ideas?
- What kinds of "doing" and "observing" experiences do the students need? Can you create rich learning experiences that allow students to pursue several learning goals simultaneously?
- What kinds of reflective dialogue will help them make sense of the content and connect it to their own lives? Can you develop multiple forms of such dialogue—one-minute papers, weekly journals, end-of-term learning portfolios?

5. WHO AND WHAT CAN HELP?

Find resources.

See Exhibit A.1 at the end of this appendix, as it can help identify the resources needed for each learning goal.

- What resources will the students need (and can you get) to support each of the learning activities listed in Decision #4? These may be people, places, or things, including media.

Intermediate Phase: Assembling the Components into a Dynamic, Coherent Whole

The next three decisions create the basic plan of learning activities. Sometimes Decision #6 (creating a course structure) will be done first, sometimes #7 (building an instructional strategy). I am presenting #6 first because it often—but not always—makes more sense to start there.

6. WHAT ARE THE MAJOR TOPICS IN THIS COURSE?

Create a thematic structure for the course.

- Identify the four to seven major ideas, topics, or themes in the course.
- Place them in an appropriate sequence.
- If possible, make sure the ideas build on one another and result in a culminating project that integrates the ideas, topics, or themes.

7. WHAT WILL THE STUDENTS NEED TO DO?

Identify the specific learning activities necessary for the desired kinds of learning and put them into an effective instructional strategy.

- An instructional strategy is a combination of specific learning activities in a particular sequence, usually laid out over a one- to three-week span of time.
- Each individual activity should build synergistically on students' past learning activities and prepare them for future activities.
- Examples of instructional strategies:

  - Continuous series of lectures and reading assignments, interrupted once or twice by a midterm exam. *Sequence of student activities:* hear—read—test.

  - Series of reading, reflective writing, and whole-class discussion assignments (sequence repeated for each topic). *Sequence of student activities:* read—write—talk. (A variation of this would be read—talk—write.)

  - Start with some field or lab work observations, followed by readings and whole-class discussions. *Sequence of student activities:* do (or look)—read—talk. (Write-ups of lab or field work are sometimes included.)

  - Lectures followed by field work or lab observations. *Sequence of student activities:* hear—see or do

  - Have students do assigned readings followed by mini-tests done individually and in small groups, then move on to group-based application projects. *Sequence of student activities:* read—individual and group tests—practice "doing" with feedback.

  - Work through a series of developmental stages lasting four to six weeks apiece: build some knowledge and skills, work on small application projects, and then work on larger, more complex projects. *Sequence of student activities:* know—build know-how—do—DO.

  - Contract for a grade—that is, set up an agreement along the lines of "read text and pass exams" to get a C, add a research paper to get a B, do extended project as well as a research paper to get an A.

It can be useful to create a diagram that illustrates the desired sequence of learning activities. A diagram of one possible sequence might look like the one in Figure A.1.

8. WHAT IS THE OVERALL SCHEME OF LEARNING ACTIVITIES?

At this time you need to dynamically integrate the course structure and the instructional strategy for the whole course.

It can be helpful to create a diagram of the course structure and the instructional strategy, and then find ways to enhance the way these two components work together. An example of such a diagram might look like the one in Figure A.2. The diagram in the figure is just an example of one possibility. It would obviously need to be adjusted to fit the circumstances of any given teaching situation.

• Good course designs and plans provide for both *differentiation* and *integration* of learning.

FIGURE A.1. SAMPLE "CASTLE TOP" DIAGRAM.

In-class activities	Lecture		Test on readings		In-class problem solving		Exam
Out-of-class activities		Reading homework		Problem-solving homework		Review	

FIGURE A.2. STRATEGY AND STRUCTURE LAYOUT.

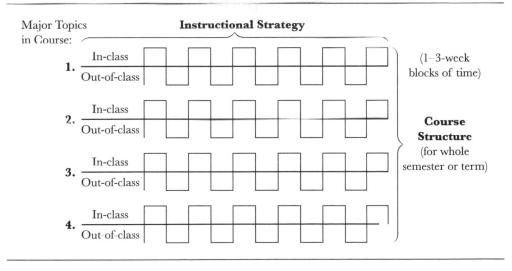

The differentiation can be reflected in variety in the type of learning activities from day to day, within each topical block of time, and in development in the complexity and challenge of the learning, from topical unit 1 through 4.

The integration should be reflected both within each topical unit of time and in the progression through each of the topical units.

- At the conclusion of this process, you should be ready to lay out a week-by-week schedule of activities for the whole term. Exhibit A.2 at the end of this handout can be useful in laying out the entire schedule or sequence of activities for the whole course. The form assumes three class sessions per week. You can adjust it as needed for courses with different time formats. As you do this, there is a helpful sequence of questions to ask:

What activities need to come first, that is, how should the course begin?

What activities do you want to conclude with, that is, how should the course end?

What should the sequence of activities be in the middle of the course?

- Developing the design or plan for the course is very important. It is also important, though, to remember that it is only a plan. Like all plans, it needs to be flexible and subject to change as it is implemented.

Final Phase: Taking Care of Important Details

9. HOW ARE YOU GOING TO GRADE?

Develop your grading system.

- It should reflect the full range of learning goals and activities. (Remember: You do *not* have to grade everything, but make sure you do grade some instances of every kind of learning you want students to retain.)
- The relative weight of each item on the course grade should reflect the relative importance of that activity.

10. WHAT COULD GO WRONG?

Debug the design by analyzing and assessing this "first draft" of the course.

- General criteria for a good course design:

Is it based on an in-depth analysis of the situational factors?

Does it include higher-level learning goals?

Do the feedback and assessment activities reflect the principles of educative assessment?

Do the teaching and learning activities include active learning?

Are the four components well integrated?

- Possible mechanical problems:

    Will the students have time to do their out-of-class assignments?

    Will they be able to obtain the necessary resources? (For instance, how many students will be trying to obtain reading material in the library reserve at the same time? Are there enough copies for all of them?)

11. LET STUDENTS KNOW WHAT YOU ARE PLANNING.

Now write the syllabus. Include at least the following points:

- General management information—instructor, office hours, phone, and so on
- Goals for the course
- Structure and sequence of class activities, including due dates for major assignments, tests, and projects
- Text and other required reading material
- Grading procedures
- Course policies: attendance, work turned in late, make-up exams, and so on

12. HOW WILL YOU KNOW HOW THE COURSE IS GOING? HOW IT WENT?

- Plan an evaluation of the course itself and of your teaching performance.
- What kinds of midterm and end-of-term feedback will you need?
- What specific questions do you have about

    The degree to which your goals for the course were achieved?

    The effectiveness of particular learning activities?

    Your ability to interact effectively with students?

- What *sources* can give you the information you need to answer these questions?

    Videotape or audiotape of the class sessions

    Student interviews or questionnaires

    Outside observers

    Test results

EXHIBIT A.1. WORKSHEET FOR DESIGNING A COURSE.

Learning Goals for Course:	Procedures for Evaluating Student Learning:	Learning Activities:	Resources:
1.			
2.			
3.			
4.			
5.			
6.			

EXHIBIT A.2. SEQUENCE OF LEARNING ACTIVITIES.

	Sessions per Week					
Week	Class Session	Between Classes	Class Session	Between Classes	Class Session	Between Classes
1						
2						
3						
4						
5						
6						
7						
8						
9						
10						
11						
12						
13						
14						
15						
Finals						

SUGGESTED READINGS

Faculty members often come up to me after my workshops and ask for a list of additional readings on specific aspects of significant learning, course design, or college teaching in general. This list is my response to that request.

While obviously not all-inclusive, it is at least one person's guide to readings that offer valuable ideas on specific aspects of teaching, organized according to some of the themes in this book:

- Particular kinds of significant learning
- Particular aspects of course design
- Particular teaching strategies
- Other key aspects of teaching:
  Developing a philosophy of teaching
  Interacting with students
- Organizational support for teaching
- Compendia of good ideas on college teaching

I. Particular Kinds of Significant Learning
    A. Learning How to Learn
        1. Lifelong self-directed learning
            • Candy, P. C. 1991. *Self-Direction for Lifelong Learning: A Comprehensive Guide to Theory and Practice.* San Francisco: Jossey-Bass.

A thorough review of the ideas and literature on lifelong learning. Has a model that takes student-directed learning beyond mini-research projects to autodidaxy and self-directed learning in life.

- Knowles, M. S. 1975. *Self-Directed Learning: A Guide for Learners and Teachers*. New York: Association Press.

  The classic work on this topic. Sets the focus on people building a learning agenda and a learning strategy.

2. Formal Inquiry
   - Novak, J. D., and Gowin, D. B. 1984. *Learning How to Learn*. New York: Cambridge University Press.

     The authors lay out their "Knowledge Vee" diagram suggesting that all structured inquiry involves a dialectic between theoretical constructs and methodological procedures. They also comment on the value of concept maps as a way of clarifying how students (or experts) understand a topic.

3. Being a Good Student

   The following two edited volumes and the review chapter in *Teaching Tips* draw on cognitive psychology to generate suggestions on what teachers can do to help students develop the motivation and skills necessary to be effective students, that is, to be self-regulated learners.
   - Schunk, D. H., and Zimmerman, B. J., eds. 1998. *Self-Regulated Learning: From Teaching to Self-Reflective Practice*. New York: Guilford Press.
   - Pintrich, P., ed. 1995. *Understanding Self-Regulated Learning*. New Directions for Teaching and Learning, no. 63. San Francisco: Jossey-Bass.
   - Weinstein, C. E., Meyer, D. K., and Van Mater Stone, G. 1999. Teaching Students How to Learn. In *Teaching Tips: Strategies, Research, and Theory for College and University Teachers*, 10th ed., by W. J. McKeachie and others. Boston: Houghton-Mifflin.

B. Caring
   - McKeachie, W. J., and others. 1999. Teaching Values: Should We? Can We? In *Teaching Tips: Strategies, Research, and Theory for College and University Teachers*, 10th ed., by W. J. McKeachie and others. Boston: Houghton-Mifflin.

     McKeachie addresses the values aspect of caring and answers both of the title questions in the affirmative. The book builds a persuasive case that teachers need to help students become more sensitive to their own values, the values of others, and the ethical implications of all personal and social decisions.

C. Human Dimension

- Baxter Magolda, M. 2001. *Making Their Own Way: Narratives for Transforming Higher Education to Promote Self-Development.* Sterling, Va.: Stylus.

  Invites teachers to a new agenda in their teaching: to be good company for college students on their journey toward "authoring" their own lives.

- Shapiro, N. S., and Levine, J. 1999. *Creating Learning Communities.* San Francisco: Jossey-Bass.

  Describes effective ways to create learning communities, a powerful tool for learning about others and how to interact with them.

D. Integration

1. Interdisciplinary Studies

   Both of these books, one single-authored and the other a collection of short essays, address the importance of interdisciplinary learning and ways to achieve it.

   - Davis, J. R. 1995. *Interdisciplinary Courses and Team Teaching.* Phoenix, Ariz.: Oryx Press.

   - Klein, J. T., and Doty, W. G., eds. 1994. *Interdisciplinary Studies Today.* New Directions for Teaching and Learning, no. 58. San Francisco: Jossey-Bass.

2. Learning Communities

   - Gabelnick, F., MacGregor, J., Matthews, R. S., and Smith, B. L. 1990. *Learning Communities: Creating Connections Among Students, Faculty, and Disciplines.* New Directions for Teaching and Learning, no. 41. San Francisco: Jossey-Bass.

     One nice feature of this collection of essays is that it addresses several of the different kinds of connections that can be made in integration learning: among students, between faculty and students, between faculty members, and among disciplines.

3. Service Learning

   Both of these collections of essays offer testimonials to the impact of service learning but also include specific suggestions as to how to employ this form of teaching and learning in a way that maximizes that impact.

   - Zlotkowski, E., ed. 1998. *Successful Service-Learning Programs: New Models of Excellence in Higher Education.* Bolton, Mass.: Anker.

   - Rhoads, R. A., and Howard, J.P.F., eds. 1998. *Academic Service Learning: A Pedagogy of Action and Reflection.* New Directions for Teaching and Learning, no. 73. San Francisco: Jossey-Bass.

E. Application
- Brookfield, S. D. 1991. *Developing Critical Thinkers: Challenging Adults to Explore Alternative Ways of Thinking and Acting.* San Francisco: Jossey-Bass.

  Noting that there are numerous definitions given to this attractive concept, Brookfield defines it as (1) identifying and challenging assumptions and (2) exploring and imagining alternatives. Then he goes on to describe strategies for helping student develop these capacities more fully.
- Paul, R. W. 1993. *Critical Thinking: How to Prepare Students for a Rapidly Changing World.* Santa Rosa, Calif.: Foundation for Critical Thinking.

  Argues passionately that we desperately need people in society who can think critically and that we are not doing a very good job of educating people for this at the present time, even when we try. Part B is titled "How to Teach for Critical Thinking."
- Sternberg, R. J., and Spear-Swerling, L., eds. 1996. *Teaching for Thinking.* Washington, D.C.: American Psychological Association.

  Lays out the triarchic perspective on thinking and offers suggestions on how to teach students multiple modes of thinking.
- McKeachie, W. J., and others. 1999. Teaching Thinking. In *Teaching Tips: Strategies, Research, and Theory for College and University Teachers,* 10th ed., by W. J. McKeachie and others. Boston: Houghton-Mifflin.

  A short essay that identifies three techniques for promoting critical thinking: student writing and discussion, explicit emphasis on problem solving with varied examples, and verbalization of methods and strategies to encourage metacognition.

F. Foundational Knowledge
- Marton, F., Hounsell, D., and Entwistle, N., eds. 1997. *The Experience of Learning,* 2nd ed. Edinburgh, Scotland: Scottish Academic Press.

  A series of stimulating essays prompted in part by the interest in "deep learning" that has emerged in educational research in Europe.

II. Particular Aspects of Course Design

A. General
- Diamond, R. M. 1998. *Designing and Assessing Courses and Curricula: A Practical Guide,* rev. ed. San Francisco: Jossey-Bass.

  Draws on the author's extensive experience in working with whole academic units as well as with professors to systematically design instruction. Is one of the few sources that focuses on designing curricula as well as courses.

- Wiggins, G., and McTighe, J. 1998. *Understanding by Design*. Alexandria, Va.: Association for Supervision and Curriculum Development. Although aimed primarily at public school teachers, this book offers a model of design based on the same principles as the one in the present book. Its authors also urge teachers to develop a good set of learning goals and then design that quality into the learning experience.

B. Situational Factors

- Diamond, R. M. 1998. Gathering and Analyzing Essential Data. In *Designing and Assessing Courses and Curricula: A Practical Guide*, rev. ed. San Francisco: Jossey-Bass.
  Diamond strongly emphasizes the importance of thoroughly gathering and analyzing data about what I call "situational factors." He offers numerous examples of how this data made a difference in the design.

- A number of Web sites contain information on learning styles:

  From Rich Felder at North Carolina State University: http://www2.ncsu.edu/unity/lockers/users/f/felder/public/ Learning_Styles.html. Access date: October 14, 2002.

  From Neil Fleming in Australia: http://www.vark-learn.com. Access date: October 14, 2002.

  From Charles Bonwell in Colorado: http://www.activel-learning-site.com/vark.htm. Access date: October 14, 2002.

C. Formulating Learning Goals

- Wiggins, G., and McTighe, J. 1998. Six Facets of Understanding. In *Understanding by Design*. Alexandria, Va.: Association for Supervision and Curriculum Development.
  The six facets of understanding offer a refreshingly original set of learning goals that is very similar to my taxonomy of significant learning.

- Gardiner, L. 1994. "What are the Critical Competencies? In *Redesigning Higher Education: Producing Dramatic Gains in Student Learning*. ASHE-ERIC Higher Education Report 7. Washington, D.C.: George Washington University.
  Although he did not label them as learning goals, Gardiner developed a list of critical competencies based on comments by civic and business leaders about what society needs in our college graduates.

- Bloom, B. S., and Associates. 1956. *Taxonomy of Educational Objectives: Handbook I: Cognitive Domain*. New York: McKay.

This taxonomy has stood the test of time extraordinarily well. It offers six major categories of cognitive learning that transcend individual disciplines: knowledge (that is, recall), comprehension, application, analysis, synthesis, and evaluation.

D. Creating Teaching and Learning Activities
   1. Active Learning in General
      • Bonwell, C. C., and Eison, J. A. 1991. *Active Learning: Creating Excitement in the Classroom*. ASHE-ERIC Higher Education Report 1. Washington, D.C.: George Washington University.
        This is *the* book that established the term and the concept of active learning solidly in the professional literature of college teaching.
   2. Experiential Learning (especially problem solving with small groups and case studies)
      • Michaelsen, L. K., Knight, A. B., and Fink, L. D. 2002. *Team-Based Learning: A Transformative Use of Small Groups for Large and Small Classes*. Westport, Conn.: Praeger.
        Team-based learning is a distinctive and unusually powerful form of teaching with small groups. It is a "strategy" rather than a "technique," and it is based on "teams," which are more powerful than "groups."
      • Millis, B. J., and Cottell, P. G. 1998. *Cooperative Learning for Higher Education Faculty*. Phoenix, Ariz.: Oryx Press.
        This is the best collection of information currently available on multiple ways of using small groups in college teaching.
      • Christensen, C. R. 1987. *Teaching and the Case Method: Text, Cases, and Readings*. Boston, Mass.: Harvard Business School Press.
        Offers advice and examples on the effective use of the case method of teaching, a form of active learning that is widely used in professional schools.
   3. Reflective Writing
      • Zubizarreta, J., ed. 2003. *The Learning Portfolio: Reflective Practice for Improving Student Learning*. Bolton, Mass.: Anker.
        Like teaching portfolios, learning portfolios are a potent device both for fostering self-awareness and for communicating something about oneself to others. This book describes the idea of learning portfolios and offers examples of different ways of using them.
      • Bean, J. C. 1996. *Engaging Ideas: The Professor's Guide to Integrating Writing, Critical Thinking, and Active Learning in the Classroom*. San Francisco: Jossey-Bass.

A rich collection of chapters that links writing to two other widespread goals in higher education: critical thinking and active learning. An excellent resource for ideas and advice.

- Zinsser, W. 1988. *Writing to Learn.* New York: HarperCollins.
  Lays out the basic arguments for the use of writing, not only as a tool for assessment but for learning as well. Through numerous examples with many different subjects, it reminds a reader that writing can be thought provoking and a joy.

E. Procedures for Educative Assessment

- Wiggins, G. 1998. *Educative Assessment: Designing Assessments to Inform and Improve Student Performance.* San Francisco: Jossey-Bass.
  This is an extremely important book because it shows how we need to change our assessment procedures if we want them to *enhance* learning as well as to audit it.

- Walvoord, B. E., and Anderson, V. J. 1998. *Effective Grading: A Tool for Learning and Assessment.* San Francisco: Jossey-Bass.
  Especially effective at laying out procedures for making our criteria and standards clearer and better. But also shows how grading and assessment need to be a more integral part of the whole educational process.

- Angelo, T. A., and Cross, K. P. 1993. *Classroom Assessment Techniques: A Handbook for College Teachers,* 2nd ed. San Francisco: Jossey-Bass.
  The classic collection of fifty techniques for assessing *learning* (the biggest set), collecting information about *learners,* and about their reaction to *instruction.*

III. Particular Teaching Strategies

My definition of a teaching strategy is a particular combination of teaching and learning activities used in a particular sequence. Using this definition, there are a few well-developed teaching strategies available that can be used by teachers in a wide range of disciplines.

A. Team-Based Learning

- Michaelsen, L. K., Knight, A. B., and Fink, L. D. 2002. *Team-Based Learning: A Transformative Use of Small Groups for Large and Small Classes.* Westport, Conn.: Praeger Press.
  A strategy that is rapidly being adopted because it is relatively easy to use and yet sophisticated enough to generate powerful forms of learning in a wide range of teaching situations. Special Web site: http://www.teambasedlearning.org. Access date: October 14, 2002.

B. Problem-Based Learning

Both of these collections of essays describe a well-developed teaching strategy that is specifically designed to promote a key form of significant learning (as well as other forms): learning how to keep on learning after the course is over.

- Duch, B. J., Groh, S. E., and Allen, D. E., eds. 2001. *The Power of Problem-Based Learning.* Sterling, Va.: Stylus.
- Wilkerson, L., and Gijselaers, W. H., eds. 1996. *Bringing Problem-Based Learning to Higher Education: Theory and Practice.* New Directions for Teaching and Learning, no. 68. San Francisco: Jossey-Bass.
- These four Web sites provide valuable information on problem-based learning and are located at universities where it has been used extensively:

  http://www.udel.edu/pbl. Access date: October 15, 2002.

  http://www.samford/pbl/pbl_main.html. Access date: October 14, 2002.

  http://edweb.sdsu.edu/clrit/PBL_WebQuest.html. Access date: October 14, 2002.

  http://chemeng.mcmaster.ca/pbl/pbl.htm. Access date: October 16, 2002.

C. Accelerated Learning

- Rose, C., and Nicholl, M. J. 1997. *Accelerated Learning for the Twenty-First Century.* New York: Dell.

  This is a relatively new strategy but it has some important features, including the fact that it starts by getting students to look at their own reasons for learning.

IV. Other Key Aspects of Teaching

A. Developing a Philosophy of Teaching

- Lowman, J. 1995. *Mastering the Techniques of Teaching*, 2nd ed. San Francisco: Jossey-Bass.

  This book goes beyond just offering useful "tips" (although it also does that) to sharing the author's own philosophy, which is based on interviews and observations with a large number of outstanding teachers.

- Leamnson, R. 1999. *Thinking About Teaching and Learning: Developing Habits of Learning with First Year College and University Students.* Alexandria, Va.: Stylus.

  The subtitle notwithstanding, this book has value well beyond teachers of first-year students. It is especially valuable in what it has to say about the importance of becoming more aware of one's philosophy of teaching and then critically examining that philosophy to make it more robust.

- Brookfield, S. 1995. *Becoming a Critically Reflective Teacher.* San Francisco: Jossey-Bass.

  For teachers ready to examine themselves as teachers, Brookfield offers four lenses through which to take a critical look at their work: their own autobiographies, their students' eyes, their colleagues' perceptions, and the theoretical literature.

B. Interacting with Students

1. Leadership and Credibility

   - Knight, A. B. *Teacher Credibility.* www.ou.edu/idp/tips/ideas/credibility.html. Access date: October 14, 2002.

     This essay takes the concept of teacher credibility and shows how teachers can use it to diagnose problems they are having in their interactions with students.

   - Kouzes, J. S., and Posner, B. Z. 1993. *Credibility: How Leaders Gain It and Lose It, Why People Demand It.* San Francisco: Jossey-Bass.

     These authors, established writers about leadership, take the same concept of credibility that Knight uses and show how it can inform the actions of anyone wanting to exert leadership. Teachers can use these ideas on "leader credibility" for thinking about how to be a leader with students.

   - Bass, B. M. 1998. *Transformational Leadership: Industrial, Military, and Educational Impact.* Mahwah, N.J.: Erlbaum.

     Another model of leadership that teachers can adapt to classroom situations. The model is based on idealized influence, inspirational motivation, intellectual stimulation, and individualized consideration.

2. Spiritual Dimension of Teaching

   - Palmer, P. J. 1983. *To Know as We Are Known: A Spirituality of Education.* New York: HarperCollins.

   - ———. 1998. *The Courage to Teach: Exploring the Inner Landscape of a Teacher's Life.* San Francisco: Jossey-Bass.

     In these two books, Palmer explores how teachers can develop the spiritual dimension of teaching by striving for wholeness, connectedness, prayerful education, love, and integrity.

   - O'Reilley, M. R. 1993. *The Peaceable Classroom.* Portsmouth, N.H.: Boynton/Cook.

- ———. 1998. *Radical Presence: Teaching as Contemplative Practice.* Portsmouth, N.H.: Boynton/Cook.
  O'Reilley presents a novel vision of teaching as contemplative practice and prophetic vocation. In such a perspective, teaching clearly has a spiritual dimension to it.

V. Organizational Support for Teaching

A. Evaluating Faculty Work

- Braskamp, L. A., and Ory, J. C. 1994. *Assessing Faculty Work: Enhancing Individual and Institutional Performance.* San Francisco: Jossey-Bass.
  Proposes that faculty assessment should be done in a way that fosters growth of both the individual faculty member and the institution. Lays out specific procedures for doing this, including a joint setting of expectations.

B. Evaluating Teaching

- Fink, L. D. 2002. Improving the Evaluation of College Teaching. In *A Guide to Faculty Development,* edited by K. H. Gillespie. Bolton, Mass.: Anker.
  Argues that, to go beyond current practices, the evaluation of teaching will require using multiple sources of information to examine multiple dimensions of teaching. Identifies specific procedures for doing this.

- ———. 1995. Evaluating Your Own Teaching. In *Improving College Teaching,* edited by P. Seldin and Associates. Bolton, Mass.: Anker.
  After presenting some reasons for the importance of good self-evaluation, this chapter identifies five kinds of information available for teachers and then argues that a thorough self-evaluation clearly requires the use of all five.

- Knapper, C., and Cannon, P., eds. 2001. *Fresh Approaches to the Evaluation of Teaching.* New Directions for Teaching and Learning, no. 88. San Francisco: Jossey-Bass.
  Offers ideas on alternative ways to evaluate teaching, including the use of student outcomes (chapter 7).

VI. Compendia of Good Ideas on College Teaching

- Davis, B. 1993. *Tools for Teaching.* San Francisco: Jossey-Bass.
  An extremely useful collection of ideas on multiple aspects of teaching. Organized in a way that makes it very easy for readers to find the topic and the level of elaboration that they are looking for.

- McKeachie, W. J., and others. 1999. *Teaching Tips: Strategies, Research, and Theory for College and University Teachers,* 10th ed. Boston: Houghton-Mifflin.

This is *the* classic collection of teaching tips. Each chapter includes both tips and a brief review of the research literature on the topic. Over the years, McKeachie has done an excellent job of modifying the chapter topics in each new edition to keep the ideas current and reflective of contemporary thinking on college teaching.

- Web sites with collections of ideas on good teaching and learning:

http://www.hcc.hawaii.edu/intranet/committees/FacDevCom/ guidebk/teachtip/teachtip.htm. The most extensive collection of specific tips for teaching on any Web site I've found.

http://php.indiana.edu/~nelson1/TCHNGBKS.html. Craig Nelson at Indiana has compiled an impressive bibliography of references on various aspects of teaching and learning.

http://www.ou.edu/idp/tips. The Web site for my program at Oklahoma has material on course design, interacting with students, assessing teaching and learning, and so on.

REFERENCES

Accreditation Board for Engineering and Technology (ABET). 1998. *Criteria 2000.* 3rd ed. Baltimore: ABET.

Alverno College Faculty. 1994. *Student Assessment-as-Learning at Alverno College.* Milwaukee, Wis.: Alverno College.

American Association of Colleges for Teacher Education (AACTE). 2000. Students Learn More from National Board-Certified Teachers. *Briefs* (AACTE Newsletter), 21 (15): 1. (Full report on this study available online: http://new.nbpts.org/press/valstudy.pdf. Access date: Aug. 29, 2002.)

American Historical Association. 1998. "AHA Statement on Excellent Classroom Teaching of History." *Perspectives* (AHA Newsletter), 36 (4): 11–12.

Amiran, M. R., with the General College Program Assessment Committee. 1989. *The GCP and Student Learning: A Report to the Campus.* Fredonia: State University College of New York at Fredonia.

Angelo, T. A., and Cross, K. P. 1993. *Classroom Assessment Techniques: A Handbook for College Teachers.* 2nd ed. San Francisco: Jossey-Bass.

Annis, L., and Jones, C. 1995. Student Portfolios: Their Objectives, Development and Use. In *Improving College Teaching,* by P. Seldin and Associates. Bolton, Mass.: Anker.

Association of American Colleges (AAC). 1985. *Integrity in the College Curriculum: A Report to the Academic Community.* Washington, D.C.: AAC.

Barr, R. B., and Tagg, J. 1995. From Teaching to Learning: A New Paradigm for Undergraduate Education. *Change,* 27 (6): 13–25.

Barzun, J., and Graff, H. F. 1992. *The Modern Researcher.* 5th ed. Boston: Houghton Mifflin.

Bass, B. M. 1984. *Transformational Leadership and Performance Beyond Expectations.* Boston: Harvard Business School Press.

————. 1994. *Improving Organizational Effectiveness Through Transformational Leadership.* Thousand Oaks, Calif.: Sage.

————. 1998. *Transformational Leadership: Industrial, Military, and Educational Impact.* Mahwah, N.J.: Erlbaum.

Baxter Magolda, M. 1992. *Knowing and Reasoning in College: Gender-Related Patterns in Students' Intellectual Development.* San Francisco: Jossey-Bass.

————. 1999. *Creating Contexts for Learning and Self-Authorship: Constructive-Developmental Pedagogy.* Nashville, Tenn.: Vanderbilt University Press.

————. 2001. *Making Their Own Way: Narratives for Transforming Higher Education to Promote Self-Development.* Sterling, Va.: Stylus.

Bean, J. C. 1996. *Engaging Ideas: The Professor's Guide to Integrating Writing, Critical Thinking, and Active Learning in the Classroom.* San Francisco: Jossey-Bass.

Beaudry, M. I. 2000. How Much Content? Are We Asking the Wrong Question? *National Teaching and Learning Forum,* 9 (4): 1–4.

Bergquist, W. H., Gould, R. A., and Greenberg, E. M. 1981. *Designing Undergraduate Education.* San Francisco: Jossey-Bass.

Berlo, D. K., Lemert, J. B., and Mertz, R. J. 1969. Dimensions for Evaluating the Acceptability of Message Sources. *Public Opinion Quarterly,* 33: 563–76.

Blackburn, R. T., Pellino, G. R., Boberg, A., and O'Connell, C. 1980. Are Instructional Improvement Programs Off Target? *Current Issues in Higher Education,* 2 (1): 32–48.

Bloom, B. S., ed. 1956. *Taxonomy of Educational Objectives. The Classification of Educational Goals. Handbook I: Cognitive Domain.* New York: McKay.

Boice, R. 1992. *The New Faculty Member.* San Francisco: Jossey-Bass.

Bonwell, C. C. 1992–93. Risky Business: Making Active Learning a Reality. *Teaching Excellence,* 4 (3): entire issue. Available from POD Network in Higher Education, P.O. Box 9696, Ft. Collins CO 80525.

Bonwell, C. C., and Eison, J. A. 1991. *Active Learning: Creating Excitement in the Classroom.* ASHE-ERIC Higher Education Report 1. Washington, D.C.: George Washington University.

Boud, D., and Feletti, G. 1998. *The Challenge of Problem Based Learning.* 2nd ed. London: Kogan Page.

Boyd, T. 1997. On Learning and Love. *Spotlight on Teaching,* 17 (2). Available online: http://www.ou.edu/idp/newsletters/archive/d2.html. Access date: October 14, 2002.

Boyer, E. L. 1990. *Scholarship Reconsidered: Priorities of the Professoriate.* Princeton, N.J.: Carnegie Foundation for the Advancement of Teaching.

Braskamp, L. A., and Ory, J. C. 1994. *Assessing Faculty Work: Enhancing Individual and Institutional Performance.* San Francisco: Jossey-Bass.

Brookfield, S. D., ed. 1985. *Self-Directed Learning: From Theory to Practice.* New Directions for Adult and Continuing Education, no. 25. San Francisco: Jossey-Bass.

————. 1995. *Becoming a Critically Reflective Teacher.* San Francisco: Jossey-Bass.

Bruner, J. S. 1960. *The Process of Education.* Cambridge, Mass.: Harvard University Press.

————. 1966. *Toward a Theory of Instruction.* Cambridge, Mass.: Harvard University Press.

Calderon, J. 1999. Making a Difference: Service-Learning as an Activism Catalyst and Community Builder. *AAHE Bulletin,* 52 (1): 7–9.

Campbell, W. E., and Smith, K. A., eds. 1997. *New Paradigms for College Teaching.* Edina, Minn.: Interaction Book Company.

Campus Compact. 1998. *Wingspread Declaration on the Civic Responsibilities of Research Universities.* Available online: http://www.compact.org/civic/Wingspread/Wingspread.html. Access date: October 14, 2002

Candy, P. C. 1991. *Self-Direction for Lifelong Learning: A Comprehensive Guide to Theory and Practice.* San Francisco: Jossey-Bass.

Carnevale, A. P., Johnson, N. C., and Edwards, A. R. 1998, April 10. Performance-Based Appropriations: Fad or Wave of the Future? *Chronicle of Higher Education,* p. B6.

Cashin, W. E., and Clegg, V. L. 1994. Periodicals Related to College Teaching. IDEA Paper no. 28. Manhattan, Kans.: Center for Faculty Evaluation and Development, Kansas State University.

Cassel, J. F., and Congleton, R. J. 1993. *Critical Thinking: An Annotated Bibliography.* Metuchen, N.J.: Scarecrow Press.

Collingwood, R. G. 1993. *The Idea of History.* rev. ed. New York: Oxford University Press.

Cooper, P. J., and Simonds, C. 1998. *Communication for the Classroom Teacher.* 6th ed. Boston: Allyn & Bacon.

Courts, P. L., and McInerney, K. H. 1993. *Assessment in Higher Education: Politics, Pedagogy, and Portfolios.* Westport, Conn.: Praeger.

Covey, S. R. 1990. *The Seven Habits of Highly Effective People.* New York: Simon & Schuster.

Creech, W. L. 1994. *The Five Pillars of TQM.* New York: Plume.

Cross, K. P. 2001. Leading-Edge Efforts to Improve Teaching and Learning: The Hesburgh Awards. *Change Magazine,* 33 (4): 30–37.

Csikszentmihalyi, M. 1990. *Flow: The Psychology of Optimal Experience.* New York: Harper-Collins.

———. 1996. *Creativity: Flow and the Psychology of Discovery and Invention.* New York: Harper-Collins.

———. 1997. *Finding Flow: The Psychology of Engagement with Everyday Life.* New York: Harper-Collins.

Davis, B. 1993. *Tools for Teaching.* San Francisco: Jossey-Bass.

Davis, J. R. 1993. *Better Teaching, More Learning.* Phoenix, Ariz.: Oryx Press.

———. 1995. *Interdisciplinary Courses and Team Teaching.* Phoenix, Ariz.: Oryx Press.

Diamond, N. A. 2002. Small Group Instructional Diagnosis: Tapping Student Perceptions of Teaching. In *A Guide to Faculty Development,* edited by K. H. Gillespie. Bolton, Mass.: Anker.

Diamond, R. M. 1998. *Designing and Assessing Courses and Curricula: A Practical Guide.* rev. ed. San Francisco: Jossey-Bass.

Dolence, M. G., and Norris, D. M. 1995. *Transforming Higher Education: A Vision for Learning in the Twenty-First Century.* Ann Arbor, Mich.: Society for College and University Planning.

Duch, B. J., Groh, S. E., and Allen, D. E., eds. 2001. *The Power of Problem-Based Learning.* Sterling, Va.: Stylus.

Duderstadt, J. J. 1999. Can Colleges and Universities Survive the Information Age? In *Dancing with the Devil,* edited by R.N. Katz. San Francisco: Jossey-Bass.

Education Commission of the States (ECS). 1994. *Quality Assurance in Undergraduate Education: What the Public Expects.* Denver, Colo.: ECS.

Ellis, D. B. 2000. *Becoming a Master Student.* 9th ed. Boston: Houghton Mifflin.

Enos, S. 1999. A Multicultural and Critical Perspective on Teaching Through Community: A Dialogue with Jose Calderon of Pitzer College. In *Cultivating the Sociological Imagination: Concepts and Models for Service-Learning in Sociology,* edited by J. Ostrow, G. Hesser, and S. Enos. Washington, D.C.: American Association of Higher Education.

Farrington, G. E. 1999. The New Technologies and the Future of Residential Undergraduate Education. *Educom Review,* 34 (4).

Fink, L. D. 1984. *The First Year of College Teaching.* New Directions for Teaching and Learning, no. 17. San Francisco: Jossey-Bass.

————. 1995. Evaluating Your Own Teaching. In *Improving College Teaching,* by P. Seldin and Associates. Bolton, Mass.: Anker.

————. 2001. Improving the Evaluation of College Teaching. In *A Guide to Faculty Development,* edited by K. H. Gillespie. Bolton, Mass.: Anker.

Flanigan, M. 2000. How to Create Writing Assignments for Students That You Actually Look Forward to Reading. *Innovation,* (4): 89–92. (An annual publication by Nottingham Trent University, England.)

Gabelnick, F., MacGregor, J., Matthews, R. S., and Smith, B. L. 1990. *Learning Communities: Creating Connections Among Students, Faculty, and Disciplines.* New Directions for Teaching and Learning, no. 41. San Francisco: Jossey-Bass.

Gardiner, L. 1994. *Redesigning Higher Education: Producing Dramatic Gains in Student Learning.* ASHE-ERIC Higher Education Report 7. Washington, D.C.: George Washington University.

Gardner, J. N., and Jewler, A. J. 1999. *Your College Experience: Strategies for Success.* 4th ed. Belmont, Calif.: Wadsworth.

Gibbs, G. P. 1992. *Improving the Quality of Student Learning.* Oxford, England: Oxford Centre for Staff Development, Oxford Brookes University.

————. 1993, April. Deep Learning, Surface Learning. *AAHE Bulletin,* pp. 10–11.

Goleman, D. 1995. *Emotional Intelligence.* New York: Bantam Books.

————. 1998. *Working with Emotional Intelligence.* New York: Bantam Books.

Gower, B. 1997. *Scientific Method: An Historical and Philosophical Introduction.* New York: Routledge.

Grow, G. 1991. Teaching Learners to Be Self-Directed. *Adult Education Quarterly,* 41 (3): 125–149.

Halpern, D., ed. 1994. *Changing College Classrooms: New Teaching and Learning Strategies in an Increasingly Complex World.* San Francisco: Jossey-Bass.

Healey, M. 1998. Developing and Disseminating Good Educational Practices: Lessons from Geography in Higher Education. Paper presented to the International Consortium for Educational Development in Higher Education's 2nd International Conference. Austin, Tex.

Heifitz, R. A. 1994. *Leadership Without Easy Answers.* Cambridge, Mass.: Harvard University Press.

Heller, S. 1989, October 11. More Than Half of Students in Survey Flunk History and Literature Test. *Chronicle of Higher Education,* p. A15.

Hestenes, D. 1999. Modeling Instruction Program. Available online: http://modeling.la.asu.edu/modeling.html. Access date: Aug. 29, 2002.

Jacoby, B. 1996. *Service-Learning in Higher Education: Concepts and Practices.* San Francisco: Jossey-Bass.

Jenkins, A. 1996. Discipline-Based Educational Development. *International Journal for Academic Development,* 1 (1): 50–62.

Johnson, D. W., Johnson, R. T., and Smith, K. A. 1991. *Cooperative Learning: Increasing College Faculty Instructional Productivity.* ASHE-ERIC Higher Education Reports, #4. Washington, D.C.: School of Education and Human Development, George Washington University.

Kegan, R. 1994. *In Over Our Heads: The Mental Demands of Modern Life.* Cambridge, Mass.: Harvard University Press.

Klein, J. T., and Doty, W. G., eds. 1994. *Interdisciplinary Studies Today.* New Directions for Teaching and Learning, no. 58. San Francisco: Jossey-Bass.

Klein, J. T., and Newell, W. 1996. Advancing Interdisciplinary Studies. In *Handbook of the Undergraduate Curriculum,* edited by J. G. Gaff and J. L. Ratcliff. San Francisco: Jossey-Bass.

Knowles, M. S. 1975. *Self-Directed Learning: A Guide for Learners and Teachers.* New York: Association Press.

Kolar, R. L., Muraleetharan, K. K., Mooney, M. A., and Vieux, B. E. 2000. Sooner City—Design Across the Curriculum. *Journal of Engineering Education*, 89 (1): 79–87.

Kotter, J. P. 1996. *Leading Change*. Boston: Harvard Business School Press.

Kouzes, J. S., and Posner, B. Z. 1993. *Credibility: How Leaders Gain It and Lose It, Why People Demand It*. San Francisco: Jossey-Bass.

Kuh, G. D. 2001. Assessing What Really Matters to Student Learning: Inside the National Survey of Student Engagement. *Change Magazine*, 33 (3): 10–17, 66.

Lazerson, M., Wagener, U., and Shumanis, N. 2000. Teaching and Learning in Higher Education, 1980–2000. *Change Magazine*, 32 (3): 13–19.

Lindbergh, C. A. 1927. *We*. New York: Putnam.

———. 1953. *The Spirit of St. Louis*. New York: Scribner.

Martinez, M. 1998. Intentional Learning and Learning Orientations. Available online: http://Mse.byu.edu/projects/elc/ilsum.htm. Access date: Aug. 29, 2002.

Marton, F., Hounsell, D., and Entwistle, N., eds. 1984. *The Experience of Learning*. 1st ed. Edinburgh, Scotland: Scottish Academic Press.

Marton, F., Hounsell, D., and Entwistle, N., eds. 1997. *The Experience of Learning*. 2nd ed. Edinburgh, Scotland: Scottish Academic Press.

McKeachie, W. J., and others. 1999. *Teaching Tips: Strategies, Research, and Theory for College and University Teachers*. 10th ed. Boston: Houghton-Mifflin.

McLeish, J. 1968. *The Lecture Method*. Cambridge, England: Cambridge Institute of Education.

Mentkowski, M. 1999. *Learning That Lasts*. San Francisco: Jossey-Bass.

Meyers, C., and Jones, T. B. 1993. *Promoting Active Learning: Strategies for the College Classroom*. San Francisco: Jossey-Bass.

Mezirow, J. 1985. A Critical Theory of Self-Directed Learning. In *Self-Directed Learning*, edited by S. Brookfield. New Directions for Continuing Education, no. 25. San Francisco: Jossey-Bass.

Michaelsen, L. K., Knight, A. B., and Fink, L. D. 2002. *Team-Based Learning: A Transformative Use of Small Groups for Large and Small Classes*. Westport, Conn.: Bergin & Garvey.

Millis, B. J., and Cottell, P. G. 1998. *Cooperative Learning for Higher Education Faculty*. Phoenix, Ariz.: Oryx Press.

National Association of State Universities and Land-Grant Colleges (NASULGC). 1997. *Returning to Our Roots: The Student Experience*. Washington, D.C.: NASULGC.

National Institute of Education (NIE). 1984. *Involvement in Learning: Realizing the Potential of American Higher Education*. Washington, D.C.: NIE.

National Science Foundation (NSF). 1996. *Shaping the Future: New Expectations for Undergraduate Education in Science, Mathematics, Engineering and Technology*. Washington, D.C.: NSF.

Novak, J. D. 1998. *Learning, Creating and Using Knowledge*. Mahwah, N.J.: Erlbaum.

Novak, J. D., and Gowin, D. B. 1984. *Learning How to Learn*. New York: Cambridge University Press.

O'Reilley, M. R. 1993. *The Peaceable Classroom*. Portsmouth, N.H.: Boynton/Cook.

———. 1998. *Radical Presence: Teaching as Contemplative Practice*. Portsmouth, N.H.: Boynton/Cook.

Palmer, P. J. 1983. *To Know as We Are Known: A Spirituality of Education*. New York: Harper-Collins.

———. 1998. *The Courage to Teach: Exploring the Inner Landscape of a Teacher's Life*. San Francisco: Jossey-Bass.

Paul, R. W. 1993. *Critical Thinking: How to Prepare Students for a Rapidly Changing World*. Santa Rosa, Calif.: Foundation for Critical Thinking.

Paul, R., Elder, L., and Bartell, T. 1997. *California Teacher Preparation for Instruction in Critical Thinking: Research Findings and Policy Recommendations*. Sonoma, Calif.: Foundation for Critical Thinking.

Paul, S. J., Teachout, D. J., Sullivan, J. M., Kelly, S. N., Bauer, W. I., and Raiber, M. A. 2001. Authentic-Context Learning Activities in Instrumental Music. *Journal of Research in Music Education*, 49 (2): 136–145.

Pintrich, P. R. 1994. Student Motivation in the College Classroom. In *Handbook of College Teaching*, edited by K. W. Prichard and R. McLaran Sawyer. Westport, Conn.: Greenwood.

Pintrich, P., ed. 1995. *Understanding Self-Regulated Learning*. New Directions for Teaching and Learning, no. 63. San Francisco: Jossey-Bass.

Porter, L. W., and McKibbin, L. E. 1988. *Management Education and Development: Drift or Thrust into the Twenty-First Century?* New York: McGraw-Hill.

Rhoads, R. A., and Howard, J.P.F. 1998. *Academic Service Learning: A Pedagogy of Action and Reflection*. New Directions for Teaching and Learning, no. 73. San Francisco: Jossey-Bass.

Roberts, M. 1997. *The Man Who Listens to Horses*. New York: Random House.

———. 2001. *Horse Sense for People*. New York: Viking.

Rose, C., and Nicholl, M. J. 1997. *Accelerated Learning for the Twenty-First Century*. New York: Dell.

Sabatini, D. A., and Knox, R. C. 1999. Results of a Student Discussion Group on Leadership Concepts. *Journal of Engineering Education*, 88 (4): 185–188.

Saunders, P. 1980, Winter. The Lasting Effects of Introductory Economics Courses. *Journal of Economic Education*, 12: 1–14.

Schmidt, P. 2000, Oct. 6. Faculty Outcry Greets Proposal for Competency Tests at University of Texas. *Chronicle of Higher Education*, p. A35.

Schön, D. A. 1983. *The Reflective Practitioner: How Professionals Think in Action*. New York: Basic Books.

———. 1987. *Educating the Reflective Practitioner: Toward a New Design for Teaching and Learning in the Professions*. San Francisco: Jossey-Bass.

Schunk, D. H., and Zimmerman, B. J., eds. 1998. *Self-Regulated Learning: From Teaching to Self-Reflective Practice*. New York: Guilford Press.

Schwab, J. J. 1962. *The Teaching of Science as Enquiry*. Cambridge, Mass.: Harvard University Press.

Shapiro, N. S., and Levine, J. 1999. *Creating Learning Communities*. San Francisco: Jossey-Bass.

Smith, F. 1998. *The Book of Learning and Forgetting*. New York: Teacher's College Press.

Spence, L. 2001. The Case Against Teaching. *Change Magazine*, 33 (6): 10–19.

Sternberg, R. J. 1989. *The Triarchic Mind: A New Theory of Human Intelligence*. New York: Penguin.

Sutherland, T. E., and Bonwell, C. C., eds. 1996. *Using Active Learning in College Classes: A Range of Options for Faculty*. New Directions for Teaching and Learning, no. 67. San Francisco: Jossey-Bass.

Svinicki, M., ed. 1999. *Teaching and Learning on the Edge of the Millennium: Building on What We Have Learned*. New Directions for Teaching and Learning, no. 80. San Francisco: Jossey-Bass.

Thelen, H. A. 1960. *Education and the Human Quest*. New York: HarperCollins.

Tough, A. 1979. *The Adult's Learning Projects: A Fresh Approach to Theory and Practice in Adult Learning*. 2nd ed. Research in Education Series no. 1, Ontario Institute for Studies in Education. Austin, Tex.: Learning Concepts.

Vaill, P. B. 1996. *Learning as a Way of Being*. San Francisco: Jossey-Bass.

————. 1998. *Spirited Leading and Learning.* San Francisco: Jossey-Bass.

"Virtual" Institutions Challenge Accreditors to Devise New Ways of Measuring Quality. 1999, Aug. 6. *Chronicle of Higher Education,* pp. A29–30.

Walvoord, B. E., and Anderson, V. J. 1998. *Effective Grading: A Tool for Learning and Assessment.* San Francisco: Jossey-Bass.

Weimer, M. 1993. The Disciplinary Journals on Pedagogy. *Change Magazine,* 25 (6): 44–51.

Weimer, M., Parrott, J. L., and Keens, M.M.K. 1988. *How Am I Teaching? Forms and Activities for Acquiring Instructional Input.* Madison, Wis.: Atwood.

Wiggins, G. 1998. *Educative Assessment: Designing Assessments to Inform and Improve Student Performance.* San Francisco: Jossey-Bass.

Wilkerson, L., and Gijselaers, W. H., eds. 1996. *Bringing Problem-Based Learning to Higher Education: Theory and Practice.* New Directions for Teaching and Learning, no. 68. San Francisco: Jossey-Bass.

Wlodkowski, R. J. 1999. *Enhancing Adult Motivation to Learn: A Comprehensive Guide for Teaching All Adults.* rev. ed. San Francisco: Jossey-Bass.

Wright, B. D. 2001. The Syracuse Transformation: On Becoming a Student-Centered Research University. *Change Magazine,* 33 (4): 39–45.

Zimmerman, B. J., and Schunk, D. H., eds. 1989. *Self-Regulated Learning and Academic Achievement: Theory, Research, and Practice.* New York: Springer-Verlag.

Zinsser, W. 1988. *Writing to Learn.* New York: HarperCollins.

Zlotkowski, E., ed. 1998. *Successful Service-Learning Programs: New Models of Excellence in Higher Education.* Bolton, Mass.: Anker.

Zubizarreta, J., ed. 2003. *The Learning Portfolio: Reflective Practice for Improving Student Learning.* Bolton, Mass.: Anker.

INDEX